VICTORIA AND ALBERT MUSEUM YEARBOOK

Number two

VICTORIA AND ALBERT MUSEUM YEARBOOK

Number two

PHAIDON

© CROWN COPYRIGHT 1970
PUBLISHED BY PHAIDON PRESS LTD, 5 CROMWELL PLACE, LONDON SW7

PHAIDON PUBLISHERS INC, NEW YORK
DISTRIBUTORS IN THE UNITED STATES: PRAEGER PUBLISHERS INC.
111 FOURTH AVENUE, NEW YORK, N.Y. 10003
LIBRARY OF CONGRESS CATALOG CARD NUMBER: 77-83519

SBN 07148 1451 2
MADE IN GREAT BRITAIN
PRINTED BY THE CAVENDISH PRESS LTD, LEICESTER

CONTENTS

The Gherardini Collection of Italian Sculpture

THE turning point in the early history of what is now the Victoria and Albert Museum was the purchase in 1854 of a group of sculptors' models known as the Gherardini Collection. Its significance was recognized in a *History of the Science and Art Department* published twenty-nine years later, which informs us that: 'The Chancellor of the Exchequer (Mr. Gladstone) purchased the Gherardini collection of models for sculpture, which was placed in the Art Museum. This collection, inasmuch as it referred to a branch of art not necessarily connected with manufactures, helped in extending the limit of the collection generally, which henceforth became "Art Collections".'[1] The purchase is amply documented, and is of interest for the light it throws first on the development of the Museum, second on the story of collecting in this country, and third on the psychology of art history in the middle of the nineteenth century.

The existence of the Gherardini Collection had come to notice not long before. The first reference to it occurs in a guide book of 1852, when it is said to have been 'lately discovered'.[2] It was housed in the Casa Gherardini in Via della Pergola in Florence, and contained 'a number of very curious models and studies of statues in wax by Michael Angelo'. Members of the public were encouraged to call there, since 'to the true connoisseur this is as interesting a collection as any in Florence'.

According to information circulated at the time, it belonged to 'a member of the Gherardini family, an aged priest, who appears either to have undervalued it or to have forgotten its existence', and at his death it was discovered by his heir, Signor Gherardini, 'in an obscure corner of his relative's house, where it had long lain neglected'.[3] It had been 'for a very long period in the possession of the Gherardini'.[4]

Before long it transpired that the collection was in fact for sale, and was fortified by certificates of authenticity from prominent members of the Florentine Academy. When the history of the certificate is eventually written, a chapter must be devoted to the rather discreditable efforts of Florentine artists in the middle of the nineteenth century to cash in on and promote the sale of works of art. This occurred with the Gherardini models. 'The leading artists of Florence', reads a report of the time,[5] 'appear to have entertained no doubt of the genuineness of, at least, the most important objects of which it consists. A catalogue raisonné in the possession of Madame Gherardini (which we have

seen), is subscribed by a number of distinguished painters and sculptors (members of the Academy of Florence and others), whose subscriptions are for the most part formally attested, and who declare that the works subscribed in the preceding catalogue are, in their opinion, what they profess to be.'

A group of Old Master drawings from Casa Gherardini was sold at this time to the Austrian Government,[6] but the disposal of the sculptors' models proved harder to negotiate. The collection was first offered to the Tuscan Government, but at a price (unrecorded) which was judged to be unreasonably high. It was then brought by Prince Poniatowski to the notice of

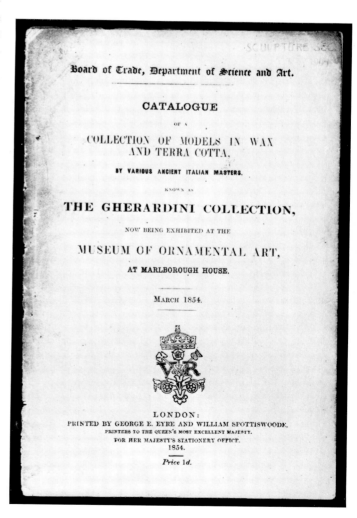

1. Title-page of the catalogue of the Gherardini Collection, as exhibited at Marlborough House in 1854.

Napoleon III.⁷ 'Madame Gherardini', who seems to have supplied the motive power through these negotiations, promptly packed up the models and moved them to Paris. But for reasons of economy the French Government, which had spent a substantial sum on buying paintings at the Soult sale, refused to purchase them. Nothing daunted, the owner moved the collection to London, and agreed that it should be exhibited for one month, from mid-March till mid-April 1854, in the Museum of Ornamental Art at Marlborough House, 'with the view of eliciting from the public and the artists of this country such an expression of opinion as to their value and authenticity as will justify the purchase or the rejection of the collection by Her Majesty's Government'.⁸ She reserved the right to accept 'any higher offer that might be made to her during this period, subject to a prior right of refusal on the part of the government to the advanced terms'. It was claimed that in London the collection was of greater value than it had been in Paris, since one of the models had belatedly been recognized as a work by Raphael, but the asking price remained unchanged at a figure of £3,000. The exhibition was promoted by Henry Cole, Secretary of the Department of Science and Art, and Richard Redgrave, Superintendent of Art; and the young Curator of the Museum of Ornamental Art, J. C. Robinson, wrote a circumspect preface to the catalogue (fig. 1). The entries in the catalogue were translated from the Italian, and at the end was a five-page extract from a report by two Royal Academicians, the painters William Dyce and John Herbert. By and large the report was unenthusiastic. 'With respect to extrinsic evidence of the genuineness of the works we have noticed', the Academicians observed,⁹ 'it must at once be stated that there is none whatever . . . Out of the thirty objects contained in the collection, it did not appear to us that more than ten or twelve were really desirable.' It may be noted incidentally that among the works whose purchase was not specially to be desired was the only model in the collection that really was by Michelangelo. The whole enterprise excited considerable curiosity, and on March 25 the models were inspected by Queen Victoria. A reference to this visit occurs in F. M. Redgrave's *Richard Redgrave: a Memoir compiled from his Diary* (London, 1891), and reads as follows: 'On a visit to Marlborough House yesterday to attend Marshall's lecture at four o'clock, I learnt that the Queen intended to come the next day to see

the Gherardini models. Cole was away in the Potteries, so I had to meet her, and, being a little nervous, I was thankful for the short notice. The Royal Party came very punctually.' It would be interesting to know how the Queen reacted to the desiccated objects that greeted her. An entry in Redgrave's diary for April 10 again refers to the purchase: 'On Monday last I was summoned to wait on the Chancellor of the Exchequer, Mr. Gladstone, on the subject of the purchase of the Gherardini models.' Following this discussion, the collection was bought at the reduced price of £2,110.

Before we pass through the portal of Marlborough House, there are two points on which some form of gloss is required. Nowadays one would think many times before showing prospective acquisitions on loan and inviting members of the public to determine whether or not they should be purchased. In the Museum of Ornamental Art, however, and later in the South Kensington Museum, the exhibition of works on loan pending eventual purchase was a not uncommon practice. The reasons for it were shortage of funds and the need to establish support for the purchasing policy of the Museum. Many of the great mediaeval works of art in the collection were, for example, secured through the agency of an early benefactor, the dealer John Webb, who placed them on loan at the Museum in return for an annual payment calculated as interest on his outlay, and who then, as money became available, sold them to the Museum outright. One of the earliest block purchases, that of the Soulages Collection from Toulouse, was treated in somewhat the same way. It was bought by a consortium of subscribers organized by Sir Henry Cole, and placed on exhibition in 1856 at Marlborough House. But the forces of enlightenment which made the Gherardini purchase possible had ebbed with the resignation of Gladstone in the preceding year, and the new purchase was vetoed by Palmerston. The subscribers managed to dispose of the collection in 1857 to the trustees of the Manchester Art Treasures Exhibition, where it was shown in the hope that the Manchester Corporation might acquire it. When this failed it was returned to London, and from 1858 was exhibited at the South Kensington Museum, the government agreeing to a compromise whereby its contents were purchased piecemeal over a six-year period from 1859 to 1865.

The second gloss relates to the collecting of sculptors' models. There is no evidence that sketch-models were collected in the fifteenth century, though the inventory of one quattrocento sculptor's studio, that made after the death of Benedetto da Majano in 1497, shows that a large number of terracotta models made at all periods in the artist's life were systematically preserved.[10] To judge from the quantity of models by Benedetto da Majano that still survive (a far larger number than with any other sculptor of the fifteenth century), this collection must have been exceptional. We know, moreover, of certain cases where models were conserved out of respect for the excellence of the completed work. One of them is Verrocchio's St. Thomas, the model for which was bought by the Università dei Mercatanti 'per non lasciare guastarsi e perire la boza e principio di si bella cosa', and another was Jacopo Sansovino's St. James, the model for which was owned by Bindo Altoviti. But these were isolated instances. Logically the collecting of preliminary studies might be expected to have begun at the point at which attention focused on the formal resolutions adopted by sculptors, since then, and then only, could interest attach to the stages by which the final resolution was reached. If this is correct, the systematic assembly of models in Florence would have been stimulated by the work of Giovanni Bologna. There are other reasons for supposing that it was in this milieu that the habit began. Two groups of models by Giovanni Bologna are mentioned in 1568 by Vasari,[11] one of them belonging to the sculptor's patron Bernardo Vecchietti, and the other to 'maestro Bernardo di mona Mattea muratore Ducale che ha condotto tutte le fabriche disegnate dal Vasari con grand' eccellenza'. Of the second we know nothing, but on the first we are relatively well informed. It is described in the *Riposo* of Borghini,[12] who mentions the models in general terms as a feature of Vecchietti's house ('di Giambologna molte figure di cera, di terra, e di bronzo in diverse attitudini rappresentanti varie persone come prigioni, donne, Dee, fiumi & huomini famosi'). A page later there occur two further references, one to a cabinet or desk with five shelves, on which were set out small figures in marble, bronze, terracotta and wax, and the other to a room on the ground floor 'tutta intorniata di modelli di Giambologna, e di statue d'altri maestri, e di pitture, e di disegni'.

Vecchietti's collection seems to have remained substantially intact until the eighteenth century, when part of it was bought by an English collector, William Lock of Norbury.[13] The transaction took place between 1767, when Lock went to Italy, and 1772, when in the Stecchi-Pagani edition of Vasari[14] we read the note: 'Il già lodato più volte Signor Lock di Londra, oltre a un buon numero di modelli originali di più insigni autori antichi; molti ha di cera, e di terracotta di Giovanbologna, esciti per la maggior parte da la celebre raccolta di Bernardo Vecchietti, che fu il suo munificentissimo mecenate.' At the same time, if a later sale catalogue[15] is to be trusted, Lock bought further models from the grandducal collection in the Palazzo Pitti. Part of his collection was disposed of by auction, under the pseudonym of Fitzhugh, at Christie's on April 16, 1785.[16] Looking through the catalogue, we find that the models fall into three broad groups. The first comprises sixteenth-century models, which might have been, probably were, bought from the Palazzo Vechietti. Some of them can still be identified, such as No. 23, 'Four Basso rilievos in wax, by Gio. di Bologna', which were bought for five guineas by Nollekens and are certainly identical with the red wax models for the Passion scenes at Genoa now divided between the Victoria and Albert Museum and the Queensland Art Gallery, Brisbane. Others are not differentiated. No. 19, for example, consists of 'Twenty-two models by Gio. di Bologna'. There are also some models by or copies after Michelangelo, which might have originated from Vecchietti's collection. The second group consists of Baroque models (e.g. No. 15, 'Model for the fountain of the Piazza Navona by Bernini, and a sketch by ditto'; No. 10, 'Child's head by Fiammingo, and Susanna after him'; No. 25, 'Samson, and half figure, by Algardi'). Unless one of Vecchietti's descendants shared his propensity for collecting models, these are unlikely to have come from the Palazzo Vecchietti, and must have been obtained from some other source. The third group, by a natural extension of the first two, is composed of eighteenth-century English sketch-models by Nollekens, Roubiliac and Delvaux. One of the purchasers at the Fitzhugh sale was Nollekens, whose own clay and terracotta *pensieri* were decisively influenced by the models of Giovanni Bologna that he knew.

Lock died in 1810, but we gain a further sidelight on his collection more than a quarter of a century later, when, on June 28, 1837, the assignees of a bankrupt named Mr. A. H. Dry put up for sale at Debenham and Storr's another group of models which had been in Lock's possession.[17] They included an alleged sketch-model for the Moses of Michelangelo, an alleged model for the Night on the tomb of Giuliano de' Medici, 'a charming terra cotta FIGURE OF PARIS, a splendid production by Michael Angelo', a 'VENUS AND CUPIDS, a fine Model, in terra cotta, executed in a beautiful and exceedingly grand and bold style by JOHN OF BOLOGNA', and 'a beautifully executed terra cotta MODEL of a TRITON, by BELLINI, in his best style' (presumably the Bernini model for the Piazza Navona fountain listed in the Fitzhugh sale catalogue). The relevance of all this to the Gherardini Collection is a double one, first that the diffusion of these sketch-models, on a scale that seems to have no parallel elsewhere in Europe, established a climate which made the Gherardini purchase possible, and second that the Gherardini models, like the models sold by Lock, included works of the seventeenth as well as of the sixteenth century, and must therefore represent an eighteenth-century amalgamation of models from a sixteenth-century collection, probably Vecchietti's, and models obtained elsewhere. At the sale of the bankrupt Mr. Dry it was affirmed that the models sold 'originally formed part of the decorations of the Ducal Palace in Florence and it is hoped that

ere long they will ornament the Sculpture Gallery of the British Museum'. Perhaps the later Gherardini models were procured from the same source.

With these points in mind, let us return to Marlborough House and set off round the exhibition with the catalogue. No. 1, a female figure in terracotta (fig. 2),[18] purports to be 'one of the numerous essays which Michelangiolo made, particularly in Carrara, where he procured the marble for the tombs of the Medici family, in the church of S. Lorenzo. The figure which he executed in marble preserves the same attitude, only it is better adapted to the pediment on which it is placed. On due consideration this model has all the appearance of having been a study made from life'. The assessors describe it as 'La Notte', though it is in fact a copy of the Dawn, but question its pretensions. 'It does not appear to us', they say, 'that the terracotta bears any distinctive character of originality', and it is indeed a sixteenth-century reduction adapted to a flat base. In reading this and other comments it must be remembered that Dyce and Herbert were in no sense specialists on Italian sculpture, and that the comparative material, mostly in the form of line engravings, was woefully inadequate. Some impressions of it can be formed by looking at the plates of Landon's and Duppa's books on Michelangelo.

2. *Dawn*, after Michelangelo. Terracotta; length 45·7 cm.

3. *Left hand*. Terracotta; height 24·9 cm.

No. 3 is a model for the group of Hercules and Cacus (fig. 4);[23] it is described by the assessors as 'a work of great excellence', and is so accepted by Robinson. In 1855 Robinson was unfamiliar with the clay model

4. *Hercules and Cacus*, after Michelangelo. Wax; height 39·4 cm.

The first cast of a work by Michelangelo to reach the South Kensington Museum, that of the colossal David, was presented by the Grand-Duke of Tuscany only in 1857.

No. 2, 'a Hand in Terra Cotta' (Fig. 3),[19] also ascribed to Michelangelo, is hailed in the catalogue entry as the recently recovered original of a work known through plaster casts. The assessors consider that it 'bears every mark of genuineness', and Robinson, in the 1855 catalogue of the contents of Marlborough House,[20] declares that it is 'probably a finished study by Michelangelo', and 'the type and model from which the mould for these (plaster) casts was made'. He was still of this opinion in 1862[21] when, after seven years intensive study of Italian sculptures, he published his great catalogue of the Italian sculptures at South Kensington, where he suggests that the hand was made by Michelangelo for didactic purposes. The hand may have been the source of the casts, but it is not by Michelangelo. Possibly it is identical with a much praised hand in terracotta that is mentioned in 1732 in a room adjacent to the Cappella de' Principi in San Lorenzo, and that disappeared in the late eighteenth or early nineteenth century.[22]

of the same group in the Casa Buonarroti (fig. 5),[24] but by 1862 he had related the two works, and had observed correctly that the Gherardini version supplied a record of two features missing in the other, the right shoulder of Hercules and the head of Cacus which were broken off.[25] The wax was in fact cast from the clay at a time when the head of Hercules was already missing, but the head of Cacus was still attached.[26] It perhaps dates from the sixteenth century, and though not directly modelled gives a clearer picture of Michelangelo's creative procedure than any model save one in the collection. The exception is No. 4,[27] the only work

5. *Hercules and Cacus*, by Michelangelo. Clay; height 41 cm. Casa Buonarroti, Florence.

owned by the Gherardini which was in fact by Michelangelo (fig. 6). The assessors acquiesced, but did not otherwise take much account of it. A wax model for the Young Slave for the tomb of Pope Julius II then in the Boboli Gardens in Florence, it is correctly identified in the catalogue and by Robinson in his catalogue of 1855,[28] though in 1862 he preferred to associate it with one of the earlier figures of Slaves in the Louvre.[29] It is by far the most important single work secured for the Museum in this purchase. The assessors none the less seem to have ranked it below No. 5 (fig. 7), which is described in the catalogue as 'a perfect gem . . . the first idea of the David'.[30] There was a disconcerting discrepancy in scale – this is one of the smallest models and the David is Michelangelo's largest statue – as well as pose; the head faced in the wrong direction and a large head of Goliath appeared between the legs, but this offered no difficulty to the cataloguers, who inferred that it represented the statue Michelangelo would have wished to carve had he not been constricted by the marble block that was available. For the assessors this elegant, nervous little figure was a work of 'great excellence', as it was for Robinson, both in 1855,[31] when he accepted its relationship to the marble David, and in 1862, when he was doubtful whether it should be connected with the marble statue or with the lost David in bronze.[32] The model is too slight and too damaged to be attributable, but seems to have been made in Florence in the late sixteenth century.

The point of reference for the next number in the catalogue, No. 6 (fig. 8), can be in no doubt; it is the Apollo carved by Michelangelo for Baccio Valori (fig. 9), which was discovered in a niche of the theatre in the Boboli Gardens not long before.[33] This identification is made in the catalogue, with the comment that 'this little sketch is more finished than the marble itself', and by the assessors. Robinson in 1855 makes the same observation,[34] and seems to have viewed it with some doubt. While admitting the possibility that it is an original study, his cautious entry recognizes that 'this fact of greater elaboration might lead to the supposition, that it is a careful after-copy by one of his scholars, destined to form the form for a bronze, the more finished appearance being simply the result of reduction to a smaller scale'. He might well have added that the academic flattening of the pose and the frontality of the head lent colour to this argument. It was left to Maclagan to draw the correct inference,[35] that the figure is cast not modelled, and was designed

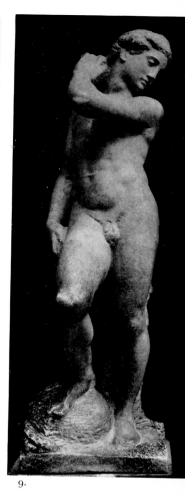

7.

8.

9.

6. *A Slave*, by Michelangelo. Red wax; height 16·7 cm.
7. *David*. Red wax; height 9·4 cm.
8. *Apollo*. Red wax; height 27·3 cm.
9. *Apollo*, by Michelangelo. Marble. Museo Nazionale, Florence.

for reproduction in bronze. There is, however, no record of a small bronze based on the design.

No. 7 (fig. 10) is presented in the catalogue as a sketch-model by Michelangelo for the Victory in the Palazzo Vecchio.[36] This identification is supported by the assessors, but not by Robinson,[37] who concludes that 'the exaggerated proportions of the principal figure in this sketch, and its hard, spiritless execution, render it probable that it is an after-study from the marble by a scholar'. Had the assessors been less mesmerized by the notion that the Gherardini models were likely to be by Michelangelo, they might have noticed that the pose was an inversion of that of the Victory, and that the right knee not the left rests on the captive beneath. On the other hand, it is possible that they had access to an engraving which showed the Victory in reverse. Even so, it should have been evident that the model shows a woman and that the Victory represents a man. This fact (which may have been responsible for Robinson's decision to delete the

model from the catalogue of 1862) might have led them to the correct conclusion, that the model is connected not with the Victory but with a group designed as a counterpart to the Victory, the Florence triumphant over Pisa of Giovanni Bologna. It is indeed the earliest record that we know of the composition of this group, and is of great importance for the study of Giovanni Bologna's attitude to Michelangelo.

The following model, No. 8 (fig. 11), shows the torso of a female figure severed through the neck, upper arms and knees, with pendulous breasts and strong contrapposto established by the opposing movement of the shoulder and the hips.[38] According to the catalogue, 'it evidently displays the energy of the artist, who sought to reproduce nature as she commonly exists, before adding those idealized forms which he would have desired'. The assessors agree that it is probably but not certainly by Michelangelo, and it seems to Robinson[39] to bear 'intrinsic evidence of the mind and manner of the great sculptor', especially when compared with the female figure in the lower left corner of the Bacchanal engraved by Nicola Beatricetto after Michelangelo.[40] In 1862 he confirmed the view that it was 'literally from the *hand* of Michelangelo, being, like the model of the Slave, rapidly blocked out

13

11. *Female torso.*
Black wax;
height 23.5 cm.

10. *Florence triumphant over Pisa,* by Giovanni Bologna. Wax;
height 22·2 cm.

in the soft wax, almost entirely with his thumb and fingers'.[41] Though the attribution in this case lingered on – it is indeed accepted by Brinckmann – the possibility that we have here to do with a Michelangelo model cannot be rated very high. None the less its quality is excellent, and we should judge from this alone that it was the work of a major artist. In the current catalogue of the Italian sculptures in London it is concluded that 'an origin in the studio or circle of Giovanni Bologna is possible'. The more closely one looks at the model, however, the less probable does the presumed connection with Giovanni Bologna seem, for the proportions of the body, especially the extended waist, differ from those usual in Giovanni Bologna, and the torsion of the figure does so too. In both respects it finds its closest parallel in the work of another contemporary sculptor, Vincenzo Danti, whose Moses and the Brazen Serpent in the Bargello offers a close parallel for the distortions in the sketch-model (fig. 12). The analogies are with male not female figures, and are therefore less than perfectly conclusive, but they are sufficiently firm to enable Danti's name to be attached, at least in a tentative way, to the wax statuette.

The rather indefinite picture of Michelangelo as a modeller which is liable to be formed from the preceding entries is still further blurred by No. 9 (fig. 13), a 'Mask in terra cotta . . . which exhibits, though in

12. Detail from the bronze relief *Moses and the Brazen Serpent*, by Vincenzo Danti. Museo Nazionale, Florence.

13. *Mask*, by Giovanni Bologna. Clay; height 7·6 cm.

small dimensions, the admirable power ('*bravura*') of Michelangelo in wild and fantastic subjects'.[42] The assessors concur in this description, and Robinson does so too, connecting it with the mask on the figure of Night in the Medici Chapel.[43] It is a tribute to the vitality of this remarkable sketch that the ascription to Michelangelo persisted in one form or another down to our own time, when it was identified independently by Mrs. Ruth Grippi[44] and Dr. Elisabeth Dhanens[45] as what it is, a sketch-model by Giovanni Bologna for a grotesque mask in the courtyard of the Palazzo Vecchietti. Its presence in the Gherardini Collection lends some plausibility to the view that Bernardo Vecchietti must have been the owner of a number of the models.

The next model given to Michelangelo, a figure of 'Marsyas(?) flayed' (No. 10) (fig. 14), is recognized in the catalogue as connected with a well-known bronze statuette,[46] but receives short shrift from Robinson, who lists it without comment in 1855[47] and omits it in 1862. Like the wax reduction of the Valori Apollo, it is cast not modelled, and depends from a version of the écorche bronze. This figure leads on to a group of five anatomical studies of arms and legs (No. 11),[48] which are identified as models for the limbs in a number of Michelangelo's early works, but

14. *Marsyas flayed*. Red wax; height 16.5 cm.

This attribution strikes even the assessors as improbable.[52] 'There is nothing in the taste or style in which it is executed', they conclude, 'to identify it as the production of Donatello, but it is probably a work of his time.' In 1855 Robinson endorses this view,[53] but by 1862 he has arrived at a different result.[54] 'From its precise resemblance in style and treatment', he writes, 'to several drawings of cows by Bandinelli, which the writer has at different times seen, he has little doubt that it is really an early study from Nature by the latter artist (see two chalk drawings attributed in the "Galerie des Dessins" at the Louvre; several others are also extant). Vasari expressly informs us that in his youthful days Baccio made, with great diligence, many studies from the cattle in his father's farm at Pinzirimonte.' The drawings Robinson had in mind can be identified as Nos. 57 and 59 in Reiset's *Notice des Dessins . . . exposés dans les salles du 1er étage*

seem rather to depend from Michelangelo and show the rather dry handling of the third quarter of the sixteenth century (figs. 15, 16). There is evidence that such models were collected at the time, for when Borghini describes the house of Ridolfo Sirigatti (who was himself a sculptor and may, for all we know, have been responsible for some of the unidentified models in this collection), he notes in the first room alongside full scale gesso casts of the allegorical figures in the Medici Chapel, 'mille teste, braccia, gambe, torsi ed altre membra di statue, di cui tutte le mura son piene, e modelli di cavalli e d'altri animali, che sopra alcuni palchetti si posano'. Of rather different character is a wax skeleton, attributed in the Gherardini catalogue to Michelangelo[50] and regarded by Robinson[51] as a study for the early Bacchus. This curious and mannered work seems to be a bona fide sculptor's model, not a work made for instructional purposes, but there are no means by which its author, be he Giovanni Bologna or some secondary artist, can be identified.

This ends the part of the Marlborough House exhibition devoted to Michelangelo. Section II consists of a single work (fig. 17), 'a cow in Terra Cotta . . . a highly finished model by Donatello . . . a real masterpiece'.

15. *Right arm écorché*. Red wax; height 23·8 cm.
16. *Right leg écorché*. Red wax; height 27·3 cm.

16

17. *An ox.* Terracotta; length 31.1 cm.

18. *Chalk drawing of a Cow* by Baccio Bandinelli. Musée du Louvre, Paris.

au Musée Impérial du Louvre of 1866, and it may be worth while to reproduce one of them here (fig. 18) to illustrate the fictitious similarity. The 'cow' is once more cast not modelled, and may have been made in the second half of the eighteenth century (witness its tell-tale interior) as the ox in a Presepio group.

Also ascribed to Donatello but not included in the catalogue is another work described by the assessors, a small marble relief of St. John the Baptist (fig. 19).[55] Initially it was looked on by Robinson as 'Italian, 15th century work',[56] but by 1862 he came to ascribe it 'with great probability . . . to some member of the Maiano family'.[57] Its real affinities are not with Benedetto da Majano, but with the late work of Antonio Rossellino, and especially with the Naples Adoration of the Shepherds of 1475, where we find, on a larger scale and more finely executed, plants like

those incised on the foreground of the little relief. Rossellino's most celebrated portrayal of the subject, the marble statuette of the Young Baptist entering the Wilderness now in the Bargello, was executed in 1477, and the Gherardini relief is likely to have been carved about the same time by some secondary artist in Rossellino's following.

19. *St. John the Baptist entering the wilderness*, style of Antonio Rossellino. Marble; 28·6 × 18·7 cm.

20. *Diana*, after Giovanni Bologna. Terracotta; height 26·7 cm.

year as reductions made in connection with bronze statuettes.[62] This is the only case in the entire catalogue where the claims of the vendors were right and the doubts of the purchasers unwarranted, for the tiny model of a male and female figure really does record an otherwise unknown phase in the development of the Rape of the Sabines, and the little figure of Hercules and the Centaur can be shown also to be autograph.

The fourth and last section is devoted to works by 'Various Authors', and opens with one of the most puzzling models in the whole collection, a little figure in pale yellowish terracotta of a seated youth (fig. 23) which was given in Paris to Jacopo Sansovino and in London to Raphael.[63] 'This judgment', declare the

21. *The Rape of the Sabines*, by Giovanni Bologna. Wax; height 12·1 cm.

Section III is devoted to Giovanni Bologna. The first item (No. 14), 'a carefully finished model, which displays all the skill of that celebrated sculptor', represents Diana (fig. 20).[58] The assessors set no store by it, and neither does Robinson.[59] It is, he says, 'a contemporary copy of the large bronze figure still extant in Florence'. Save that the bronze represents Venus not Diana (it lacks the crescent moon over the forehead), is small not large, and is a hundred and fifty years earlier than the copy, this analysis is correct. The next two items are of much greater interest. The first (No. 15) is described in the catalogue as a sketch-model for the Rape of the Sabines (fig. 21),[60] and the second (No. 16) as a 'first conception' of the Hercules and Cacus (fig. 22).[61] Both were dismissed by Robinson in the following assessors, ' . . . was unhesitatingly, and at the first glance, pronounced by one of us who happened to be the first to see the collection, and before learning to whom, either in Italy or France, the model has been attributed.' Today we are bound to enquire why the assessors should have linked the figure with the Jonah in the Chigi Chapel of S. Maria del Popolo (fig. 24). Part of the answer is implicit in the eighteenth-century literature of Raphael. According to Vasari, the sculptor Lorenzetto was instructed by Raphael to carve this and the companion figure for the Chapel ('a Lorenzetto scultor fiorentino fece lavorar due figure'). In 1790, however, when enthusiasm for Raphael was at its height, there appeared a forged life of Raphael by

23. *Seated youth*. Terracotta; height 29·8 cm.

22. *Hercules and the Centaur*, by Giovanni Bologna. Wax; height 13·3 cm.

Comolli, in which a more explicit account was given of this as of other transactions.[64] It is referred to in the Gherardini catalogue, which quotes the words: 'He worked also in sculpture, and executed some statues; I have seen one in the hands of Giulio Pippi, which represents a child; the model of Jonah, which is in the Church del Popolo, is equally by him.' As late as the middle of the nineteenth century Comolli's life was accepted as first-hand testimony, and proof of its influence is found in Riepenhausen's engraved illustrations of the life of Raphael,[65] in one of which (fig. 25) we see the artist proffering the imaginary

24. *Jonah*, by Lorenzetto. Marble. S. Maria del Popolo, Rome.

model for the Jonah to Pope Leo X. In the eighteen-fifties, therefore, it would have been assumed that such a model had existed and was liable to reappear. But why did the Gherardini model not look more like the statue? The assessors gain full marks at least for ingenuity. The model, according to their argument, represented the statue Raphael wished to make, but the niche in the chapel was not deep enough to take it. The painter therefore cut off the left foot and part of the left leg, and only when this surgery proved inefficacious, flattened the pose as the dimensions of the niche required. The result of this wrong decision was that 'the Raffaellesque character of form and attitude so strongly marked in the terracotta has, to a great degree, evaporated in the marble of the Cappella Chigi', and the model was thus the only valid index to Raphael's intentions for the figure and 'the only existing specimen of sculpture by his hand'.

Thirty years ago this figure had the rare good fortune to exchange an attribution to one great artist for an attribution to another. When Benvenuto Cellini's Narcissus was rightly identified by Kriegbaum with a

25. *Raphael proffering the model for the Jonah to Pope Leo X*. Plate from Riepenhausen, *Vita di Raffaelle*, Rome, 1833.

statue in the Boboli Gardens, this statuette was wrongly cited as Cellini's preparatory sketch.[66] The figures have points in common, of course, among them the downturned head and the placing of the left arm, but the legs are set differently, and the pose, which is fully circular, postulates a block of marble of quite different proportions from the block Cellini had available. Moreover the morphological peculiarities of the statuette – the large right forearm, for example – do not recur in Cellini's authenticated works. How then is the model to be explained? That it does represent Narcissus and was conceived as a projected garden statue is very probable. It must, moreover, have been inspired by the same class of Hellenistic statue on which the Jonah was based. This is evident both in the raised left arm and in the rock on which the figure sits. But the posture is weak and insecure – the figure slithers round its base – and the anatomy, whether in the deep crevice that does service for the spine or in the area of the chest or knees, suggests that it should properly be looked upon as a late sixteenth-century pastiche, in the style of Caccini or Sirigatti, by a relatively unskilled sculptor. In the nineteenth century this quality of amateurishness was held to corroborate its ascription to a painter, and today it is responsible for the fact that the statuette is unattributed. Especially when it is placed alongside genuine terracotta models by known artists, its defects, both as a sculptural concept and as an artefact, are very marked.

There follows (No. 18) a 'model of the statue representing Architecture upon the monument of Michelangiolo, in the church of Santa Croce, sculptured either by Lorenzi or Giovanni dell' Opera, it is not certain which'.[67] The assessors considered this beautiful figure (fig. 26) unworthy of notice, but Robinson deals with it in both catalogues, first as a work of either Giovanni Bandini or Battista Lorenzi,[68] and then in 1862 more decisively as a study for Bandini's figure of Architecture on the Michelangelo monument.[69] In the event this represented the wrong option, for a hundred years later a study for the companion figure was traced in the Soane Museum, and proved to be Giovanni Bandini's model for the Architecture, whereas the Gherardini model was that made by Battista Lorenzi for the Sculpture when this was to be set on the left of the sarcophagus.[70]

Next to it, No. 19 (fig. 27) is a 'male figure, recumbent on the ground in an academic attitude, which probably

26. *Sculpture*, by Battista Lorenzi. Terracotta; height 34·1 cm.

27. *Recumbent youth*, by Pietro Francavilla. Terracotta; length 41.9 cm.
28. *Meleager*. Bronze; height 76.5 cm. Skulpturensammlung, Dresden.

was accompanied by a corresponding female figure as a *pendant*, that both might serve for architectural ornaments, as is inferred from various similar examples. The style is that of the school of Michelangiolo, but without more certain data it is impossible to ascertain decidedly by whom it was modelled'.[71] Robinson in 1855 was non-committal,[72] but by 1862 decided that it had 'considerable resemblance to the style of Ammanati'.[73] This splendid model was fated to be pushed by twentieth century art historians from pillar to post, from Vincenzo de'Rossi to Vincenzo Danti, until it was finally ascribed, with a fair measure of confidence, to Giovanni Bologna's pupil, Francavilla.[74]

The basis of this attribution was first its technical resemblance to Francavilla's models of Moses and Aaron in the Bargello for the sculptures in the Niccolini Chapel, and second its stylistic connection with the prisoners from the monument of Henry IV in the Louvre. More convincing still are its affinities with a bronze figure of Meleager at Dresden (fig. 28), for which Francavilla must have been responsible, though it was shown in 1967 in the Bode-Museum in East Berlin as the work of an unknown Italo-Flemish artist of the early seventeenth century.[75] The bronze is almost twice the size of sketch-model, and the modelling is therefore less particularized, but the congruence of the heads would be inexplicable if the same artist were not at work.

Many sculptors' studios in the eighteenth century contained casts from Duquesnoy, and it is to this artist that the three succeeding models are ascribed.

29. *Female figure*, possibly by François Duquesnoy. White wax; height 11.3 cm.

frequently copied. A 'Susanna after Fiammingo' appears, for example, as No. 13 of the Lock models in the Fitzhugh sale. In 1855 the present model was regarded by Robinson as a 'sketch with variations for the statue',[77] but in 1862 it was omitted from his catalogue. Once more the reason for this may have been the fact that the sketch-model represented a pose like that of the statue but in reverse, with the weight on the left not the right leg, the left arm not the right extended at the side and the right arm raised. There is no means of telling whether it is by Duquesnoy, nor whether it is a sculptor's or a painter's model (some very similar figures appear in landscapes by Claude Lorrain), but the original ascription cannot be excluded on grounds of quality. The two other models are more straightforward. The first (No. 21), 'Child in terra cotta' (fig. 30),[78] is a typical Duquesnoy sketch-model of enchanting spontaneity, and the second, No. 22 (fig. 31), claimed in the Gherardini catalogue as 'the model of one of the many little angels, which this most skilful artist executed so admirably as to rival in marble the incarnations of the

One (No. 20) is a very small model of excellent quality (fig. 29) described as sketch for the St. Susanna (here called S. Martina) in S. Maria di Loreto.[76] In the middle of the nineteenth century the St. Susanna was still one of the most popular sculptures in Rome (it remained at the top of the charts till it was ousted from its place by the cult of Bernini) and it was

30. *Seated child with a book*, by François Duquesnoy. Terracotta; height 9·4 cm.

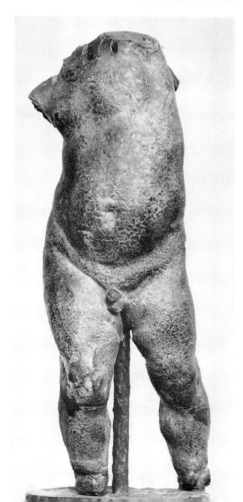

31. *Torso of a child*, probably by François Duquesnoy. Red wax; height 14.5 cm.

magic pencil of Titian in the sister art',[79] is also probably by Duquesnoy, though it is so mutilated that there must remain some element of doubt.

The last two entries in the catalogue, a wax Nativity 'in a more modern style than the others' (No. 23)[80] and a poor version of a well-known bronze plaquette of the Rape of Ganymede (No. 24)[81] do not merit notice, but they are followed by two excited notes, the first signalizing the addition of four further models, a Madonna[82], a 'kneeling friar'[83], 'a sketch of one of the Caricature Statues of the Boboli Gardens'[84] and 'a basso rilievo sketch representing the Rape of the Sabines'[85], attributed to Giovanni Bologna, and the second identifying yet another model as a study for the St. Luke of Giovanni Bologna at Or San Michele.[86] The much damaged terracotta sketch of the Rape of the Sabines has the distinction of being the largest of the Gherardini sculptures, but the possibility that it originated with or near Giovanni Bologna can be ruled out. Finally, after the catalogue was printed there turned up one more model, in red wax over a plaster core, of a bull baited by two dogs (fig. 32), loosely deriving from the animal groups of Giovanni Bologna and Susini and seemingly made as a model for a stopper or seal-handle.

The Gherardini purchase brought to the South Kensington Museum, among much dross, a genuine wax model by Michelangelo, four models by Giovanni Bologna of great historical and artistic interest, two exceptionally fine Florentine terracotta models by

32. *Bull baited by two dogs*, style of Giovanni Bologna. Red wax over plaster; height 7.6 cm.

Francavilla and Battista Lorenzi, and two genuine but unimportant works by Duquesnoy. When filled out, as they were soon to be, with other purchases – such as the Giovanni Bologna model for the Neptune on the Bologna fountain, which was bought at the Woodburn sale on May 19 of the same year; a large wax model for the Rape of the Sabines, which had belonged to Lawrence and was secured on the same occasion; the three Giovanni Bologna wax Passion scenes, which had belonged to Lock and entered the Museum in 1879; the clay model for a River God at Pratolino, bought direct from Florence in 1876; and the Descent from the Cross of Jacopo Sansovino, which arrived with the Gigli-Campana sculptures in 1861 – they formed, as they still form, the richest, most representative collection of High Renaissance sculptors' models in the world.

Notes

1. *History of the Science and Art Department*, London, 1883, p. lix.
2. *The 'Lions' of Florence and its environs*, by an Artist. 2nd ed., Florence, 1852, p. 108.
3. *Catalogue of a Collection of Models in Wax and Terra Cotta by various ancient Italian masters known as the Gherardini Collection, now being exhibited at the Museum of Ornamental Art at Marlborough House*, London, 1854, p. 11. Hereafter referred to as *Gherardini*.
4. *Gherardini*, p. 3.
5. *Gherardini*, p. 11.
6. The drawings are not in the Graphische Sammlung Albertina, nor is there a record of their purchase for the National Library or for the Oesterreichische Museum für Angewandte Kunst. Dr. Walter Koschatzky, to whom I am indebted for this information, has pointed out that at this date the term Austrian government could also have been used of the Austrian authorities in Milan.
7. *Gherardini*, p. 11.
8. *Gherardini*, p. 3.
9. *Gherardini*, p. 15.
10. G. Baroni, *La Parocchia di S. Martino a Majano*, Florence, 1875, pp. lxvii f.
11. Vasari, *Vite*, ed. Milanesi, vii, Florence, 1881, p. 630.
12. R. Borghini, *Il Riposo*, Florence, 1584, pp. 13–14.
13. R. Lightbown, 'England and Italian Sculpture', in *Apollo*, lxxx, 1964, pp. 16, 19n.
14. Vasari, *Vite*, ed. Stecchi & Pagani, vii, Florence, 1772, p. 171n.
15. See note 17 below.
16. *A Catalogue of a valuable Collection . . . consisting of the Antique Statue called Discobolus also a fragment of a Venus and a female bust, allowed to be among the most perfect specimens of ancient art, with the intaglio of Hercules and the Nemean Lion brought from Smyrna, by the late Mr. Fitzhugh, likewise . . . Bronzes and Terra Cottas &c. . . .*, Christie's, April 16, 1785 (Lugt No. 3861).
17. *A Catalogue of a Collection of Models by Michael Angelo, purchased in Florence and brought to this Country by that celebrated Antiquarian, the late Mr. Locke of Norbury Park. These Models form some of Michael Angel's noblest productions, executed by his own hand, and originally formed part of the decorations of the Ducal Palace in Florence . . .*, Debenham & Storr, June 28, 1837.
18. *Gherardini*, pp. 1, 11. J. Pope-Hennessy and R. Lightbown, *Catalogue of Italian Sculpture in the Victoria and Albert Museum*, ii, London, 1964, no. 446, pp. 424–5, iii, fig. 446.
19. *Gherardini*, pp. 5, 12–13.
20. J. C. Robinson, *Catalogue of the Museum of Ornamental Art at Marlborough House*, i, London, 1855, no. 195, p. 37.
21. J. C. Robinson, *Italian Sculpture of the Middle Ages and Period of the Revival of Art*, London, 1862, pp. 147–8.
22. Pope-Hennessy and Lightbown, ii, no. 461, p. 433, iii, fig. 515.
23. *Gherardini*, pp. 5, 12–13.
24. Robinson, 1855, no. 199, p. 39.
25. Robinson, 1862, pp. 131–4.
26. Pope-Hennessy and Lightbown, ii, no. 445, pp. 423–4, iii, fig. 442. The two heads and the left arm of the standing figure were identified and reattached in 1926.
27. *Gherardini*, pp. 6, 12–13. Pope-Hennessy and Lightbown, ii, no. 444, pp. 421–3, iii, figs. 444–5a.
28. Robinson, 1855, no. 208, pp. 41–42.
29. Robinson, 1862, pp. 140–2.
30. *Gherardini*, pp. 6, 12–13. Pope-Hennessy and Lightbown, ii, no. 452, pp. 427–8.
31. Robinson, 1855, no. 197, p. 38.
32. Robinson, 1862, pp. 137–9.
33. *Gherardini*, pp. 6, 12–13. Pope-Hennessy and Lightbown, ii, no. 452, pp. 428–9, ii, fig. 452.
34. Robinson, 1855, p. 41.
35. E. Maclagan, 'The wax models of Michael Angelo in the Victoria and Albert Museum', in *Burlington Magazine*, xliv, 1924, p. 12.
36. *Gherardini*, pp. 6–7, 12–13. Pope-Hennessy and Lightbown, ii, no. 489, pp. 467–8, ii, fig. 487.
37. Robinson, 1855, no. 209, p. 42.
38. *Gherardini*, pp. 7, 12–13. Pope-Hennessy and Lightbown, ii, no. 454, p. 429, iii, fig. 459.
39. Robinson, 1855, no. 196, p. 38.
40. For the engraving to which Robinson refers see M. Rotili, *Fortuna di Michelangelo nell'incisione*, Benevento/Rome, 1965, no. 38, fig. 22.
41. Robinson, 1862, p. 147.
42. *Gherardini*, pp. 7, 12–13. Pope-Hennessy and Lightbown, ii, no. 496, pp. 473–4, iii, fig. 488.
43. Robinson, 1855, no. 198, p. 39.
44. R. Grippi, 'A sixteenth century bozzetto', in *Art Bulletin*, xxxviii, 1956, pp. 143–7.
45. E. Dhanens, *Jean Boulogne: Giovanni Bologna Fiammingo*, Brussels, 1956, pp. 222–4.
46. *Gherardini*, pp. 7, 12–13. Pope-Hennessy and Lightbown, ii, no. 462, p. 434, iii, fig. 460.
47. Robinson, 1855, no. 205, p. 40.
48. *Gherardini*, pp. 7, 12–13. Pope-Hennessy and Lightbown, ii, nos. 456–60, pp. 430–3, iii, fig. 454–8.
49. Borghini, op. cit., p. 20.
50. *Gherardini*, pp. 7, 12–13. Pope-Hennessy and Lightbown, ii, no. 455, pp. 429–30, iii, fig. 453.
51. Robinson, 1855, no. 204, p. 40; 1862, p. 136.
52. *Gherardini*, pp. 8, 14.
53. Robinson, 1855, no. 194, p. 37.
54. Robinson, 1862, p. 152.
55. *Gherardini*, p. 13. Pope-Hennessy and Lightbown, i, no. 181, p. 199, iii, fig. 190.
56. Robinson, 1855, no. 193, p. 37.
57. Robinson, 1862, p. 81.

58. *Gherardini*, pp. 8, 14. Pope-Hennessy and Lightbown, iii, no. 501, pp. 476–7.

59. Robinson, 1855, no. 215, p. 43.

60. *Gherardini*, p. 8. Pope-Hennessy and Lightbown, ii, no. 490, p. 468, fig. 489.

61. *Gherardini*, p. 8. Pope-Hennessy and Lightbown, ii, no. 497, p. 474, fig. 491, 492.

62. Robinson, 1855, nos. 216, 217, pp. 43–44.

63. *Gherardini*, pp. 8–9, 14–15. Pope-Hennessy and Lightbown, ii, no. 518, pp. 491–1, iii, fig. 514.

64. *Vita inedita di Raffaello da Urbino illustrata con note da Angelo Comolli*, Rome, 2 ed. 1791, pp. 75–77: 'Lavorò anchora in scultura, havendo fatto qualche statua, et una ne ho veduta in mano di Giulio Pipi, che presenta un putto, et anche il Giona del popolo è modello suo.'

65. G. Riepenhausen, *Vita di Raffaelle da Urbino*, Rome, 1833, pl. IX.

66. F. Kriegbaum, 'Marmi di Benvenuto Cellini ritrovati', in *L'Arte*, n.s. xi, 1940, p. 21.

67. *Gherardini*, p. 9. Pope-Hennessy and Lightbown, ii, no. 483, pp. 455–6 (as Giovanni Bandini), iii, fig. 482.

68. Robinson, 1855, no. 212, p. 42.

69. Robinson, 1862, pp. 158–9.

70. J. Pope-Hennessy, 'Two models for the tomb of Michelangelo', in *Studien zur Toskanischen Kunst: Festschrift für L. H. Heydenreich*, 1964, pp. 237–43, reprinted in *Essays on Italian Sculpture*, London, 1968, pp. 132–5.

71. *Gherardini*, p. 9.

72. Robinson, 1855, no. 213, pp. 42–43.

73. Robinson, 1862, p. 148.

74. Pope-Hennessy and Lightbown, ii, no. 510, p. 482, fig. 509.

75. Skulpturensammlung no. H.156/53, *Italienische Bronzen der Renaissance und des Barock*, Berlin, Bodemuseum, 1967, p. 26, no. 90, repr. p. 24.

76. *Gherardini*, p. 9. Pope-Hennessy and Lightbown, ii, no. 657, pp. 622–3, iii, fig. 627.

77. Robinson, 1855, no. 220, p. 44.

78. *Gherardini*, p. 9. Pope-Hennessy and Lightbown, ii, no. 634, p. 594, iii, fig. 623.

79. *Gherardini*, p. 10. Pope-Hennessy and Lightbown, ii, no. 635, p. 595, iii, fig. 624.

80. *Gherardini*, p. 10. Robinson, 1855, no. 225, p. 45. Robinson, 1862, p. 182. Pope-Hennessy and Lightbown, ii, no. 615.

81. *Gherardini*, p. 10, Robinson, 1855, no. 211, p. 42.

82. *Gherardini*, p. 10. Robinson, 1855, no. 226, p. 45. Pope-Hennessy and Lightbown, ii, no. 507, p. 480, iii, fig. 499.

83. *Gherardini*, p. 10, Robinson, 1855, no. 218, p. 44. Pope-Hennessy and Lightbown, ii, no. 614, p. 578, iii, fig. 600.

84. *Gherardini*, p. 10, Robinson, 1855, no. 223, p. 44. Pope-Hennessy and Lightbown, ii, no. 613, pp. 577–8, iii, fig. 599.

85. *Gherardini*, p. 10. Pope-Hennessy and Lightbown, ii, no. 612, p. 577, iii, fig. 601.

86. Robinson, 1855, no. 224, p. 45. Pope-Hennessy and Lightbown, no. 508, p. 481, iii, fig. 500.

A Manuscript of Petrarch's Rime and Trionfi

IN the sixties and seventies of the fifteenth century a group of scribes and illuminators in north-east Italy began to experiment in their manuscripts with a new type of script and decoration. Both were based more closely than anything preceding them on classical models. The new style thus created was a distinctive achievement of the Italian Renaissance and it soon spread to other centres both in Italy and beyond. Its influence continued to be felt even in the decoration of the printed book.

The inspiration was partly imaginative and partly archaeological, involving in particular a study of classical inscriptions. James Wardrop has written of this phenomenon as it applies to script, emphasizing the importance of such antiquarians as Ciriaco of Ancona, Giovanni Marcanova of Padua and Fra Giocondo of Verona, and of the outstanding scribes employed by them, especially Felice Feliciano and Bartolomeo Sanvito.[1] These men were all connected with the Veneto, particularly with Venice, Padua and Verona.

In the figurative arts the same archaeological classicism has long been recognized in the work of Andrea Mantegna.[2] Whether or not Mantegna ever himself worked at book illumination, undoubtedly many of the artists who did were from his circle, and were strongly influenced by the same humanistic culture as he was.[3]

An important example of this type of manuscript was acquired by the Victoria and Albert Museum in 1947.[4] It contains Petrarch's *Rime* and *Trionfi* written on parchment. Fols. 1–7 contain the usual index of first lines and are followed by a bifolium, fols. 8–9, which is stained green. On fol. 9ᵛ is a frontispiece to the *Rime* painted in green, silver and gold (fig. 1). It shows a classical figure with a lyre standing before what appears to be a funeral monument with a man and a woman sculpted on it half-length. The man holds a palm and hands a book to the woman. To either side are winged *genii* holding torches symbolizing death. In the foreground on a bush is a cardinal's hat in red surmounting an erased coat of arms. On fol. 10 recto which is not stained, the first sonnet, 'Voi ch'ascoltate', is written in epigraphic capitals in lines of gold alternating with blue, pink, green and purple (fig. 2). The initial 'V' is a faceted capital in pink with gold shredding, placed in a landscape with two rabbits. Below the text is a deep plinth, or perhaps sarcophagus, painted blue, on which a plant scroll in

green forms three roundels in which are water-birds. Above on either side pink square pillars surmounted by blue spiral columns support the entablature, which is also blue.

On fol. 106 the poems on the death of Laura are prefaced by another monument (plate 3). This is left white but surrounded by blue shredding and flanked by green swags with bucrania. At the top, painted in gold chiaroscuro on black, a woman is shown falling headlong from a chariot. Below, the beginning of the poem 'Iovo pensando' is written in blue capitals and introduced by a faceted capital 'I' with blue vine

1. Victoria and Albert Museum, L.101–1947, fol. 9ᵛ. Petrarch and Laura. Apollo (?).

27

2. L.101–1947, fol. 10. Frontispiece to Petrarch's *Il Canzoniere*.

scroll on a crimson ground. Fols. 148–9 are a purple stained bifolium, and on fol. 149ᵛ a third frontispiece introduces the first of the *Trionfi*, the triumph of Love (fig. 3). A winged naked putto in a chariot drawn by two horses is about to fire a flaming arrow. Beside the chariot walks a crowned monarch and behind is a group of men and women captives, all with arms bound behind their backs. Another figure on the ground is crushed by the chariot wheels. In the fore-ground is a pool with two swans swimming in it and beside it the reclining figure of an antique river God. The scene is painted in gold and silver. The gold appears to have been painted in liquid form with a brush, but the lines of silver, which has tarnished and is therefore very hard to see, are always incised as if with a hard point.

On fol. 150 recto the text is again written in lines of gold and coloured epigraphic capitals with a similar faceted initial 'N', this time accompanied by a hind. The plinth is bronze-coloured and on it a reclining figure is painted in chiaroscuro. This has flaked

unfortunately and is very indistinct. The flanking pillars are blue and the entablature pink and blue. Each of the *Trionfi* is introduced by an historiated initial, on fol. 162 a 'Q' with 'Chastity' firing an arrow at 'Love', on fol. 166 a 'Q' with 'Chastity' falling from her chariot (reflecting the composition on fol. 106), on fol. 175 a 'D' with 'Fame' on horseback blowing a trumpet, on fol. 182 a 'D' with 'Time' as a winged naked man holding a dragon, which bites its tail, and on fol. 184ᵛ a 'D' with 'Divinitas' represented as a bearded God the Father with two cherubs.

Unfortunately the Petrarch is not dated and the original owner is unknown since the arms on fol. 9ᵛ have been thoroughly erased. We depend, therefore, entirely on the script and decoration in our attempts to date and place the manuscript. Some evidence of date is provided by the script which has already been attributed by James Wardrop to Bartolomeo Sanvito of Padua.[5] Sanvito was born in 1435 and the earliest dated manuscript connected with him so far is a Virgil in which the capitals of the rubrics are attri-buted to him, the main text being by a different scribe. The colophon states that the Virgil was written 'per Franciscum de Camuciis' – i.e. for, or possibly by, Francesco, in 1463. This was probably in Padua, since the type of white-vine stem decoration used is found in manuscripts written at Sta. Giustina, Padua.[6] Sanvito next appears, again only as a rubricator, in a group of manuscripts datable to the years 1469–71. By then, however, he had moved to Rome, since the manuscripts were written there by Pomponio Leto for Fabio Mazzatosta.[7] It is in Rome that Sanvito's main activity as a scribe took place over the next thirty years or so. At the end of his life he returned to Padua, where he kept a day-book during the years 1505–11, and he was still alive in 1518. He is known to have suffered from arthritis and a shakiness is apparent in the script of his later manuscripts, for example the Cicero now at Eton College, written at Rome in 1498. Many question-marks still attach to Sanvito's earliest activity. In particular another scribe, who had already been discovered by Wardrop and whose *oeuvre* has since been enlarged, Antonio Tophio, wrote a hand which is very hard to distinguish from Sanvito's. Tophio signed a Macrobius in Cambridge as written in Rome in 1466. He was a member of the household of Pope Paul II (1464–71), for whom he wrote another manuscript, which is documented though not signed, in 1469–70.[8]

3. L.101–1947, fol. 149ᵛ. Triumph of Love.
Frontispiece to Petrarch's *Trionfi*.

It is clear from this that the attribution of the script has an important part to play in the dating and placing of the Petrarch. Dr. A. C. de la Mare, who has kindly given me her views on these problems, is in agreement with Wardrop's attribution of the Petrarch to Sanvito.[9] It should be noted that it has the Greek sigla used by Sanvito (though also by other scribes), in the margins on fols. 48 and 50, for example. Since there is no sign of shakiness in the script, the Petrarch must date from the earlier part of Sanvito's career.

In considering the illumination we may start with the technique and the subject matter of the miniatures.

The use of stained parchment in the Petrarch and of a technique of painting in lighter colour, either gold or silver, on darker is a feature of many manuscripts of this group.[10] Such late antique manuscripts as the *Codex purpureus* at Brescia or the Gospels written in silver and gold on purple, which was admired at Verona by St. Bernard of Siena, may have been the model.[11] An interesting sidelight on the technique is provided by Matteo dei Pasti's letter to Piero di Cosimo de'Medici written in Venice in 1441. He has learnt, he says, a most valuable technique, that is to paint with gold using it just like any other colour.[12]

4. Rome, Vatican, Galleria Lapidaria, 80A. Augustan grave relief.

Two of the three frontispieces are modelled on classical prototypes. That to the *Rime* (fig. 1) recalls a very common type of classical grave relief. One such relief of the Augustan period, now in the Vatican, achieved a certain fame in the Renaissance (fig. 4).[13] It was copied for the epitaph of Stefano and Maddalena Satri in S. Omobono, Rome, *c.*1495, and a little later received the inscriptions 'Fidei simulacrum' 'Amor', 'Honor' and 'Veritas'. If these ideas, which Mrs. Williams Lehmann traces to the influence of Marsilio Ficino, could have been associated with this or other similar monuments even earlier, the use of such a model for this frontispiece would be explained.

The monument was later included in various printed collections of inscriptions, and Mrs. Williams Lehmann has suggested that a woodcut of it in one of these is 'strongly influenced by Northern Italian painting probably of the Paduan region' and that the cut 'probably derives from an illustrated antiquarian text in which the now famous Vatican monument was reproduced and discussed'. When we consider that Sanvito was a friend of the antiquarian Fra Giocondo of Verona and made a dozen or so copies of his *Sylloge* of classical inscriptions,[14] we can easily see how the artist might have known this very monument, though since it was so common a type, one cannot, of course, be sure of this.

The lyre-playing figure on fol. 9ᵛ (fig. 1) is clearly also classical in spirit and is to be interpreted either as an 'Apollo Musagetes' or by comparison with a

Virgil in Paris (fig. 5)[15] as Orpheus, in either case an obvious classical counterpart of Petrarch as poet. Comparison with the Virgil manuscript suggests that the two lyre-playing figures might have a common model, though it seems unlikely that this was an antique figure, since in classical examples the lyre is usually either played by a seated figure or, if by a standing figure, is rested on a pillar or other object.[16]

The falling female figure on fol. 106 which symbolizes the death of Laura (plate 3), on the other hand, certainly derives from a classical composition of

5. Paris, Bibliothèque Nationale, latin 11309, fol. 4ᵛ. Frontispiece to Virgil's Georgics. Orpheus charming the beasts.

the fall of Phaethon from the chariot of the sun. The actual model used may be reflected in a Renaissance cameo now in Florence (fig. 6).[17] In the surviving classical carved reliefs Eridanus, the Po, into which Phaethon fell, is shown as a classical river God. In the cameo, presumably for reasons of space, only the river God's urn is included and this appears as an otherwise unexplained detail in the Petrarch miniature. A river God does, however, appear on fol. 149ᵛ of the Petrarch (fig. 3, lower left) unconnected with main scene, so that the artist may also have known of the reliefs. The chariot is also very similar to that in the cameo.

The use of the Phaethon iconography to symbolize the death of Laura is not motivated by any specific comparison in the text. Petrarch, however, refers frequently to Laura as his 'sun' and in the famous note concerning her death made in his copy of Virgil (now in the Ambrosiana, Milan) he writes 'ab hac luce lux illa subtracta est'.[18]

In his diary kept in the years 1505 to 1511 Sanvito refers to a representation of Phaethon by 'Gasparo' owned by himself.[19] The description of it as a 'phetonte . . . tochato de aquarella' can hardly apply to the present miniature drawn in gold, and suggests a single sheet not a manuscript. Perhaps it was a copy of the cameo or of one of the reliefs. It may even have been used for his composition by our artist.

Whilst the theme of a triumphant procession is a classical one, the scene of the Triumph of Love as on

7. Venice, Biblioteca Marciana, Lat. II. 39 (2999), fol. 7.ᵛ

fol. 149ᵛ (fig. 3) is fairly standard in illuminated manuscripts of the *Trionfi* and is probably not based on any particular classical model. In Florentine examples the chariot is usually shown frontally, whereas the procession in file with a King at the head with arms bound behind his back is found more often in examples from north Italy.[20]

Before considering the identity of the artists of the Petrarch, we may note the two types of architectural frontispiece and the type of initials, both features of many manuscripts made in north-east Italy. Mrs. Corbett has charted the development of the architectural frontispiece. She points out that the earlier form used is a small aedicule with the title written on it copying many actual classical monuments (fig. 7).[21] Later a larger triumphal arch surrounds the whole first page of text including its title or heading. I have suggested elsewhere that this may have been in part due to the introduction of printing, since the artist was then faced with a pre-ordained block of type with only the margins to embellish.[22] Certainly

6. Florence, Museo degli argenti. Cameo showing the fall of Phaethon (after Furtwängler).

several early examples occur in incunables printed in Venice, and two artists seem to have pioneered the style about 1470, Giovanni Correnti and the so-called 'Maestro dei Putti'.[23] The use of both the earlier type and of the later, still in a rather simple form, suggests a date around 1465–70 for the Petrarch.

The initials of the Petrarch are of the faceted type which have been studied by Professor Meiss and which appear already in a Ptolemy, Cosmography, of 1457 and in the Albi Strabo of c.1458–59.[24] On fol. 106 of the Petrarch the initial 'I' (plate 3), is entwined with a classical-looking vine scroll in blue on a crimson background which is very reminiscent of that in the Albi Strabo. This again leads us to the same Veneto-Paduan milieu in the 1460's to early 1470's.

The illumination of the Petrarch is by two artists. The first painted the frontispieces on fols. 10 (fig. 2) and 150 and all the historiated initials. A clue to his identity is given by the landscape of the initials on fols. 10 and 150. The little hills and the wavy clouds painted in gold on blue have a Lombard flavour and recall the style of Belbello da Pavia. A very similar type of landscape occurs in the work of Franco dei Russi and can be seen in a signed cutting in the British Museum (fig. 8).[25] Commenting on this landscape style Professor Levi D'Ancona suggested an early contact between Franco, who was born at Mantua, and Belbello, who was at work there on the illumination of a Missal for Barbara of Brandenburg in 1461.

Franco first appears in company with Taddeo Crivelli as one of the two illuminators to whom the main part

of the decoration of the great Bible of Borso d'Este, duke of Ferrara, was assigned in 1455. Already by that date he must have been an established artist. The last payment recorded to him was in 1465, the Bible having been finished in 1461.[26] In addition to this documented work there are three signed miniatures, the cutting in the British Museum already mentioned, another signed cutting in a private collection in Milan, and a frontispiece to a Bible printed by Vindelinus de Spira in Venice in 1471, which is now in Wolfenbüttel.

Another manuscript in the British Museum, with two illuminated architectural frontispieces, has also been attributed to Franco by comparison with these signed works (fig. 9).[27] It contains an *oratio panegyrica* delivered on behalf of Padua University by Bernardo Bembo on the occasion of the accession of Cristoforo Moro, Doge of Venice 1462–71. The manuscript bears the arms of Cardinal Ludovico Scarampi (whose portrait, now in Berlin, was painted by Mantegna), and it may have been presented to the cardinal in 1462 when he was enrolled as a Venetian patrician. It must certainly date before Scarampi's death in 1465. It has the same fine coloured epigraphic capitals as the Petrarch, and Bartolomeo Sanvito is again almost certainly the scribe.

If we compare the Petrarch frontispieces and initials with these manuscripts, in addition to the similar landscape already commented on, we find similar figure types, for example the God the Father on fol. 184[v] and the Creator on fol. 1 of volume I of the Wolfenbüttel Bible. The rabbits on fol. 10 with their

8. London, British Museum, Add. 20916, fol. 1. Triumph of a scholar (?).

EIVSDEM FRANCI
SCI PETRARCAE DE
MORTE DOMINAE
LAVREAE RHŸTHMI
INCI PIVNT·

O VO PENSANDO ET
NEL PENSIER M'ASSALE
VNA PIETA SI FORTE
DI ME STESSO
CHE MI CONDVCE SPES
SO·

PLATE I.
L 101-1947 fol. 106
Allegorical
representation of the
Death of Laura

9. London, British Museum, Add. 14787, fol. 6ᵛ. Bernardo Bembo, Oratio gratulatoria to Doge Cristoforo Moro. Copy presented to Cardinal Scarampi.

slit ears and the ducks with their odd swelling necks can also be exactly paralleled in the Bible and in the signed cutting (figs. 2, 8).

The next datable manuscript so far attributed to Franco is a copy of Libanius' Letters translated by Francesco Zambecari written by Matteo Contugi for Federigo da Montefeltro at Urbino. This is almost certainly the copy made for presentation in 1475.[28] That Franco was still in Venice in 1471 or soon after is suggested both by the Wolfenbüttel Bible and by two illuminated copies of Tortelli's *de orthographia* printed by Nicholas Jenson in Venice in that year.[29] One of these has a triumph scene of classical type painted in gold on purple (fig. 10) which is comparable in

technique to fol. 149ᵛ of the Petrarch (fig. 3). We may bear in mind, therefore, the years 1462–75 as the most likely time for Sanvito and Franco dei Russi to have collaborated on the Petrarch.

The second artist, who painted fols. 9ᵛ, 106 and 149ᵛ (figs. 1, 4 and plate 3), is much closer in style to Mantegna than is Franco dei Russi. He copies Mantegna's drapery with its clinging folds based on antique sculpture, and also his rocky terrain with its outcrops and pebbles and overhanging precipices. The conventional bushy-topped trees of fol. 10 (fig. 2) are replaced by twisting trunks and branches silhouetted against the background, and by foliage in which each leaf is picked out separately (fig. 3). The second artist's compositions are more subtle and complex than Franco's, and the quality of the miniatures is much more classical than anything Franco achieved.

Two closely related miniatures are both in manuscripts now in the Biblioteca Ambrosiana, Milan. They occur in a Caesar, A. 243 inf., and a Book of Hours, Sp.13. On fol. 3ᵛ of the Caesar there is an architectural structure with a plinth supported by eagles with the title of the work written on it (fig. 11).[30] Below there is a battle scene with cavalry and foot soldiers in a *mélée*. This, like fol. 149ᵛ of the Petrarch, is painted in gold and silver on a purple-dyed leaf, which makes it hard to see in the photograph, and even in the original, since the silver has tarnished. In the Hours a frontispiece on fol. iiiᵛ shows the 'Adoration of the Magi' with again an inscribed plaque (fig. 12).[31] This is also painted in gold and silver on a pink-stained bifolium.

Comparison with the Petrarch miniatures reveals stylistic and technical similarities which show they are by the same artist. The stance of the left hand of the three Magi is nearly identical with that of the lyre-playing figure on fol. 9ᵛ of the Petrarch, for example, and so is their drapery (figs. 1, 12). The details of the pilasters on the same folio of the Petrarch are almost identical with those in the frontispiece of the Caesar. In all the scenes the figures move in a space like a shallow stage platform.

Unfortunately there is no evidence for the date or the original owners of either of the two Ambrosiana manuscripts. The Book of Hours is closely related to the Petrarch in another way, since its main decoration has for long been attributed to Franco dei Russi.[32] All the features of Franco's style noted above recur in the Hours. Some of the miniatures and initials have an identical type of vine-scroll to that on fol. 10 of the Petrarch, and in this Franco appears to be influenced by Paduan models.

The Book of Hours is somewhat unusual in having been written in humanistic script. This is again the formal round script with coloured epigraphic capitals of which we have already spoken. It was thought to be written by Sanvito by Professor Levi D'Ancona following Professor Millard Meiss, and with their verdict Dr. de la Mare is in agreement.[33]

The Book of Hours and the Petrarch were produced by the same scribe and the same two artists in collaboration, therefore, probably at the same moment, and quite possibly for the same patron.[34]

Dr. de la Mare would also attribute the script of the Caesar to Sanvito. Here a problem arises, however. The first page of text of the Caesar has a rich border of plant scroll in gold and silver with red flowers set on a black background (fig. 13). In this are set medallions with vignettes with city or landscape views or with animals. The border is unusual and there is no difficulty in recognizing the same hand in two other manuscripts. The first of these is the Cambridge Macrobius already referred to as written by Antonio Tophio in Rome in 1466. It has a similar scroll and medallions with a background of scarlet and black. The second is an Aulus Gellius in the British Museum whose script has also been attributed to Tophio by Mr. Alfred Fairbank.[35] Here again there is the unusual feature of a black background to a similar scroll in gold and silver in initials on fols. 180 and 195. I do not know of anything like these borders in documented Venetian manuscripts and since the Macrobius was written in Rome, it seems probable that the Caesar was too, and that the border on fol. 4 and the initials were painted there by this, probably Roman, illuminator.

Another manuscript with a bearing on our problem is now in Venice and was written for Ludovico Trevisan, patriarch of Aquileia, who died in 1465.[36] It is very small and is written throughout in gold on purple-stained parchment. Once again the scribe is probably Bartolomeo Sanvito. The title of the work, the *Vita Malchi* ascribed to St. Jerome, is written on a little aedicule of the type mentioned earlier (fig. 7). On the plinth there is an unusual form of decoration to simulate marbling, and an identical convention is used on fol. 9ᵛ of the Petrarch (fig. 1). The other details of this and a second frontispiece in the Venice manuscript agree, so far as they can be compared, with the Petrarch frontispiece. These are small matters for comparison, but nevertheless it seems likely that the illumination of the *Vita Malchi* is by the second artist of the Petrarch. It displays the same archaeological learning and it is still very early to find this kind of decoration.[37]

From what has been said, it is evident that both the place where the Petrarch was illuminated and the identity of the second artist remain problematic. The evidence points to the Petrarch having been made in just those years when artists and scribes from the Veneto might have gone to Rome to seek the patronage of the Venetian Pope Paul II (1464–71), and in which we know that Sanvito himself went to Rome. On the whole it seems likely that the Petrarch was made in Venice or Padua since we know independently that Franco dei Russi illuminated another manuscript, the Bembo *oratio*, written by Sanvito in Venice or Padua. Though the stained leaves in the Petrarch might have been added later, this cannot have been so of fol. 106 which is also illuminated by the second artist, and which is integral to the book. It is clear that Franco knew this miniature on fol. 106 since he copied it in his historiated initial on fol. 166. The Petrarch must have been illuminated by the two artists in the same centre concurrently and since we have no evidence that Franco was in Rome at this time, that place is likely to have been Venice. The *Vita Malchi* and the Ambrosiana Hours are no doubt contemporary or a little earlier. The Ambrosiana Caesar on the other hand was perhaps written and decorated in Rome a little later, since it can be connected with the Macrobius written by Tophio in Rome in 1466. In that case our second artist may, like Sanvito, have moved to Rome from Venice and illuminated the frontispiece of the Caesar there.

This gives us some information to work on, in trying to identify this second artist. Nevertheless, the possibility of such an identification will have to await further study of script and illumination both in Venice and in Rome during this period. The names of a number of artists active in these years are known, but art historians have not yet succeeded in finding works securely documented as being by them. One such artist is Gasparo Romano, who is known from contem-

---

10. Paris, Bibliothèque Nationale, vélins 526. Frontispiece of Tortelli, *de orthographia*, printed Venice, 1471.

IOANNIS TORTELLII ARRETINI COMMENTARIORVM GRAM
MATICORVM DE ORTHOGRAPHIA DICTIONVM E GRAECIS
TRACTARVM PROOEMIVM INCIPIT AD SANCTISSIMVM
PATREM NICOLAVM QVINTVM PONTIFICEM MAXIMVM.

OPERAM OLIM BEATISSIME
pater Nicolae.v.summe pontifex com
mentaria quædam grammatica condere:
qbus omnem litterariam antiquitatem
& orthographiæ ratione cũ opportunis
historiis pro poetarum declaratione cõ
nectere conabar:pfuturus sane pro mea
uirili studiosis linguæ latinæ. interim
ab aliis studiis negociisq; familiaribus
interceptus illa prorsus relinquere: at
que longo tempore abiicere uisus sum.
Sed nuper cum apud Alatrium campa
niæ oppidum ex aeris romani molestia
secessisse:ea absoluere quorundam ami
corum rogatu conatus sum:ac sic quoq;
ad calcem ux usque perduxi opus magnum uarium & diffusum:atque illud tuæ
sanctitati a qua uelut fonte omnia mea bona fluxerunt : dedicare constitui . non
quidem ut nstitutionibus grammaticis poetarumq; historiuculis tua beatitudo
indigeat: qui cæteros in doctrinis oibus etiã minutis ex sũma igenii memoriæq;
felicitate præellis:Sed ut i tua illa bibliotheca:quam omnium quæ fueꞃt præstã
tissimam comparas aliquo pacto collocare possis. Nã lic& ex magnificétia animi
tui:qui nõ nii clarissima in litteris ædificiisque:& rebus cæteris aggrederis: uiros
utriusq; linguæ eruditissimos ex omnibus fere terris ueluti ad uirtutis quoddam
asylum conuicaueris:quos ut suum possint excolere ingenium:laudemq; sibi pa
rare :& aliquid conficere:quod posteritati prodesse possit maximis premiis affe
ceris.nõ tamé eterrebor : et ego aliquid pro mea paruitate tuæ bibliothecæ offerre.
Quam tameti ex clarissimis altissimarum doctrinarum auctoribus fulcire cupis:
quia tamé & minores aliquando facultates necessariæ sunt:nõ dedignaberis pro
tua sapientia:eiã minorum facultatũ libros inserere. Video enim quãtis impéfis
et sumptibus qiantaq; diligentia græca oratorum uolumina:historicorũ et phi
losophorũ atq; umorum theologorũ in latinam liguam traduci procuras. Video
quantam adhie s curam in antiquorũ nostrorum operibus exquirendis:quæ de
perdita credebatur:Ita ut non nullos ad diuersas extremasq; mundi partes pro
re hac:multis cũ difficultatibus et impésis destinaueris. Quæ cum magnis in
rebus effeceris ncpigebit etiã minorum facultatum libros in ipsa tua bibliotheca
reponere:& maxime illos:qui de grammaticæ facultate loquuntur. Quæ auctore
Quintiliano:nisi oratoris futuri fundaméta fideliter iecerit:quicqd superstruxerit
corruet.Et nisi æqo longior essem:complura possem i medium exempla afferre:
quibus facile cogbsceret:quot ex huiusmodi artis negligentia in poetis oratori
bus:& historicis qutidie errores insurgunt:quot in iure ciuili:medicinæque arte:
et cæteris facultatibus interpretationes ineptissimæ singulis afferũt diebus : quot

porary references to have worked in Rome as illuminator for Cardinal Giovanni d'Aragona.[38] If he were identical with the Gasparo from whose hand Sanvito possessed the drawing of Phaethon 'tochato d'aquarella' he might be a possible candidate for identification as

12. Milan, Biblioteca Ambrosiana, MS. SP.13, fol. iii. Adoration of the Magi. Frontispiece to Book of Hours.

11. Milan, Biblioteca Ambrosiana, MS. A.243 inf., fol. 3ᵛ. Frontispiece to Caesar.

the second artist of the Petrarch. Works so far attributed to him, however, do not seem compatible with such an identification. The same is true of Lauro Padovano, who was an illuminator and was connected with and probably a contemporary of Sanvito.[39]

An attribution to a third, equally problematic, figure is recorded in the Victoria and Albert Museum's typescript catalogue. This is Jacometto Veneziano, who is known to have been an illuminator as well as a painter.[40] Comparison here is with two small portraits formerly in the Liechtenstein collection, now in the Robert Lehman collection, New York. In spite of certain difficulties, these are generally accepted as being the portraits described by Marcantonio Michiel in the house of Alvise Contarini in 1543 and ascribed by him to Jacometto. On the reverse of the portrait of the male sitter is a figure seated in a landscape (fig. 14). It is painted in gold chiaroscuro on purple and is technically rather similar to the third frontispiece of the Petrarch (fig. 3). The reverse is damaged and even in the original is difficult to see. The treatment of the landscape, however, and of the drapery both here and in the portraits is more impressionistic than is the detailed linear drawing of the miniatures. Even granted that the portraits are considerably later, dating presumably from *c*.1480, it would be difficult to maintain with any confidence that the artist is the same.[41]

In the circumstances any identification of our second artist would be premature. His importance is not to be denied, however. His miniatures are an early instance of a very sophisticated kind of antiquarianism. At the same time in the miniature of the death of Laura there is a hint of a more personal and elegiac interpretation of classical mythology, which in some ways looks forward to the later classical and allegorical pictures of Giovanni Bellini and of Giorgione.[42]

13. Milan, Biblioteca Ambrosiana, MS. A.243 inf., fol. 4. Caesar.

14. New York, Robert Lehman collection. Reverse of a portrait ascribed to Jacometto Veneziano.

Notes

1. J. Wardrop, *The script of humanism*, 1963, pp. 13 ff.

2. P. Kristeller *Andrea Mantegna* (English edition by S. A. Strong), London, 1901, ch. I, and for Mantegna's study of classical inscriptions, *ib.* pp. 175–6, and of statuary, M. Meiss, *Andrea Mantegna as illuminator*, Hamburg, 1957, p. 21.

3. Meiss, *op. cit.*, attributes two mss. to Mantegna's studio and in part to his own hand, though the attribution has not been universally accepted. For illuminators in the Mantegna circle see M. Bonicatti, *Aspetti dell'umanesimo nella pittura Veneta dal 1455 al 1515*, 1964, especially for Giorgio Culinović (Schiavone); G. Mariani Canova, 'Le origini della miniatura rinascimentale Veneta e il maestro dei Putti (Marco Zoppo?)', *Arte Veneta*, xx, 1966, pp. 73–86; M. Bonicatti, 'Contributi marginali alla pittura Veneta della Rinascita', *Rivista dell'Istituto nazionale d'Archeologia e Storia dell'Arte*, N.S. VII, 1958, pp. 248–91 for Giovanni Correnti; J. J. G. Alexander, 'A Vergil illuminated by Marco Zoppo', *Burlington Magazine*, CXI, 1969, pp. 514–7; G. Mariani Canova, *La miniatura Veneta del rinascimento, 1450–1500*, 1969.

4. L.101–1947. Sotheby's, 16–18 Dec. 1946, lot 560, pl. x, 'the property of a gentleman'. The MS. contains the book label of C. W. Dyson Perrins (no. 135) but was not included in G. F. Warner's catalogue. Fol. 10 is reproduced in *Roman Lettering. A book of alphabets and inscriptions*, London, Victoria and Albert Museum, 1958, pl. 9. The MS. has been rebacked and resewn and the panels remounted. They have cameo type medallions of Pompey and Diana. The binding was described as Milanese (?), *c.*1500, in the Sotheby collection. Comparisons can, however, also be made with bindings attributed to Rome by T. De Marinis, *La legatura artistica in Italia nei secoli XV e XVI*, I, 1960, nos. 454, 473, 606.

5. *Script of Humanism*, p. 51.

6. London, British Museum, Harley MS. 2726. A. Fairbank, 'More of Sanvito', *Journal of the Society of Scribes and Illuminators*, no. 42, 1965, pl. 1. For the decoration cf. J. J. G. Alexander, A. C. de la Mare, *The Italian manuscripts in the library of Major J. R. Abbey*, 1969, no. 41, pl. LIIIa, from Sta. Giustina.

7. See J. Ruysschaert, 'Miniaturistes "romains" sous Pie II', in *Enea Silvio Piccolomini – Papa Pio II* (Atti del convegno per il quinto centenario della morte e altri scritti raccolti da Domenico Maffei), Siena, 1968, pp. 274–5.

8. For Tophio see A. Fairbank 'Antonio Tophio', *Journal of the Society for Italic Handwriting*, no. 45, 1965, pp. 8–14 and A. C. de la Mare, *op. cit.*, (note 6 above) p. xxx. The script of the Cambridge Macrobius is reproduced by Wardrop, *Script of Humanism*, pl. 4. The unidentified coat of arms does not appear to be that of the original owner.

9. Wardrop, *Script of Humanism*, p. 34.

10. Coloured vellum is referred to in Sanvito's day-book from which extracts were published by S. de Kunert, 'Un padovano ignoto ed un suo memoriale de'primi anni del Cinquecento (1505–11)', *Bolletino del Museo Civico di Padova*, x, 1907, pp. 1 ff.

11. *Codices Latini Antiquiores*, ed. E. A. Lowe, III, 1938, no. 281, IV, 1947, no. 481. The earliest mention of the practice quoted by Th. Birt, *Das antike Buchwesen*, Berlin, 1882, p. 108, is St. Jerome's condemnation of the extravagance of such books whilst beggars starve: 'inficiuntur membranae colore purpureo, aurum liquescit in litteras, gemmis codices vestiuntur: et nudus fores earum Christus emoritur', Ep. XVIII ad Eustochium, IV.2.

12. The letter is printed in *Il Buonarroti*, ser. ii, IV, 1869, pp. 78–9: 'oro masinato, ch'io lo dipingho come ogni altro collore'. Matteo was painting some *Trionfi* for Piero! He is known to have worked at illumination but nothing by him has so far been identified. Another source for such gold chiaroscuro paintings may have been late antique and early Christian gold glass medallions.

13. Vatican, Galleria lapidaria 80A. P. L. Williams, 'Two Roman reliefs in Renaissance disguise', *Journal of the Warburg and Courtauld Institutes*, IV, 1940–1, pp. 47–66, pl. 11a. A somewhat similar title piece introduces Pontano, *de principe*, Vat. Urb. Lat. 225, showing Duke Alfonso of Calabria on the monument. T. De Marinis, *La biblioteca napoletana dei re d'Aragona*, II, Milan, 1947, p. 134, IV, tav. 199.

14. Wardrop, *op. cit.*, pp. 27 ff.

15. Bibliothèque nationale, latin 11309. See Alexander, *op. cit.*, (note 3 above) suggesting a date of *c.*1463. At least some of the classical looking details may derive from other renaissance artists. For example F. Wittgens pointed out that the sphinx throne of the Virgin in the Ambrosiana Hours (fig. 12) copies Donatello's bronze of the Virgin in the Santo at Padua. See below note 31.

16. M. Wegner, *Die Musensarkophage*, Berlin, 1966.

17. A. Furtwängler, *Die antiken Gemmen*, I, 1900, Taf. LVIII.2, II, p. 263. E. Kris, *Meister und Meisterwerke der Steinschneidekunst in der Italienischen Renaissance*, 1929, pp. 30, 153, pl. 14, fig. 43. C. Piacenti Aschengreen, *Il Museo degli Argenti a Firenze*, 1968, p. 178, no. 883. I am grateful to Dr. Piacenti for informing me of the Cameo's whereabouts and for the references cited. Kris dates the Cameo to the early 16th Century. Possibly both it and the miniature derive from a lost source therefore. For the iconography in general and especially the classical sculptured reliefs see C. Robert, *Die antiken Sarkophag – Reliefs*, III. 3, Berlin, 1919, pp. 405–35, Abb. 332–50. One of these reliefs was copied in the *Codex Escurialensis* on fol. 40, see H. Egger, *Codex Escurialensis*, 1906. The pose of the falling figure with arms above the head was never quite lost sight of in the Middle Ages, though divorced from its context. To give two examples: the fall of Simon Magus in a 10th century Sacramentary from Fulda, Göttingen, Univ. bibl., theol. fol. 231, fol. 93; and St. Cuthbert reproved by the Angel, Bede, Life of Cuthbert, Oxford, University College MS. 165, p. 8. Actually used in the Phaethon scene it occurs in an Ovid moralizatus in Gotha, Landesbibliothek, I.98, Padua or Bologna, early 15th century, and in the Caxton Ovid, Magdalene College, Cambridge, which will be studied by Mrs. K. M. Scott. I am grateful to her for discussing this iconography with me.

18. I am very grateful to Professor C. Grayson, Oxford, for suggesting this interpretation of the miniature to me. In 1533 Michelangelo made three drawings of the fall of Phaethon for presentation to Cavalieri. He interpreted the fall as the pre-

sumptuous Phaethon being consumed by the thunderbolts representing the strength of his passions. E. Panofsky, *Studies in iconology*, Harper Torchbooks, 1962, pp. 219–20. Ch. de Tolnay, *Michelangelo III. The Medici Chapel*, Princeton, 1948, pp. 112–5. If the artist of the Petrarch had had some such thought in mind he would surely have represented Petrarch not Laura as thrown from the chariot. Petrarch's dreams foretelling the death of Laura by a series of allegorical images (poem no. 323) are illustrated in two copies of the *Rime* both probably written by Sanvito. Cf. Alexander and de la Mare, *op. cit.*, (note 6 above) p. 110.

19. S. de Kunert, *op. cit.* and also 'Due codici miniati da Girolamo Campagnola?', *Rivista d'Arte*, XII, 1930, p. 68. The 'Phetonte' was lent to Guilio Campagnola in Venice on June 14, 1507. On August 30, 1508 a 'triompho' also by Gasparo was lent to Fra. Bernardino at S. Pietro Viminario (Monselice).

20. V. Massena, prince d'Essling, E. Müntz, *Pétrarque. L'illustration de ses écrits*, Paris, 1902. Alexander and de la Mare, *op. cit.*, (note 6 above), pp. 106–10, pl. XLVIII. A classical triumphal procession winding through the Arch of Titus is shown in a Caesar written by Sanvito, Biblioteca Casanatense, Rome, MS. 453, fol. i, another purple dyed leaf.

21. M. Corbett, 'The Architectural Title-Page', *Motif*, XII, 1964, pp. 49–62. See also Ch. Mitchell, 'Felice Feliciano Antiquarius', *Proceedings of the British Academy*, XLVII, 1961, pp. 197–221, espec. pl. XXXVIII.

22. Alexander and de la Mare, *op. cit.* (note 6 above), pp. xxxviii–ix.

23. See G. Mariani Canova and M. Bonicatti, *op. cit.* (note 3 above).

24. Meiss, *op. cit.*, ch. III.

25. Add. 20916, fol. 1. For Franco see M. Bonicatti, 'Aspetti dell'illustrazione del libro nell' ambiente padano del secondo '400', *Rivista D'Arte*, XXXII, 1957, pp. 119–20, fig. 8; M. Levi D'Ancona, 'Contributi al problema di Franco dei Russi', *Commentari*, XI, 1960, pp. 39–40, tav. XIII, fig. 3; Bonicatti, *Aspetti dell'umanesimo, op. cit.* (note 3 above), pp. 11 n.1, 12–13, 46 n.2, 47, 168, fig. 19; L. Michelini Tocci, *Il Dante Urbinate della Biblioteca Vaticana (Codice Urbinate Latino 365)*, (Codices e Vaticanis Selecti XXIX), 1965; G. Mariani Canova, *Miniatura veneta, op. cit.*, pp. 104–6.

26. H. J. Hermann, 'Zur Geschichte der Miniaturmalerei am Hofe der Este in Ferrara', *Jahrbuch der Kunsthistorischen Sammlungen des allerhöchsten Kaiserhauses*, XXI, 1900, pp. 249–53 prints the accounts.

27. Add. MS. 14787. *British Museum. Reproductions from illuminated manuscripts*, II, 1923, pl. XLVII; Levi D'Ancona, *op. cit.*, p. 35, tav. XII, fig. 1; Mariani Canova, *Miniatura veneta*, fig. 20–1.

28. Urb. Lat. 336. Bonicatti, *op. cit.*, pp. 118–9, fig. 7 and Levi D'Ancona, *op. cit.*, p. 40, tav. XII, fig. 2; Exh., *Miniature del Rinascimento*, Vatican, 1950, no. 58, tav. VII.

29. Paris, Bibliothèque Nationale, vélins 526, 527. Exh., *Trésors des bibliothèques d'Italie*, Paris, Bibliothèque Nationale, 1950, nos. 221, 220; Mariani Canova, *Miniatura veneta*, pp. 105–6, 146, pl. 25–6. Vélins 526 bears the arms of Malatesta and on the carriage on the elephant's back appear the initials 'A.R.' (Ariminensis?).

30. R. Cipriani, *Codici miniati dell'Ambrosiana*, (Fontes Ambrosiani XL), 1968, pp. 159–60, with earlier literature. I have only seen fols. 3ᵛ–4 since the MS was on exhibition when I was in Milan and depend on photos for the rest. The added arms on fol. 4 are of Borromeo.

31. F. Wittgens, 'Illuminated manuscripts in the Ambrosiana', *Burlington Magazine*, LXIII, 1933, p. 63, pl. 1 c.

32. Wittgens says 'Russi inspired the miniaturist'. Bonicatti ascribes the MS. with query dating it to c.1470–80. Levi D'Ancona unequivocally attributes it to Franco and places it in date between Add. 14787 and Urb. Lat. 336. Mariani Canova attributes only fol. 1 to Franco and the rest to an inferior hand. For bad colour reproductions see D. Formaggio, C. Basso, *A Book of Miniatures*, London, 1962, pl. 102–3. A modern inscription states the MS. was owned by Bianca Maria Sforza, but there is no evidence for this. See E. Pellegrin, *La Bibliothèque des Visconti et des Sforza*, 1955, p. 374.

33. *Commentari*, XI, 1960, p. 40 n. 21. Proposing a date c.1470–5, by which time, however, Sanvito was, as we have seen, in Rome.

34. The most likely candidate is Cardinal Francesco Gonzaga (1461–83) for whom Sanvito wrote part of a Homer in 1477, Vat. Gr. 1626. Other cardinals for whom Sanvito wrote MSS. were Scarampi, d.1465 and Raphael Riario cr. 1477, d.1521. For the library of Cardinal Francesco Gonzaga see *Mostra dei codici Gonzagheschi*, Mantua, Biblioteca comunale, 1966 (catalogo a cura di Ubaldo Meroni), pp. 59–60. There is an unpublished inventory of 1483.

35. *Journal of the Society for Italic Handwriting*, no. 45 (*op. cit.* note 8 above). The Burney manuscript was later owned by Lodovico Maria Sforza, Il Moro. See E. Pellegrin, *op. cit.*, p. 365.

36. Venice, Marciana, Lat. II. 39 (2999), Jerome, Lives of Sts. Malchus and Paulus. *Mostra storica, nazionale della miniatura*, Rome, Palazzo Venezia, 1954, no. 631.

37. Three MSS. and a drawing seem to me also to be close to our artist. They are i) Oxford, Bodleian Library, MS. D'Orville 11, erased arms of a cardinal. See O. Pächt, J. J. G. Alexander, *Illuminated manuscripts in the Bodleian Library*, II. *Italian school*, 1970, no. 617. ii) London, Victoria and Albert Museum, L.2464–1950. Ars Geomantiae. Erased coat of arms. The script is probably by Sanvito. There is an historiated initial by a weak hand on fol. 1. It should be compared with the miniatures in a Greek Gospels written for Cardinal Francesco Gonzaga in 1478, British Museum, Harley 5790. In addition on fol. 1 there is a border with zodiac signs painted in gold on purple. I suspect this is by our artist but it is too damaged to be certain. The text connects the MS. with the Gonzaga library. iii) Vienna, Nationalbibliothek, Cod. 1591 is partly by the so-called 'Maestro dei Putti'. Fol. 16 seems to be by our artist, however, and has an architectural frontispiece incorporating a miniature of Christ's entry into Jerusalem. Above are two eagles with swags, a detail found also in the Ambrosiana Caesar, which is copied from the column of Trajan. See H. J. Hermann, *Beschreibendes Verzeichnis der illuminierten HSS. in Oesterreich*, Bd.VI.2, *Oberitalien: Venetien*, 1931, pp. 190–200. iv) A drawing of tritons and sea horses which is now in the Ecole des

Beaux-Arts, Paris. See K. T. Parker, *North Italian drawings of the Quattrocento*, 1927, pl. 16 and F. Heinemann, *Giovanni Bellini e i Belliniani*, 1963, fig. 875 (V. 215).

38. T. De Marinis, *La biblioteca napoletana dei re d'Aragona*, I, 1952, pp. 86, 156. See also M. Levi D'Ancona 'Un libro d'ore di Francesco Marmitta da Parma', *Bolletino dei Musei Civici Veneziani*, XII. 4, 1967, p. 27 n. 16 and J. J. G. Alexander, 'Notes on some Veneto-Paduan illuminated books of the Renaissance', *Arte Veneta*, XXIII, 1969, p.20 n. 36.

39. See G. Robertson, *Giovanni Bellini*, 1968, ch. III. The most likely group of illuminations that might be attributed to him is that listed in Alexander and de la Mare, *op. cit.* pp. 107–10, in MSS. many of which are written by Sanvito. Lauro is also mentioned in Sanvito's diary, 4 October 1510, as the illuminator of a 'David in charta rossa' and a 'Nunciata in charta tenta' for a Book of Hours.

40. The attributions made so far and the literature is conveniently summarized by Mariana Canova, *Miniatura veneta*, pp. 111–2. See also M. Davies, *The Earlier Italian Schools* (National Gallery catalogues), 2nd edn. revised, 1961, pp. 257–60.

41. A rather similar problem occurs in regard to Giovanni Bellini and the attribution and dating of the Caritá and St. Vincent Ferrer altar-pieces in relation to his later work. See Robertson, *op. cit.*, ch. III.

42. I should like to express my gratitude to Mr. John Pope-Hennessy, Professor O. Pächt and Dr. A. C. de la Mare for their help and criticism, and to Mr. J. Harthan and Miss I. Whalley for facilitating my study of the Petrarch.

ROBERT SKELTON

Mughal Paintings from Harivaṃśa Manuscript

AN important addition to the Museum's collection of Mughal paintings was made recently when six illustrations from a manuscript of the *Harivaṃśa*, were acquired as a part of the bequest of the late Lady Macnaghten. The manuscript had previously been known only from a few dispersed pages, largely in American collections, which have been published in recent years.[1] It has been obvious that these were from a manuscript of the highest quality but until now no attempt has been made to bring a number of miniatures from this copy of the *Harivaṃśa* together in one publication. The Museum's newly acquired pages provide an opportunity for this and for an assessment to be made of the paintings in relation to another important copy of the same work.

Before acquiring this new group, the Museum had, of course, already owned an outstanding collection of Mughal paintings. However, in their subject matter, the paintings bequeathed by Lady Macnaghten add a new dimension to the collection. This is because, until now, almost all the important early Mughal manuscript illustrations in this country have either been from historical works or devoted to subjects taken

from Persian literature.[2] The newly acquired pages, however, depict some of the most popular Indian legends. Thus visitors to the Museum can now see for the first time just how brilliantly Hindu artists at the early Mughal court responded to the stimulus of illustrating their own myths in terms of the newly evolved realism of the Mughal style.

This impact of the new stylistic means of expression on the depiction of Hindu myths can clearly be seen if one of the newly acquired paintings is compared with a typical pre-Mughal illustration of the same subject, in which the child Krishna is tied to a mortar to keep him out of mischief (figs. 1 and 2). In the earlier picture (fig. 1) we merely see the captive child admonished by his mother in a simple stylized landscape. The drawing is lively and direct but the means at the painter's disposal did not enable him to bring the scene to life in a convincing manner. By contrast, the Mughal picture enlarges the stage and graphically shows the consternation of the mother's neighbours when the peaceful routine of the village is shattered by the unexpected outcome of this apparently trivial domestic incident (fig. 2). The difference between these two pictures is so great that it seems almost as if the Indian pictorial imagination had been suddenly freed after centuries of restraint. Events portrayed in a conceptual and symbolic manner in the late medieval period were suddenly imbued with a dramatic power and actuality that calls to mind the treatment of such themes at such early sculptural sites as Elura.

The events which led to this revival of a powerful dramatic vision in Indian painting are well known. In 1526, the crumbling Muslim sultanate of Delhi was taken over by Bābur, a prince from Turkistan, descended from Tīmūr, the Central Asian conqueror, whose exploits more than a century earlier had included the capture of Delhi. Thus the first Mughal Emperor reasserted his family's control over this far-off segment of his great ancestor's empire.

In the next reign, the newly established dynasty was overtaken by a misfortune which turned out to be of the greatest significance for the development of Mughal painting. Bābur's son, Humāyūn, lost his kingdom to an Afghan usurper and fled to Persia. In exile, he was entertained by the Persian ruler, Shāh Ṭahmāsp, whose earlier zeal for the art of painting was becoming eroded by a growing bigotry in religion and involvement in affairs of state. As a consequence, Persian artists, whose work had reached unprecedented levels

1. KRISHNA TIED TO A MORTAR. Illustration to the *Balagopālastuti*. Western India, 15th century. Victoria and Albert Museum. $4\frac{3}{16} \times 4\frac{3}{8}$ in. (10·6 × 11·1 cm.). (I.S.82–1963)

of elegant naturalism by the time of Humāyūn's arrival in Persia, were beginning to look elsewhere for patronage. Two of these, Mīr Sayyid 'Alī and Khwāja 'Abd al-Samad, entered Humāyūn's service and when he finally regained his kingdom they followed him to Delhi. At first, they must have worked in comparative isolation but with the accession of Akbar in 1556, soon after his father's return to India, the dynasty's fortunes began to prosper and in due course the Persian masters found themselves at the head of a large artistic establishment. In this newly founded studio painters of varied ethnic and artistic backgrounds developed a common style that was employed to illustrate manuscripts for the royal library.

Many of these books were copies of the well known Persian classics, which one would expect to find in the library of any cultured ruler of the period for whom the Persian language provided a literary background. However, Akbar was unusual among the Muslim rulers of India for the breadth of his political vision and his tolerance towards other religions. The contents of his library reflected this. His initial enquiries into the doctrines of Islam gradually extended to an interest in other faiths, including Hinduism. As a pragmatic statesman concerned with the consolidation of power, he formed marriage alliances with Hindu rājās, who attained high office at his court and gained both his respect and friendship. His Hindu wives no doubt furthered his understanding of the religious views of the majority of his subjects, whom most orthodox Muslims saw only as idolatrous infidels. Quite apart from seeing the advantage of having powerful Hindu friends in a land where his fellow Muslims were split into dangerous factions, Akbar was a genuine idealist with a concern for the welfare of his subjects regardless of their religious persuasions. Furthermore, he firmly believed that some progress could be made towards communal integration if he led the way.

It is not surprising, therefore, that the royal library, as a repository of information, was connected with the very nerve centre from which the Emperor's revolutionary ideas were being generated. Thus in addition to the usual standard works on Islamic theology, jurisprudence, history, poetry, *belles-lettres* and the sciences, the Emperor also commissioned translations of works concerning other religions. With these and with the help of representatives of the religions concerned, he and his associates were able to familiarize themselves with the doctrines of the Parsees, Jains, Christians and, perhaps most important of all, the Hindus, who formed the largest element in the population. Abū'l-Faẓl, the Emperor's friend, minister and historian, lists some of the more important books in the chapter on the royal library in his remarkable descriptive and statistical account of the Empire – the *Ā'īn-i Akbarī* ('Institutes of Akbar').[3] He states that 'Philologists are constantly engaged in translating Hindī, Greek, Arabic and Persian books into other languages'[4] and among the Hindī (i.e. Sanskrit) works that he mentions perhaps the most significant is the *Mahābhārata*, India's national epic, to which Akbar gave the Persian title, *Razm nāma* or 'Book of Wars'. It was of this enormous work that the great Muslim encyclopaedist, Al-Birūnī, had observed five centuries earlier that the Hindus 'firmly assert that everything which occurs in other books is also found in this book, but not all that occurs in this book is found in other books'.[5]

Not only was the *Mahābhārata* a vast repository of Hindu religious knowledge but it embodied this in a framework of myths and bardic legends whose heroic and fantastic exploits have formed the staple repertoire of Indian story-tellers throughout at least two thousand years of constant repetition. As a subject for pictorial illustration it provided enormous opportunities for exercise of the imagination. Nobody who has been privileged to turn the pages of Akbar's royal copy of the translation (*Razm nāma*), now in the Jaipur City Palace, could avoid being impressed by the vividness with which his artists visualized the events of the narrative. One cannot fail to wonder whether they were perhaps recreating the visions which had filled their minds in childhood during the spoken and acted reiteration of stories from the epic which is still a regular feature of Indian village life. It could no doubt be argued that before working on the *Razm nāma* they had already shown similar powers of imagination in their work on the *Ḥamza nāma* – that giant illustrated romance of early Islamic heroism. Yet there is no doubt that for the Hindu painters, who greatly outnumbered their Muslim colleagues, the task of illu-

2. KRISHNA, TIED TO A MORTAR, UPROOTS TWO TREES. Illustration to the *Harivaṃśa*. Mughal, *c.*1590. Victoria and Albert Museum (Lady Macnaghten Bequest). $7\frac{5}{16} \times 11$ in. (18.5×27.9 cm.). (I.S.2–1970)

43

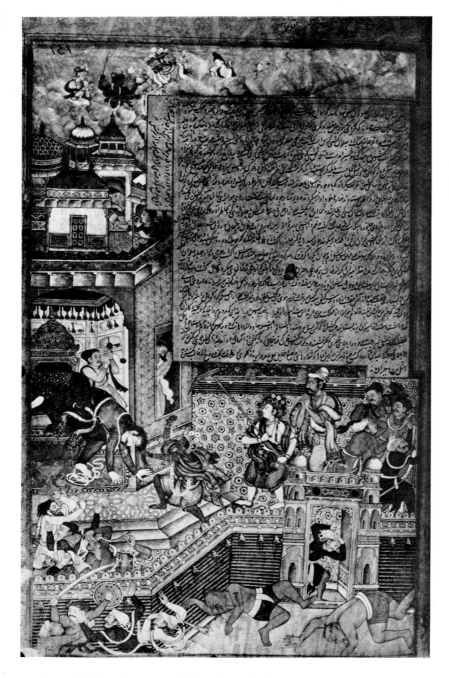

3. KRISHNA KILLS RAJA KANSA. Illustration to the *Harivaṃśa*. Mughal, *c.*1586. Coll. of H.H. the Maharaja of Jaipur (after Hendley)

strating the stories on which they had been reared since infancy must have been an occupation very close to the heart.

Although the paintings bequeathed to the Museum by Lady Macnaghten are not exactly comparable with those of the great Jaipur copy of Akbar's translation of the *Mahābhārata*, they stand much closer to it than many other paintings of the period. Their subject, the *Harivaṃśa*, is closely connected with the *Mahābhārata* although it is actually an independent work, which has become attached to the epic as an appendix.[6] This close relationship between the two texts is demonstrated in the Jaipur copy of the epic, which concludes with a copy of the *Harivaṃśa*, written and illustrated

as part of the main project. By contrast, the copy from which the present pages have been separated was evidently prepared as a separate self-contained entity, since no illustrated copy of the main epic can now be linked with it.

Whereas the actual epic is devoted to the central theme of a great war between rival branches of an ancient kingly race, the *Harivaṃśa* 'Genealogy of Hari'[7] deals in greater detail with the lineage and career of Vāsudeva Krishṇa, who appears in the *Mahābhārata* as a non-combatant adviser to its heroes, the five Pāṇḍava brothers. It is already apparent in the epic itself that Krishṇa was regarded as something more than mortal even in a context in which humans

4. KRISHNA RECEIVED BY RAJA BHISHMAKA. Illustration to the *Harivaṃśa*. Mughal, *c*.1590. Victoria and Albert Museum (Lady Macnaghten Bequest). $7\frac{13}{16} \times 12\frac{5}{8}$ in. (19·8 × 32 cm.). (I.S.4–1970)

5. KRISHNA'S COMBAT WITH INDRA. Illustration to the *Harivaṃśa*. Mughal, *c.*1590. Victoria and Albert Museum (Lady Macnaghten Bequest). $7\frac{1}{4} \times 11\frac{5}{8}$ in. (18·4 × 29·6 cm.). (I.S.5–1970.)

themselves were conceived as having remarkable attributes. Certain passages, in fact, leave no question as to his divinity. In the *Harivaṃśa*, as in the *Purāṇas*,[8] which also elaborate on his career, Krishna's divine nature as an incarnation of the god Vishṇu is far more explicit. In these texts, which appear to have found their final form later than the epic, no opportunity is lost of glorifying this popular deity, whose devotional cult steadily increased during the later medieval period.

The story of Krishṇa, as outlined in the second of the three sections of the *Harivaṃśa*, contains episodes of great charm, particularly those which deal with his childhood in a cowherds' village. The cause of Vishṇu's intervention in the affairs of mankind on this occasion was the excessive power obtained by an evil king, Kaṃsa, who reigned in Mathura after deposing his father, Ugrasena. It was prophesied that Kaṃsa's relative Devakī would give birth to a child, who would grow up to destroy the king. Kaṃsa thereupon took the precaution of confining her and killing her children as they were born. The eighth baby, Krishṇa, was carried from the palace with divine assistance and substituted for the child of Nanda, a cowherd, who lived in the neighbouring village of Gokul. There he was reared by his foster-mother, Yasodā, together with his brother, Balarāma, who was also a divine incarnation saved from the king's clutches.

During his childhood in the village Krishṇa endeared himself to the villagers, especially the womenfolk, by his mischievous pranks and on several occasions confused them by his manifestations of supranormal powers. An example of this already noticed is the occasion when he was tied to a mortar (fig. 2). When Krishṇa crawled off dragging the heavy mortar behind him, it became lodged between two trees and they were uprooted. On various occasions during their childhood, demons were sent by Kaṃsa to harm the brothers but these were all successfully overcome. At Krishṇa's instigation the cowherds moved to the village of Brindaban on the river Jumna near Mathura and were persuaded by him to worship a local hill, Mount Govardhan, in place of their annual festival in praise of the god Indra. Indra retaliated with a devastating series of rain storms but Krishṇa supported the mountain as an umbrella over the heads of his admiring friends. Indra thereupon acknowledged Krishṇa's superiority.

With approaching manhood, Krishṇa charmed the

6. KRISHNA'S COMBAT WITH INDRA. Illustration to the *Harivaṃśa*. Mughal, *c*.1586. Coll. of H.H. the Maharaja of Jaipur (after Hendley)

villagers with his flute-playing and danced with the enamoured milkmaids in the moonlight. Hearing of the brothers' exploits, Kaṃsa lured them to Mathura to compete in a festival with his wrestlers. An elephant was loosed upon the youths but was destroyed. The wrestlers were defeated in the contest and finally the king was dragged by the hair from his throne and killed (colour plate). Kaṃsa's father, Ugrasena, was then restored to the throne and supervised the education of the two young cowherds for their future role as princes.

Reaching manhood, Krishṇa determined to marry and learned that Rukmin, the son of king Bhīshmaka of Vidarbha, had arranged a ceremony in which the king's daughter, Rukmiṇī, would select a husband.[9] Krishṇa appeared among the assembled princes and was courteously received by king Bhīshmaka (fig. 4) but owing to the plotting of Krishṇa's enemies the king made his apologies and the ceremony was not held. Later, Rukmiṇī was betrothed to another king but Krishṇa abducted her. In the meanwhile, Krishṇa removed his family's capital from Mathura, where it was subject to attack by Kansa's enraged father-in-law, to Dwarka, where a golden city was built on the sea coast.[10]

As Rukmiṇī's husband, Krishṇa fathered ten sons and later married seven other queens and sixteen thousand other wives. Nevertheless he still found time to perform heroic feats of battle. A demon was killed at the request of Indra, the king of the gods, and following this Krishṇa found himself in conflict with Indra himself. This was due to the jealousy of his wife Satyabhāmā after he had given Rukmiṇī a blossom from the Pārijāta tree growing in Indra's heaven. In response to Satyabhāmā's sulky demands Krishṇa promised to bring her the tree. This resulted in a battle between Krishṇa on Vishṇu's eagle, Garuḍa, and Indra on his elephant (fig. 5). The dispute was eventually settled through arbitration. Following this, Krishṇa again fought battles with demons and finally destroyed the demon king, Nikumbha (fig. 7). This took place in a cave, where the other heroes of the Yādava race had been imprisoned. The *Harivaṃśa* then gives an account of another demon, who was born with the prophesy that he could only be killed by Śiva, the divine yogī, who shares with Vishṇu a supreme role among the gods. This demon, Andhaka, was tempted by a sage to steal a flowering creeper from a garden created by Śiva. Heedless of his own temerity, the demon defied the great god but his host was routed by Śiva's followers and he was destroyed (fig. 8). The narrative then deals with the adventures of Krishṇa's son, Pradyumna, and finally lapses into a series of loosely arranged legends and religious passages, which are not important in the present context.

In order to determine the place of the Macnaghten paintings in relation to the work of Akbar's studio as a whole, one must inevitably make comparisons with the *Harivaṃśa* illustrations forming the last part of the great Jaipur manuscript. There seems little reason to suppose that the two versions are very far removed from each other in date but there are significant differences in the treatment of the subjects which call

for discussion. There is also scope for confusion over the date of the Jaipur manuscript, which bears no colophon. In consequence, various suggestions have been put forward regarding the period of time in which it was completed. These suggestions are all founded on three known facts. Firstly, there is a contemporary statement that the work of translating the *Mahābhārata* was started in A.D. 1582.[11] This information is supplemented by a remark by one of the translators, which has been noticed in a manuscript of the work in the British Museum.[12] This tells that the translation took eighteen months to complete and was finished in August–September 1584 (Sha'ban, 992 A.H.). Thirdly, the current year (995 A.H. = 1587 A.D.) is mentioned in the preface, which was added after the translation had been made.[13] Armed with these facts and the additional, but irrelevant, information that part of the work was re-cast in A.D. 1589, scholars have come to different conclusions about the date of the Jaipur copy of the work.[14] Fortunately, an examination of the manuscript itself, instead of reliance merely upon references to it, enables us to clear the matter up. Several of the miniatures between numbers 73 and 118 are dated in the year 993 A.H., which corresponds with A.D. 1585. Another miniature (No. 145) appears to be dated in the following year and thus appears to have been finished after December 23, 1585. However, the preliminary sketches for thirty of the miniatures were carried out by the painter, Daswanth, who committed suicide in 1584.[15] Thus although the final execution of the miniatures went on until at least the beginning of 1586, the work of preparing the preliminary drawings had already reached an advanced stage in 1584, the year in which the translation itself was completed. So far as the *Harivaṃśa* section of the Jaipur manuscript is concerned, I have discovered no dates under the miniatures but as there are only seventeen of them it seems probable that they were completed in 1586 along with the last few miniatures of the third volume of the *Razm nama*. After this, the royal artists went on to illustrate the translation of India's other great epic, the *Rāmāyana*, which contains over 170 miniatures and was completed in November 1588.

Of course, the fact that one can at last be certain that work on the Jaipur *Harivaṃśa* was carried out in 1586 does not automatically give a date for the dispersed copy of the work. It would be surprising indeed if it were completed before the principal royal copy of

PLATE 2.
KRISHNA KILLS
RAJA KANSA.
Illustration to the
Harivaṃśa.
Mughal, *c.*1590.
Victoria and
Albert Museum
(Lady
Macnaghten
Bequest).
$8\frac{1}{16} \times 12\frac{3}{4}$ in.
(20·4 × 32·3 cm).
(I.S.3–1970)

7. KRISHNA KILLS THE DEMON, NIKUMBHA, IN A CAVE. Illustration to the *Harivaṃśa*. Mughal, *c*.1590.
Victoria and Albert Museum (Lady Macnaghten Bequest). $7\frac{5}{16} \times 12\frac{1}{8}$ in. ($18\cdot7 \times 30\cdot7$ cm.). (I.S.6–1970)

8. SIVA KILLS THE DEMON ANDHAKA. Illustration to the *Harivaṃśa*. Mughal, *c*.1590. Victoria and Albert Museum (Lady Macnaghten Bequest). $7\frac{1}{4} \times 12\frac{5}{16}$ in. (18·5 × 31·2 cm.). (I.S.7–1970)

the text. Therefore a date before 1585 is unlikely. This is borne out by a comparison of miniatures from the two copies, which suggests that the artists of the dispersed manuscript borrowed from the earlier compositions and worked them out more carefully.

In place of the excitement and tension which pervade the miniatures of the Jaipur copy, the dispersed *Harivaṃśa* pages show a broader and more considered treatment of the subject matter. The approach is rational rather than declamatory. Whereas the Jaipur pictures often suggest the bucolic atmosphere of a festive occasion and may have been partly inspired by the enactment of mythological scenes in the great seasonal festivals, the pages of the dispersed copy show a less ephemeral approach to the drama of the myths, which take on more of their underlying cosmic significance.

This is largely achieved by adjustment to the compositional arrangement of the scenes, showing a much more thoughtful exploitation of the available picture surface. The reserved panels of text which often cramp the compositions in the Jaipur copy are dispensed with and the action is often organized along swiftly moving diagonals. This enables the gods to move with ease against their adversaries, leaving no doubt about the outcome of events, which consequently develop with pre-ordained inevitability.

In the scene of Kaṃsa's death (compare fig. 3 and colour plate), the introduction of diagonal steps to the throne reinforces the downward thrust of Kaṃsa's figure as Krishṇa drags him from it. The arrangement of the architecture and the placing of Balarāma's figure in a position just below that of Krishṇa adds to this effect. Krishṇa's prowess is also emphasized by a greater attention paid to those hazards which were overcome immediately before the moment of final victory. The dead wrestlers look more powerfully built and the artist has also introduced the inert bulk of the dead elephant as well as the distorted corpse of a courtier who had barred the brothers' progress.

In the case of the combat between Krishṇa and Indra, the composition already has a strong diagonal thrust in the Jaipur version (fig. 6) and this is retained (fig. 5). The cosmic nature of the encounter is, however, brilliantly suggested by the action being taken up into the sky. The drama of the situation is also heightened in other ways. Instead of meeting each other in a single plane against an intrusive background of rocks, the two gods almost burst forth from the picture as

they collide at an angle amid billowing clouds. Indra's temporary discomforture as his elephant lurches downwards is admirably suggested, and instead of confusing the action by including members of Indra's army moving forwards at a tangent, the artist has caused the bottom of the picture to be occupied by a charming landscape, seen from above, in which two boatloads of Europeans land near a coastal town. With the text panel removed at the top, the watching gods in the heavens are far more convincingly disposed and their slightly concave alignment accentuates the bold convex arc formed by the main protagonists.

A similar rationalizing intelligence is displayed in the revision of the composition in which Śiva and his host destroy Andhaka and his fellow-demons (compare figs. 8 and 9). As in other cases, the main combatants are now placed in a diagonal relationship and the landscape is altered to support the action. Thus the arrangement is again clarified and the assault of Śiva and his followers against the cowering forces of evil appears more purposeful. Clearly the issue is not in doubt as destiny unfolds its inexorable course. Andhaka was born to be slain and despite his theatrical bravado he is no more than a paper tiger.

It is interesting to compare the way in which the two sides of the combat have been treated in these two versions. In the earlier picture (fig. 9) the demons are wonderfully represented as creatures of nightmare fantasy. The battle is more frenzied and the difficulties of the battle are reflected in the tense facial expressions of Śiva and his forces. In the other version (fig. 8) Andhaka himself is more boldly represented, in a fashion reminiscent of the buffoon-like villains of popular drama, while his followers have neither the weird fiendishness with which they are invested in the Jaipur picture (fig. 9) nor the corporeal vigour of their adversaries (fig. 8). At the top, especially, the defeated group is not really conceived in depth and lacks the strong three-dimensional relationship of the militant yogīs who harass it. It is also perhaps significant that in this later version Śiva and his host show no particular emotions as they perform their predestined role.

There is little evidence for speculation as to the reasons for the differences between the two copies and it is unfortunate that re-margination has deprived us of the artist's names, which might have given some clue as to the personalities involved in the creation of the later versions of these compositions. It is possible,

9. SIVA KILLS THE DEMON ANDHAKA. Illustration to the *Harivaṃśa*. Mughal, *c*.1586. Coll. of H.H. the Maharaja of Jaipur (after Hendley)

however, that the removal by suicide of the unstable but clearly influential artist, Daswanth, in 1584 may have something to do with the change of emphasis from Dionysiac to Apollonian qualities that has been observed.

Daswanth was the particular pupil of 'Abd al Samad, whose son, Muhammad Sharīf, supervised the illustration of the Jaipur *Razm nāma* and appears to have entrusted his father's star pupil with an important role in planning the work. This is evident from the large number of pictures in the Jaipur manuscript for which Daswanth produced the preliminary drawings.[16] Unfortunately, with one exception,[17] all of Daswanth's surviving output is in this form and it is not easy to appraise his qualities. Accepting this limitation, however, a close examination of these miniatures in the original suggests that their often obsessive and expressionistic qualities are a peculiar characteristic of Daswanth's artistic personality. This is also consistent with what Abū'l-Faẓl tells of Daswanth's madness and eventual suicide during an attack of melancholy.[18] Nevertheless his work was greatly admired and as one who was considered at the time to have surpassed his fellows in the art[19] he was almost certainly a profound influence upon his colleagues. This may account for the subordination of compositional logic in favour of imaginative expressiveness (bordering in some cases on hallucinatory excitement), which can be detected in many pictures of the Jaipur manuscript irrespective of their precise authorship.[20] It is in this manuscript, after all, that we find almost all of Daswanth's surviving work and his final breakdown occurred before its completion. Thus his influence is likely to have been strongest at this time, when his life was near its tragically unsettled end. After his death, more rational personalities are likely to have impressed themselves upon the studio's work and it is perhaps this circumstance which accounts for the differences between the miniatures of the two copies.

The length of time which intervened between the production of the two manuscripts is difficult to assess but the second version is certainly not later than the mid-fifteen-nineties, when the Mughal style again changed course – perhaps in response to a growing interest in painting on the part of the heir-apparent. A date near to 1590 seems not unlikely for the Museum's *Harivaṃśa* pages and this accords well with opinions expressed elsewhere.[21]

Notes

1. The text portion of this copy including both the opening and the undated conclusion was acquired in 1957 by the State Museum, Lucknow (No. 57.106.12). It contains about 200 folios and 9 miniatures of which 6 are original and the remaining 3 are much later additions. The opening and one miniature are published by S. M. Naqvi, 'Persian and Urdu manuscripts related with Lord Kṛṣṇā's life in the State Museum, Lucknow', *The Bulletin of Museums and Archaeology in U.P.*, 2, Dec. 1968, pp. 41–42. The page size of the manuscript is 35·0 × 22·0 cm. and the text is written in Nasta'līq script, 17 lines to the page in an area measuring 23·0 × 13·5 cm.
Of the remaining miniatures, at least 12 were formerly in the collection of the late A. C. Ardeshir, who published one in 'Mughal miniature painting', *Roopa-Lekha* I (sic), 2, 1940, pl. I, p. 32. The present whereabouts of these is unknown apart from two pages now in the Los Angeles County Museum of Art (see *The Arts of India and Nepal: The Nasli and Alice Heeramaneck Collection*, catalogue of an exhibition held at the Museum of Fine Arts, Boston, 1966–67, pp. 144 and 147) and two pages in the Edwin C. Binney, 3rd, collection (see *Islamic Art from the Collection of Edwin Binney, 3rd*, catalogue of a Smithsonian Institution travelling exhibition, 1966, No. 67 and *Persian and Indian Miniatures from the collection of Edwin Binney, 3rd*, Supplement to the catalogue of an exhibition held at the Portland Art Museum, 1962, No. 56a).
Other pages from the manuscript, not formerly in the Ardeshir collection, are in the Metropolitan Museum of Art, New York (S. C. Welch, *The Art of Mughal India*, 1963, pl. 13; *Catalogue of highly important oriental manuscripts and miniatures*, Sotheby & Co., 6/12/1967, lot 115; M. S. Dimand, 'Three Indian Paintings of the Early Mughal Period', *Metropolitan Museum of Art Bulletin*, XXIII, 1928, pp. 124–127, fig. 1; *idem*, *A Handbook of Mohammadan Decorative Arts*, 1930, fig. 23, pp. 54 and 56); Freer Gallery of Art, Washington (R. Ettinghausen, *Paintings of the Sultans and Emperors of India*, 1961, pl. 5); the Bharat Kala Bhavan, Benares (A. Mookerjee, *The Arts of India from pre-historic to modern times*, 1966, pl. 126) and the Chester Beatty Library, Dublin (M.S. 32, vol. 2, f. 12).
It appears from this list that the manuscript originally contained at least 29 miniatures as against 17 in the Jaipur copy of the work. I am most grateful to Prof. Pramod Chandra for drawing my attention to the Lucknow portion of the MS. and to Dr. N. P. Joshi for sending information about it. Prof. Richard Ettinghausen also very kindly sent details of the paintings in New York.

2. Fable books, such as the *Anwār-i Suhaylī* are, of course, Indian in origin but when they reappeared in India in Persian guise they had lost their specifically Indian character. The only substantial group of early Mughal illustrations to a truly Indian text are those in a copy of the Mahābhārata, completed in the Imperial studio in 1007/1598 A.D., which is divided between the British Museum, India Office Library and this Museum. It seems certain from its quality, however, that this was not made for the royal library but was simply one of the copies made for members of the leading nobility. See G.

Meredith-Owens, '*A Persian translation of the Mahabharata*', The British Museum Quarterly, XX, 1955–56, p. 62.

3. Abul Fazl 'Allami, *The Āīn i Akbarī* tr. by H. Blochmann, I, 1873, pp. 103–6.

4. *Ibid.*, p. 104.

5. E. Sachau, *Albiruni's India*, I, 1888, p. 132.

6. In some copies of the epic, the *Harivaṃśa* is treated as a part of the main text, of which it then forms the 19th and final book. Akbar's Persian translation was made by Maulānā Sherī, a poet and minor official, who died in battle in 994 A.H./ 1586 A.D., see Abul Fazl 'Allami, *op. cit.*, I, pp. 106, 197, 202, 204, 610.

7. 'Hari' is a name of the god Vishṇu. The word is now familiar in the West through the chant 'Hare Krishna'.

8. The word *Purāṇa* signifies 'old narrative' and comprises a class of sacred writings which contain mythological accounts of the origin and nature of the universe together with legends of the gods, heavenly sages and early rulers of mankind. Although not included among the 18 principal *Purāṇas*, the *Harivaṃśa* itself really belongs to this class of literature and its version of the life of Krishṇa overlaps those which appear in the *Bhāgavata, Vishṇu, Brahma* and *Brahmavaivarta Purāṇas*.

9. The account of this episode differs in some respects from the circumstances related in the popular *Bhāgavata Purāṇa*. I notice, also, from the Persian text on the back of our miniature, that the translation by Maulānā Sherī appears to follow a different version of the original from that used for the English translation of the *Harivaṃśa* edited by D. N. Bhose (Calcutta, no date).

10. An impressive illustration of Krishṇa's golden city is in the Freer Gallery of Art, Ettinghausen, *loc. cit.*

11. Al-Badāonī, *Muntakhab-ut-Tawārīkh*, tr. by W. H. Lowe, II, 1884, p. 329 (year mentioned, p. 325). Text (Bibliotheca Indica, vol. 51), II, pp. 319–320 (year mentioned, p. 315).

12. C. Rieu, Catalogue of the Persian Manuscripts in the British Museum, I, 1879, p. 57, referring to MS. Add. 5642.

13. *Loc. cit.* It is unfortunate that most writers have followed T. H. Hendley (*Memorials of the Jeypore Exhibition 1883*, IV, 1884, p. 1) who equates 995 A.H. with 1588 A.D. It actually runs from 12 Dec. 1586 to 1 Dec. 1587.

14. P. Brown, *Indian Painting under the Mughals*, 1924, p. 12 – '*cir*. A.D. 1580': I. Stchoukine, *La peinture indienne a l'époque des Grands Moghols*, 1929, p. 38 – 'terminé en 1588': R. Pinder-Wilson, 'A note on the miniatures' appended to Meredith-Owens, *op. cit.*, p. 64 – 'probably the copy which was presented to Akbar soon after the translation was completed in 1584': W. G. Archer, *The Loves of Krishna*, 1957, p. 98 – 'The abridgement . . . was probably completed in 1588 but illustrated copies, including the great folios now in the palace library at Jaipur, were probably not completed before 1595': D. Barrett and B. Gray, *Painting of India*, 1963, p. 83 – 'its production is likely to have extended over the years 1584 to 1589'.

15. Abū'l Faẓl, *Akbar nāma*, tr. by H. Beveridge, III, 1939, p. 651. It is curious that the actual date of this very celebrated artist's death has been generally overlooked: see, for example, W. Staude, 'Daswanth', *Encyclopedia of World Art*, IV, 1958, p. 235, also Barrett and Gray, *loc. cit.*

16. He made the preliminary drawings for almost one in four of the first 125 pictures, after which his contribution ceased completely: as a result, no doubt, of his death.

17. S. E. Lee and Pramod Chandra, 'A Newly Discovered Tūti-Nāma and the Continuity of the Indian Tradition of Manuscript Painting'. *The Burlington Magazine*, cv, 729, 1963, p. 553, and fig. 33. Another miniature in the MS. is attributed to Daswanth by the authors of the article.

18. Daswanth's mental breakdown is mentioned by Abu'l Fazl (*A'in i Akbarī*), tr., i, p. 108.

19. *Loc. cit.*

20. Compare, for example, the imaginative but disordered representation of Krishna raising mount Govardhan in the Jaipur manuscript (Hendley, *op. cit.*, pl. CXXXIV) with the less original but far more carefully conceived version in the later manuscript (S. C. Welch, *op. cit.*, pl. 13).

21. For example, S. C. Welch, *op. cit.*, p.164, No. 13, and E. J. Grube, *The Classical Style in Islamic Painting*, 1968, p. 203, Nos. 95 and 96.

Medieval and Renaissance embroidery from Spain

A MAGNIFICENT Renaissance altar frontal, acquired in 1969, is without doubt the finest Spanish embroidery to enter the Museum during a century of collecting in this field (fig. 1). The nucleus of the Museum's holdings of medieval and Renaissance embroidery from Spain was a group of some thirty or forty examples purchased from Sir J. C. Robinson in 1880, to which several dozen more have been added from time to time as opportunities arose; they formed a reasonably representative collection, but since many of them are small or damaged the addition of a large and impressive frontal in splendid condition is particularly welcome. Early Spanish embroidery is a rather unfamiliar subject and it seems best to place the new piece in its historical context by discussing it, not in isolation, but in conjunction with some other characteristic examples from the collection.

Spanish church embroidery emerges from obscurity in the Romanesque period with a group of three pieces from northern Catalonia, namely the great wool-embroidered hanging of the Creation at Gerona Cathedral,[1] the silk-embroidered banner of St. Oth in the Barcelona Museum,[2] and another silk-embroidered piece in the Victoria and Albert Museum (fig. 2).[3] This last is a much damaged hanging of undyed linen embroidered in tones of red, pink, yellow and white with Christ in the mandorla (inscribed VIA VERITAS),

the twelve apostles (APOSTOLI DOMINI NR̄I IHESV XRISTI) and three of the four evangelist-symbols (SC̄S MAR̄C, S IOH and S LV̄C); no doubt the fourth symbol appeared at the bottom of the hanging, which has been ruthlessly cut away. The piece has been described hitherto as an altar frontal, and it may well have served as such since its mutilation, but its original height of about four feet (122 cm.) was too great for this use; it must certainly have been made as an altar dossal and it appears to be the earliest known example of this class of liturgical furnishings.[4]

It was bought in 1904 in Cologne, at the auction of the stock of the art-dealer Bourgeois, and was described in the sale-catalogue as German work of about 1200.[5] Following the same line of thought the Museum continued until the 1950s to label it as Rhenish work of the 13th century. In view of its provenance the attribution seemed reasonable and it was supported, first, by the existence in Germany of copper-gilt altar frontals likewise showing Christ in the mandorla, the evangelist-symbols and the twelve apostles arranged in four groups of three,[6] and, second, by the presence in the Museum of parts of another 12th century embroidered altar hanging from north Germany with the same elements, though in a different arrangement;[7] admittedly these are basic elements of Christian iconography, very widely used for the adornment of church

1. Altar frontal of crimson velvet, embroidered in gold, silver and silk with the Baptism of Christ, the Virgin and Child with the infant St. John the Baptist, and other subjects. Formerly in the church of San Juan de los Reyes, Toledo, the frontal was probably made in that city about 1530.

2. Altar dossal, embroidered in silk with Christ in Majesty, the twelve Apostles, the symbols of the Evangelists, and the rivers of Paradise. Formerly at La Seo de Urgel in northern Catalonia, the dossal is Catalan work cf the 12th century.

sanctuaries and altars. In 1956, however, Dr. José Gudiol of Barcelona threw an entirely new light on the matter when he very kindly informed me that, some thirty years before, he had shown a photograph of the dossal to Dr. Paul Tachard of Toulouse, who thereupon stated that he himself had purchased this embroidery at La Seo de Urgel in northern Catalonia, and had subsequently sold it outside Spain.[8] There can be no doubt of the authenticity of this testimony, particularly since the banner of St. Oth, likewise from La Seo de Urgel, is so like the dossal in execution and colouring that an origin in the same embroidery workshop seems more than likely. The banner is signed (ELISAVA ME FCIT), but the date and location of the workshop, whether at Urgel or elsewhere, remain uncertain. Despite its name, there is no secure evidence that the banner dates from the lifetime of St. Oth, who was Bishop of Urgel from 1095 to 1122, but it is natural to suppose that the two embroideries were most probably commissioned during the period of

greatest artistic activity at Urgel, from the commencement of work on the new cathedral in 1116 until the sack of the town in 1195.[9] A painters' workshop established there about the middle of the century produced wall-paintings and altar frontals depicting Christ in majesty, evangelist-symbols and apostles, but these were the commonest iconographical elements in Catalan painting of the time, and the style of the embroideries, in so far as it can be evaluated in their present damaged condition, hardly justifies an attribution of their designs to painters of the Urgel workshop rather than another.[10] The arrangement of the apostles in four groups of three, as in the dossal, does not occur in paintings of the Urgel workshop, though it was not unusual elsewhere in Catalonia.[11] Some compositional features of the dossal – the processional movement of the apostles towards the centre, and the placing of the evangelist-symbols on the arms of the jewelled cross which divides the field – have no parallel in Catalonia and recall the golden paliotto of S.

3. Altar frontal of patterned silk, embroidered in gold and silk with the arms of Aragon-Barcelona and stems of columbine. The frontal was probably embroidered in Barcelona or Valencia in the late 14th or early 15th century.

4. Altar frontal of red velvet, embroidered in gold and silk thread with the Virgin and Child and two angels. The frontal was probably embroidered in Valencia in the first half of the 15th century.

Ambrogio in Milan;[12] but they are by no means surprising in Catalan art, which incorporated a variety of elements from Italo-Byzantine, Romanesque and Carolingian sources. The most unusual features of the iconography, the nude figures holding urns and representing the rivers of paradise (FISON, GION in the upper corners and doubtless two others, now lost, below) find a parallel in the great Creation embroidery at Gerona, which also shows various stylistic affinities with the two pieces from Urgel, though it differs from them in materials, technique and colouring and was evidently produced in a different workshop. Considered together, these three works clearly demonstrate the existence of a Catalan school of Romanesque embroidery, parallel with the Catalan school of Romanesque painting.

In the early Gothic period, on the other hand, although a number of embroideries exist which were probably made in Spain, they do not coalesce to form a recognizable Spanish school. In fact, all the finest embroideries of the 13th and early 14th century in Spain were imported from elsewhere, notably the Florentine altar frontal at Manresa,[13] and the three great copes in Madrid, Toledo and Vich,[14] all of English work, or, as a 14th century Toledo inventory describes it, *orofres de Londres*.[15] This phase of imported embroideries is represented in the Museum by a set of English chasuble orphreys, formerly in an unidentified Spanish church, which have now returned to the city where they were made six and half centuries ago.[16]

The period of the International Gothic or soft style produced, parallel with the development of Spanish painting, a marked resurgence of embroidery, especially in the Kingdom of Aragon, where a number of embroiderers, both native and foreign, are recorded in Barcelona and Valencia from the late 14th century onwards.[17] Apart from orphreys and other minor works this phase is represented in Spain by an altar frontal of 1393 at Vich[18] and two altar frontals at Gerona,[19] all of which are likely to have been made in the Barcelona workshops. Their various pictorial styles are characteristic of Catalan painting, with traces of influence from both northern Europe and Italy. The figure subjects, coats of arms and plant motifs are finely executed in silk and gold thread on pieces of silk or linen, cut to shape and applied to backgrounds of silk or velvet.

The Museum owns two altar frontals of this period. One, acquired in 1893 from the Paris dealer Stanislas Baron, is an armorial piece worked in silk and gold thread on pieces of silk and linen, which have been cut to shape and applied to a silk background; the latter, woven with a pattern of Oriental type in gold on pink, is datable to the late 14th or early 15th century (fig. 3).[20] The embroidered motif, thrice repeated, consists of twined stems of columbine – reminiscent of the flowers on the Vich frontal of 1393 – surrounding the arms of Aragon-Barcelona (or four pallets gules) in a lozenge, as borne chiefly by the city and kingdom of Valencia. Thus the frontal may well be Valencian work, though an origin in Barcelona can hardly be excluded. The second frontal has a symmetrical composition – again reminiscent of the 1393 frontal – consisting of figures embroidered in silk and gold thread on pieces of silk and linen which have been cut to shape and applied to a red velvet background, now much worn (fig. 4).[21] The central group, the Virgin and Child enthroned, is badly damaged, but the angels who kneel on either side are still well enough preserved, despite the loss of the scrolls which they held, to reveal a quality of design which can only be due to one of the best Spanish painters of the early 15th century (fig. 5). Their facial types, with blunt but attractive features, their exuberantly serpentine locks encircled with curious diadems, and the mellifluously curving folds of their draperies recur in a number of paintings of the Valencian school – the St. Barbara altarpiece in Barcelona, the St. Martin altarpiece in Valencia, the St. Michael in Edinburgh, and others – which have

5. Detail, an angel, from the altar frontal in fig. 4.

been grouped under the name of Gonzalo Pérez or the Master of the Martin de Torres family.[22] If the design of the frontal is attributable to a Valencian painter, then it seems highly probable that the embroidery likewise was executed in a Valencian workshop. Unfortunately there seem to be no authenticated Valencian embroideries of this period with which the Museum's two frontals can be compared, and in technique and execution they are hardly distinguishable from the presumed products of the Barcelona workshops which have been cited above.

From the middle and late 15th century, besides many orphreys, a number of altar frontals have been preserved which include some of the most sumptuous embroidery produced in Europe at that period. Their styles show an evolution, parallel with that of Spanish painting, from the smoothly flowing lines of International Gothic to a tormented angularity derived from Flanders. In the Kingdom of Aragon, examples preserved at Barcelona,[23] Gerona,[24] Tarragona,[25] Tortosa[26] and Vich[27] are probably from the Barcelona workshops, while two fine frontals formerly in Valencia cathedral, but destroyed in the Spanish Civil War, were presumably Valencian products.[28] In the Kingdom of Castile, an embroidered frontal and retable from El Burgo de Osma, now in Chicago,[29] and several frontals at Guadalupe[30] and Cordoba[31] may represent the work of Toledo and Seville, both of which possessed embroidery workshops from the early 15th century onwards.[32] While most of the frontals here attributed to Barcelona still adhered to the earlier formula of a single scene silhouetted against a background of silk or velvet, the general tendency was towards a series of scenes on backgrounds completely embroidered with gold thread. The Museum has no really worthy example of this period, but in order that it shall not be entirely unrepresented here a detail of one of the minor pieces in the collection is reproduced (fig. 6); work of ordinary commercial quality, not attributable to any particular centre, it shows angular drapery, luxuriant foliage and fanciful architecture characteristic of the late 15th century.[33]

The unification of the entire country under Ferdinand and Isabella, the discovery and conquest of the Americas, and Charles V's choice of Spain as his political base, all contributed to make it, in the 16th century, the richest and most powerful country in Europe. The church enjoyed an ample share of the new wealth and many workshops were employed in supplying it with embroideries. These, though preserved in considerable numbers, have not yet been adequately studied, so that their dating and attribution remains at present somewhat speculative. Strongly

6. Detail, St. Peter, from an orphrey embroidered in Spain in the late 15th-century.

7. Detail, the Baptism of Christ, from the altar frontal of *c.*1530 shown in fig. 1.

8. Detail, the Virgin and Child with the infant St. John, from the same altar frontal.

influenced, like other branches of Spanish art, by the Italian Renaissance, they tended to become more ornamental and less pictorial in character; figure subjects were frequently confined to medallions, while the remaining surfaces were overspread with gold-embroidered ornament, at first closely based on Italian models, but soon developing characteristically Spanish traits. The most favoured background materials for this gold embroidery were silk velvets of superb quality, woven in Spain and often dyed with costly crimson dye.

Probably the most important centre in the early 16th century was Toledo, where there is a good deal of documentary evidence concerning the embroidery workshops, and where the cathedral still possesses a number of superb embroideries in the shaded gold (*or nué*) technique which were made between 1513 and 1526 (or later) by members of the Covarrubias family and others for Cardinals Cisneros and Fonseca.[34] Also associated with Toledo is the altar frontal which provides the pretext for the present article (fig. 1).[35] This altar frontal was acquired in 1969 from French and Company, New York, who state that it comes from the collection of William Butterworth, Moline, Illinois, from the San Donato (i.e. Demidoff) collection, Florence, and from the church of San Juan de los Reyes, Toledo. Although it has not been possible to

verify this provenance from independent evidence, there is no reason to doubt its correctness. San Juan de los Reyes, the church of a Franciscan convent founded by Ferdinand and Isabella and originally intended as their burial-place, was erected during the last quarter of the 15th century to the design of Juan Guas. A drawing attributed to Guas shows, on the high altar of the church, an armorial altar frontal with a large central medallion, five small medallions in the frontlet above, and a single small medallion in each of the two side panels;[36] the arrangement resembles that of the Museum's frontal (which must be considerably later than the drawing) but is too common to have any evidential value. The interior of the church was much damaged by the French in 1808 and it is possible that its altar frontals and other furnishings were removed at that time.

The Museum's frontal, of rich crimson velvet, is embroidered with gold, silver and silk threads in a variety of techniques and textures; four objects of rosette shape, which have left an imprint on the velvet but are no longer present, were possibly metal ornaments. The two large medallions (figs. 7, 8), most of the smaller ones, and much of the embroidered ornament are worked on applied pieces of silk textiles woven with metallic wire, which is now blackened but was no doubt bright when new; some pieces of

9. Detail, Christ, from the scene of the Baptism in fig. 7.

10. Detail, St. John the Baptist, from the same scene.

this metallic tissue are white in colour (e.g. the large medallion on the left), while others are yellow (e.g. the large medallion on the right), producing marked and evidently intentional differences of tonality in the embroidered subjects. The *or nué* technique of the Covarrubias embroideries in Toledo cathedral is here very sparingly used, principally in six small cherub-heads, but the execution is of extremely high quality throughout, and especially so in the heads and flesh-parts in the large medallion on the left (figs. 9, 10), where the embroiderer seems to have reproduced the designer's style with such fidelity as to raise hopes of identifying the artist responsible. The present writer's knowledge of Spanish art of the period is insufficient for this purpose, but both the pictorial and the ornamental style of the frontal point to the generation of artists who were introducing Italian formal ideas into Spain during the first half of the 16th century. In the Toledo school of painting this means Juan de Borgoña and his successors,[37] while among sculptors active in the city Vasco de la Zarza, Felipe Vigarny, Alonso Berruguete and others employed a comparable Italianate vocabulary of forms.[38] The main panel of the frontal shows pictorial and ornamental styles related to those of the *or nué* embroideries in the cathedral, but probably slightly later in date; they seem to fit most naturally within a few years of 1530, and can hardly be much later than the middle of the

century. The ornamental style of the frontlet and side panels could be somewhat later than that of the main panel, but this is by no means certain.

Iconographically the frontal makes a confused impression. The large medallions depict two meetings of Christ and St. John the Baptist, which one might have expected to be shown in chronological order from left to right, rather than the reverse. On the frontlet, the small medallion in the centre depicts Christ carrying the cross; the two on either side show a nimbed eagle with chalice and quill, the symbol of St. John the Evangelist, the titular saint of San Juan de los Reyes; that on the extreme left depicts the martyrdom of St. John the Evangelist, and that on the extreme right the same saint with his eagle and two angels. The small medallion on the left side-panel represents the Stigmatization of St. Francis, that on the right St. Catherine of Siena with heart, flowers, cross and crown of thorns; these are two saints who enjoyed a miraculous sympathy with the Passion of Christ.[39] It is very curious indeed that the seven small medallions, concerned with the Passion and with St. John the Evangelist, have no apparent iconographical relationship with the two large medallions, concerned with St. John the Baptist.

The work most nearly comparable with the present frontal is an embroidered altar frontal of similar size in Chicago, which appears, however, to be later

11. Lectern cover of green velvet, embroidered in gold, silver and silk with scenes from the life of St. John the Baptist. Formerly in the church of La Madre de Dios, Seville, the cover was probably made in that city about 1570–75.

in style, probably from the late 16th century. This frontal is said to have been made for the cathedral of La Seo de Urgel;[40] it has also been stated that it was made in Toledo.[41] By a strange coincidence it presents the same iconographical confusion as the Museum's frontal, only in reverse. Its main panel has three large medallions depicting the Agony in the Garden, the Last Supper and the Entombment, i.e. three subjects from the Passion story in which St. John the Evangelist plays a prominent role; the seven small medallions on the subsidiary panels, however, are mainly concerned with the story of St. John the Baptist. It is very tempting to imagine that the subsidiary panels in Chicago were originally intended for the main panel in London, that the subsidiary panels in London were meant for the main panel in Chicago, and that at some stage of their existence the various panels have been confused and interchanged. On the other hand it must be acknowledged that this idea may be nothing but a red herring, for at the present moment there is no evidence to show that the two frontals have ever been together. It may or may not be relevant that in the 19th and 20th centuries there have been in the north transept of San Juan de los Reyes an altar and retable devoted to St. John the Baptist and in the south transept an altar and retable devoted to St. John the Evangelist;[42] it is uncertain whether this arrangement already existed there in the 16th century, though similar arrangements are known in other Spanish churches of that period.[43]

The history of the newly acquired frontal is evidently a tangled skein which will require further time and study to unravel. For the present, however, it can be admired as an outstanding example of Spanish embroidery of the 16th century, probably from the workshops of Toledo.

Seville, like Toledo, had possessed embroidery workshops since the early 15th century, but it was in the late 16th and early 17th century, as the wealth of the Americas flowed into the city, that they attained their greatest activity and distinction.[44] The Museum owns a handsome example of their work in a lectern cover from the church of the Dominican convent of La Madre de Dios in Seville (fig. 11).[45] Of green velvet, it is embroidered with gold, silver and silk threads in a variety of techniques. The design comprises foliage ornament and small oval strapwork medallions showing the arms of the Dominican order, the head of St. John the Baptist on a charger, and various other motifs; two square panels at the ends are embroidered, on a ground of white silk, with the Birth of the Baptist, surrounded by the four Doctors of the Church, and the Baptism of Christ, surrounded by the four evangelists (figs. 12, 13). In this case it seems unlikely that the designer can be identified, but there is no reason to doubt that he belonged to the Seville school in the latter half of the 16th century.[46] The church of La Madre de Dios was completed in 1572; a number of its fittings date from the early 1570s, which also seems a likely date for the lectern-cover. The latter may have been associated with an altar and carved retable on the south side of the church devoted to St. John the Baptist; the retable also includes representations of the Birth, the Baptism and the four Evangelists, and the treatment of the Birth scene is similar to that in the embroidery.

The collection includes other interesting examples but those described and illustrated here will suffice to suggest an outline history of Spanish church embroidery as it develops through various styles, with its centres shifting progressively from north-east to south-west of the peninsula: Romanesque in Catalonia, Gothic in the Kingdom of Aragon with its centres at Barcelona and Valencia, early Renaissance in Toledo, late Renaissance in Seville. Yet, even though the collection is fairly comprehensive, it would be a mistake to suggest that it covers every aspect of this exceedingly rich and varied tradition. The absence of any adequate example of the Flemish-influenced style of the late 15th century has already been mentioned. Among other desiderata the Museum would do well to acquire one of the splendid late Renaissance embroideries produced in the workshop of the Escorial.[47]

12. Detail, the Birth of St. John the Baptist, and the four Doctors of the Church, from the lectern cover in fig. 11.

13. Detail, the Baptism of Christ, and the four Evangelists, from the same lectern cover.

Notes

1. P. de Palol, 'Une broderie catalane d'époque romane', *Cahiers archéologiques*, VIII, 1956, pp. 175–214, IX, 1957, pp. 219–51.

2. Antonio C. Floriano Cumbreño, *El bordado*, 1942, pp. 40–41, fig. 6.

3. 1387–1904; 3 ft. × 5 ft. 7½ in. (91 × 172 cm.).

4. On dossals, see Joseph Braun, *Der christliche Altar*, II, 1924, pp. 534–40.

5. *Collection Bourgeois Frères*, I, 1904, p. 256, Lot 1385.

6. Braun, *op. cit.*, II, p. 97, pl. 131.

7. 8713–1863, 1252 and A–1864, from the abbey of Huysburg, near Halberstadt.

8. The provenance had been mentioned in José Gudiol Ricart, *Arte de España*: *Cataluña*, 1955, p. 42. Dr. Gudiol's letter of July 3 1956 provided the evidence: 'Cuando yo traje de Londres en 1925 la fotografía del frontal bordado que se conserva en ese Museo, Tachard me afirmó haber comprado aquella pieza en la Seo de Urgel y haberla vendido en el extranjero'.

9. Edouard Junyent, *Catalogne romane*, II, 1961, pp. 40–41.

10. On the Urgel workshop, see C. R. Post, *A History of Spanish Painting*, I, 1930, pp. 105–07, 221–23; W. W. S. Cook and J. Gudiol Ricart, *Ars Hispaniae. VI. Pintura e Imagineria Románicas*, 1950, pp. 69, 193, figs. 45, 46, 163–65; W. W. S. Cook, *La pintura romanica sobre tabla en Cataluña*, 1960, pp. 14–15, pls. 1–3.

11. Post, *op. cit.*, figs. 51, 62, 63; Cook and Gudiol Ricart, *op. cit.*, figs. 162, 191, 201, 206, 311, 329, 332, 346, 349.

12. Braun, *op. cit.*, I, p. 113.

13. M. Salmi, 'Il paliotto di Manresa e l'opus florentinum', in *Bollettino d'Arte*, XXIV, 1930–31, pp. 385–406.

14. A. G. I. Christie, *English Medieval Embroidery*, pp. 135–138,

156–58, 165–67, pls. LXXXVIII–XC, CIX–CXI, CXXII–CXXIV; D. King, *Opus anglicanum* exhibition catalogue, London, 1963, pp. 43–44.

15. Antolín P. Villanueva, *Los ornamentos sagrados en España*, 1935, p. 155; the inventory is given in full in *Boletín de la Academia de la Historia*, LXXXIX, 1926, p. 382ff.

16. T.72 and A–1922; Christie, *op. cit.*, pp. 118–20, pls. LXX, LXXI; King, *op. cit.*, p. 34.

17. El Conde de la Viñaza, *Adiciones al Diccionario Histórico*, I, 1889; José Sanchis y Sivera, *La catedral de Valencia*, 1909, pp. 48–50, 565–66, and 'El arte del bordado en Valencia en los siglos XIV y XV', *Revista de Archivos, Bibliotecas y Museos*, XXXVI, 1917, pp. 200–23; Villanueva, *op. cit.*, p. 159; Floriano Cumbreño, *op. cit.*, pp. 70–72.

18. *Catálogo del Museo Arqueológico-artístico episcopal de Vich*, 1893, p. 238; Gudiol Ricart, *op. cit.*, p. 63, fig. 359; *Europäische Kunst um 1400* exhibition catalogue, Vienna, 1962, p. 479–80, no. 534, pl. 100; Marie Schuette and Sigrid Müller-Christensen, *The Art of Embroidery*, 1964, p. 315, figs. 274–78.

19. Lamberto Font, *Gerona: La Catedral y el Museo Diocesano*, 1952, pp. 46, XXVII, fig. 100; Gudiol Ricart, *op. cit.*, p. 63, figs. 358, 360; *Europäische Kunst um 1400*, pp. 480–81, no. 535, pl. 101.

20. 792–1893; 2 ft. 11 in. × 6 ft. 10 in. (89 × 208 cm.).

21. 257–1880; 2 ft. 6 in. × 7 ft. 1 in. (76 × 216 cm.). This frontal, formerly divided into three pieces, has recently been re-assembled; the imprint on the velvet of the scrolls originally held by the angels shows that a few inches of the length were lost when the frontal was divided.

22. C. R. Post, *op. cit.*, III, 1930, pp. 75–83, 95–104, and IX, pt. II, 1947, pp. 759–64; José Gudiol Ricart, *Ars Hispaniae, IX, Pintura Gótica*, 1955, p. 156, figs. 116–18, pl. IV.

23. Floriano Cumbreño, *op. cit.*, pp. 101–02, fig. 32; Juan Ainaud, José Gudiol Ricart and F.-P. Verrié, *Catálogo Monumental de España: La Cuidad de Barcelona*, 1947, p. 276, figs. 1156–67 (including associated vestments); F.-P. Verrié, *Barcelona Antigua*, 1952, pp. 97–98; Schuette and Müller-Christensen, *op. cit.*, p. 315, figs. 280–82.

24. Braun, *op. cit.*, II, p. 66; Font, *op. cit.*, pp. 46, XXVIII, fig. 99.

25. El Marqués de Lozoya, *Historia del Arte Hispánico*, III, 1940, p. 391, fig. 398; J. Gudiol Ricart, *Arte de España: Cataluña*, 1955, p. 63, fig. 362.

26. Braun, *op. cit.*, II, p. 67; Lozoya, *op. cit.*, p. 391, fig. 399.

27. *Catálogo del Museo . . . de Vich*, 1893, pp. 238–41; Braun, *op. cit.*, II, pp. 66–67, pl. 128; Villanueva, *op. cit.*, pl. XII; Schuette and Müller-Christensen, *op. cit.*, p. 315, figs. 284, 285.

28. J. Sanchis y Sivera, *La catedral de Valencia*, 1909, pp. 435–36; Lozoya, *op. cit.*, p. 391, figs. 394–97; Schuette and Müller-Christensen, *op. cit.*, pp. 315–16, figs. 286, 287.

29. Floriano Cumbreño, *op. cit.*, pp. 90–93, fig. 25; Mildred Davison, 'An Altarpiece from Burgo de Osma', in *Museum Studies* (The Art Institute of Chicago), III, 1968, pp. 108–24.

30. Floriano Cumbreño, *op. cit.*, pp. 79–89, 95–96, 106–108, figs. 22–24, 28–30, 38, 39; Carlos Callejo, *El monasterio de Guadalupe*, 1958, pp. 119–26; Schuette and Müller-Christensen, *op. cit.*, pp. 315–16, figs. 279, 288–91.

31. Braun, *op. cit.*, II, pp. 67–68; L. Torres Balbás, *La mezquita de Córdoba*, 1952, pp. 129–30; Santiago Alcolea, *Córdoba*, 1963, pp. 94–95.

32. José Gestoso y Pérez, *Sevilla monumental y artistica*, II, 1890, p. 409f., and *Ensayo de un Diccionario de los artifices que florecieron in Sevilla*, I, 1899, pp. 27–46; Madrid, Junta para ampliación de estudios, *Datos documentales para la Historia del Arte español*, I, 1914; Floriano Cumbreño, *op. cit.*, pp. 72–74.

33. 601–1898, acquired from Louis de Farcy, Angers.

34. Madrid, Junta, *Datos documentales*, I and II, 1914–16; Villanueva, *op. cit.*, pp. 196–98; Floriano Cumbreño, *op. cit.*, pp. 140–42; J. Gudiol Ricart, *La catedral de Toledo*, n.d., pp. 136–37; Jean François Rivera, *La cathédrale de Tolède*, 1957, figs. 264, 265.

35. T.141–1969; 3 ft. 7¼ in. × 8 ft. (110 × 244 cm.).

36. *Exposición Conmemorativa del V Centenario del Matrimonio de los Reyes Católicos*, Valladolid, 1969, no. 563, pl. CIX.

37. C. R. Post, *op. cit.*, IX, pt. I, 1947, pp. 162–382. The style of the Baptism in the frontal seems not unlike that of Juan de Borgoña's *Last Supper* in Toledo Cathedral (Post, fig. 58).

38. J. M. Azcárate, *Ars Hispaniae, XIII, Escultura del Siglo XVI*, 1958, pp. 42–46, 96–102, 149–153. On the general question of Italian influence in Spain, see A. de Bosque, *Artistes Italiens en Espagne*, 1965, with excellent illustrations.

39. The representation of St. Francis is natural in an altar frontal destined for a Franciscan convent such as San Juan de los Reyes; the representation of the Dominican St. Catherine seems less so.

40. Christa Charlotte Mayer, *Masterpieces of Western Textiles from the Art Institute of Chicago*, 1969, p. 127, pl. 99.

41. Villanueva, *op. cit.*, p. 235.

42. El Vizconde de Palazuelos, *Toledo*, 1890, pp. 658–59. The altar and retable of St. John the Baptist can be seen in Leopoldo Torres Balbás, *Ars Hispaniae, VII, Arquitecture Gótica*, 1952, fig. 275.

43. E.g., the church of La Madre de Dios, Seville, source of the next embroidery to be discussed here, has an altar and retable of St. John the Evangelist on the north side and an altar and retable of St. John the Baptist on the south side.

44. Isabel Turmo, *Bordados y Bordadores Sevillanos* (Siglos XVI a XVIII), 1955.

45. 529–1877; 9 ft. 6 in. × 2 ft. (290 × 61 cm.).

46. Diego Angulo Iñiguez, *Ars Hispaniae, XII, Pintura del Renacimiento*, 1954, pp. 196–222, 314–27.

47. Paulina Junquera de Vega, 'El Obrador de Bordados de el Escorial', in *El Escorial*, II, 1963, pp. 551–82; Sabine Jacob, 'Bemerkungen zu einer Kasel aus dem Escorial', Berliner Museen, N.F.XVIII, 1968, pp. 46–53.

The altar-piece of St. George from Valencia

I. THE ALTAR-PIECE

On the 18th October 1864, J. C. Robinson, the Art Referee of the Science and Art Department, wrote in some excitement from Paris to Henry Cole, director of the South Kensington Museum: 'A work of art of unusual interest has just been brought to Paris and I beg to report on it herewith in order that their Lordships may be informed at the earliest moment.'[1] Robinson, to whom the Museum owes some of its most splendid purchases, went on to describe the object: 'a Spanish "retable" or altar-piece of great size', not later than 1430 and in an excellent state of preservation. He subsequently reported that it had been 'brought from a destroyed church in Valencia'.

Robinson was unable to complete his inspection of the retable before his return to London as it was dismantled in seventeen pieces, but he authorized John Webb, dealer, collector and antiquarian, to do so at the earliest opportunity. On the 27th October, Webb reported: 'To-day is the first fine day I have been able to catch Baur [the dealer concerned] to have the retablo put into the courtyard to see it together.' Webb confirmed Robinson's favourable report, but Baur's price, 20,000 francs (some £840), threatened to halt the proceedings, especially when Baur turned down successive offers of £500 and 15,000 francs. However, thanks to Robinson's advocacy, the purchase was subsequently authorized at £840 and the retable reached London before the end of 1864.[2]

Painted in tempera and gilt on panels of pitch pine, it reaches to a height of 21 ft. 9 in. (6.60 m) and a width of 18 ft. (5.50 m) (figs. 1–16). The large central panels show St. George fighting the dragon; a Christian army under James I of Aragon defeating the Moors, with the help of St. George, at the battle of Puig (October 18, 1237), and, at the top, the Virgin nursing the Child and crowned by Christ and angels – 'Our Lady of Victory'.[3] This is surmounted by Christ with the orb, flanked by Moses and Elijah, and the holy dove at the very top. On the two sides are sixteen scenes of the life and martyrdom of St. George, with the four evangelists surrounded by angels in the upper register. Each compartment has an elaborate carved, gilt frame. In the pilasters between these compartments are twenty-four prophets,[4] each standing under a trefoil arch surmounted by an elaborate pinnacle. The outer frame contains compartments with the twelve apostles[5] separated from each other by panels,

containing blank squares, which are 19th century replacements. Only the four squares at the top, which appear dark in the photograph, still contain the original arms (figs. 1, 30). Below, there is a much damaged predella consisting of ten scenes of the Passion (of which the outer two have been cut down by a third): the Agony in the Garden, the Betrayal, Christ before Caiaphas, the Flagellation, the Mocking, Christ bearing the cross, the Crucifixion, the Lamentation, the Entombment and the Resurrection.

The general appearance of the altar-piece is unmistakably Spanish. While it is true that painted retables with compartments, gothic pinnacles and arcading originated in Italy, in this case the shape – with the striking protrusion of the central compartment at the top – the great size, the large number of compartments and figures in columns, the predilection for gold, all indicate a Spanish origin. Specifically and uniquely Spanish, also, are the so-called 'dust-guards' (guardapolvos) that form the outer frame. The guardapolvos habitually consisted of strips of wood slanting outwards at the sides, and upwards at the top. They were often painted with figures and coats of arms, as they are here.[6]

This type of Spanish retable nearly always had a predella. In the case of the Museum's retable, the scenes of Christ's Passion are probably intended to form a parallel to those of St. George's martyrdom above, but this choice of scenes is not uncommon on Catalan and Valencian predellas. A closely similar series of six scenes appears, for example, on the predella of the retable from Rubió of c.1350, now in the Museum at Vich.

An early example of the fully developed Spanish retable, including guardapolvos, or outer frame, is that of the Virgin and Child from Sigena attributed to Jaime Serra and dated about 1360–70 (Barcelona Museum). In the late 14th and 15th centuries there tended to be an increase in the number of compartments and the size of these retables, and they often covered the whole end wall of a chancel or chapel. The basic features remained constant until the early 16th century, though towards the end of the period the painted surface was often embellished with carved figures.

In general terms the St. George retable belongs to this Spanish type, but in detail its construction, or what may be termed its carpentry, points unmistakably to Valencia.[7] The wide guardapolvos, painted with large

65

1. Marzal de Sas (?) (active in Valencia 1393–after 1410). Retable of St. George, *c*.1410–20. Tempera and gilt on pine, 21 ft 9 in × 18 ft (6·6 m × 5·5 m). Victoria and Albert Museum, 1217–1864.

66

2. Proposed reconstruction of the retable:

1	2	3	4
5	6	7	10
8	9	11	12
13	14	15	16

3. St. George
retable: *St. George
and the Dragon.*
(Before cleaning)

figures, and the angels and prophets painted on blue ground alongside the pinnacles at the top occur more regularly in Valencia than elsewhere. But it is above all in the carving and gilding of the cusped arches and compartmental frames that the Valencian origin becomes most apparent. The carving is intricate and the gilding even more so. Many of the rosettes and interstices are decorated with deeply punched floral designs, painted blue over the gold. The effect of the carved and gilt framework is sumptuous from a close view, as it is dazzling from afar.

The retable, then, may be placed in a particular category of Spanish altar-pieces, and it is an outstanding example of its kind. Nothing of like importance remains in Valencia – considering its size, completeness, quality and relatively early date – and even in Catalonia, where the number of such retables is still considerable, there are few to equal it on all these counts. It is, therefore, hardly surprising that it has been discussed and reproduced in nearly every book on Spanish painting published in the last sixty years,[8] and Valencians have expressed some bitterness at the loss of this major work.[9] In the Ceramics Museum at Valencia there is a copy on tiles of the central panel, the battle of Puig, made some forty years ago by Gonzales Marti, the founder of that Museum.[10]

Yet, even if the picture's importance has long been recognized, it is only with the cleaning carried out in 1969–70 by the Museum's Conservation Department that its spectacular quality and remarkable state of preservation were fully revealed (figs. 7, 8, 10–12, 14, 15). It is this conservation work which has prompted the writing of these notes, and it must be admitted at once that they raise more problems than they solve.

4. St. George retable: *The Battle of Puig* (1237). (Before cleaning)

II. THE ATTRIBUTION OF THE ALTAR-PIECE TO MARZAL DE SAS

Valencia, after its reconquest from the Moors by James I of Aragon in 1238, became a kingdom under the Crown of Aragon. The city itself received a charter from James I granting a considerable degree of autonomy, and in the later Middle Ages it enjoyed a period of prosperity as one of the major sea ports of Europe. Its population, which rose from 40,000 in 1418 to 75,000 in 1483, was much greater than that of Barcelona and was, with Seville, the largest in Spain.[11] To-day it is a city most famed for its baroque past, but its great Gothic buildings of the 14th and 15th centuries remain as visible evidence of the city's early greatness, and the sky-line is still dominated by the 'Micalet', the octagonal belfry begun in 1381.

An independent school of painting appears to have developed at about this time – at least nothing much earlier has survived – initially as an offshoot of the Catalan school. Catalonia had a distinguished tradition of panel painting stretching back over two hundred years. In the 14th century the Catalan school was represented by artists of the calibre of Ferrer Bassa (active 1324; d.1348); the brothers Jaime (active 1361–after 1375) and Pedro (active 1363–c.1400) Serra, and Luis Borrassá (active 1388–after 1424), all, to varying degrees, subject to Italian influence.[12] Among the earliest extant Valencian paintings is a group that includes the panels from a retable of St. Luke in the Museum at Valencia and the retable of the Blessed Sacrament in the Ermita S. Bartolomé at Villahermosa. These have been attributed to Francisco Serra II, who was active in Barcelona from 1376 and recorded in Valencia in 1382 and 1394.[13] This attribution is in itself an indication of the debt of these early Valencian paintings to the Catalan school. At the same time it seems likely that the young Valencian school had direct links with Italy, not surprisingly in view of the close trading and political connections. Certainly, the altar-piece commissioned by Bonifacio Ferrer (Valencia Museum), brother of St. Vincent Ferrer, who became prior of Portaceli Abbey in 1400, is a very Italianate work, while the carving and gilding of the framework attests its Valencian origin.[14]

It is against this background of a growing and increasingly prosperous city without a strong native tradition of painting that we must see the arrival, before 1393, of a German painter, Marzal de Sas, who was to be the leading exponent of his art in Valencia for over a decade. He is recorded in seventeen documents dating from 1393 until 1410.[15] 'Sas' may presumably be identified with Saxony, for in a document of 1396 he is described as 'Mestre Marçal de Sas, pintor Alamany', or the 'German painter', which effectively disposes of the suggestion that Sas may have referred to Saragossa or elsewhere in Spain. The documents refer to his paintings in the Torre de Serranos (1393–94), the Consistory (1396), the Cathedral (1399–1400) and the Church of the Holy Cross (1399), and to a retable commissioned by Petrus Torella (1404–05). Several of these works were produced in collaboration with other artists, among whom Pedro Nicolau, Gonzalo Perez and Gerardo Gener are named in the documents. Pedro Nicolau and Gonzalo Perez were Valencians; Gerardo Gener came from Barcelona and a large retable by him may still be seen in the Cathedral of that city.

From the nature of the commissions alone it is clear that Marzal de Sas was one of the leading painters in Valencia in the period round 1400, and it is, therefore, lamentable that of the eight major works recorded in the documents only one small fragment survives. This is a panel of the *Incredulity of St. Thomas* in the Valencia Cathedral Museum, which has been traditionally identified as having formed part of a retable of St. Thomas painted by Marzal de Sas for St. Thomas's chapel in the Cathedral in February–March 1400 (fig. 17). This identification was tentatively accepted by the historian of the Cathedral in 1909[16] and accepted as 'probable' by Chandler Post who, in his monumental study of Spanish painting, was the first to throw light upon the early history of the Valencian School.[17]

Post examined the *Incredulity of St. Thomas* and found in its style sufficient confirmation of the German origin of the artist. He pointed to the angular, contorted draperies and, in particular, to the 'ill favoured physiognomies, Teutonic in the cast of features . . . close to the border of caricature'. There can, indeed, be no doubt that these very naturalistic and expressive facial types stand out as a strange phenomenon in Spanish painting around 1400, but it is almost equally difficult to find close parallels in Germany. Marzal must have received his training in Germany before his appearance as a 'Master' in Valencia in 1393, but at that period German painting is not notably more naturalistic or prone to 'ill favoured physiognomies'

5. St. George retable:
The Virgin and Child;
above: *Christ flanked by
Moses and Elijah.* (Before
cleaning)

6. St. George retable: *St. George armed*; *the dragon fed*; above: *St. John and St. Luke*. (Before cleaning)

than that of any other school. However, a comparison can be made with Bohemian art, in particular with the Třeboň (Wittingau) retable of c.1380 (National Gallery Prague).[18] The long-nosed, bearded and hooded figure in the upper right of the St. Thomas panel (fig. 17) may be compared with the apostle holding Christ's head in the Třeboň *Entombment*, and some of the other faces can be paralleled in the Třeboň *Agony in the Garden* (fig. 18). As there was considerable Bohemian influence on German painting at this time, Post's theory remains inherently acceptable. And once Post had established the 'Germanic nature' of the St. Thomas panel he was able to point to many similarities with the St. George retable in the V. & A. Museum and hence to attribute this and several other paintings to Marzal de Sas. His attribution has been accepted by all subsequent scholars in this field.[19]

The most striking individual characteristic of the St. George retable is the naturalism and expressiveness of the figures. Most of the compartments are crowded with some eight or ten figures engaged in lively discussion or violent action. Their faces are sharply individualized and no two are alike in physiognomy or expression. The 'good' characters – notably St. George himself, the people of Silene in the upper registers and the prophets and apostles in the borders – are individually characterized as recognizable human types; the evil torturers and companions of the Roman provost Dacian – shown as a King – are caricatured in varying degrees. In caricaturing the torturers the artist is following the medieval tradition of giving them grotesquely ugly and occasionally negro faces to express evil. This tradition can be traced continuously in the depiction of Christ's Passion; some of the most splendid caricatures may be found in English art, for example in the Flagellation in the Winchester Psalter of the mid-12th century.[20]

A consistent feature of the figures in the retable is the prominent long nose, broad at the base with a white highlight on the tip. The long-nosed type has been seen as the hall-mark of Marzal de Sas' style, though in the St. George retable it appears with endless variation. The facial colours consist of pink with an undercoat of green for the shadows and contrasting white highlights. The fullness of the modelling combined with expressive, highly individualized features produce an effect of naturalism unusual at this early date. The faces of the prophet Daniel and of the adviser to Dacian in the adjoining

compartment (fig. 14), for example, present a degree of realism almost more reminiscent of the age of Jan van Eyck than of the International style.

Realism is also not too strong a word to describe the treatment of the Saint's tortures. Even the most horrible of these (plate 3 & fig. 12) are explicitly portrayed down to the last gruesome detail, so that one can almost feel St. George being scraped, pierced and sawn asunder. The International style is more aptly connected with courtly elegance than gruesome realism, and yet the period round 1400 did see important attempts to portray nature – in particular, plants and animals – with greater accuracy than hitherto.[21] Nor should it be forgotten that there was also what Panofsky described as the 'nocturnal' aspect of the International style; the pronounced stress on the gruesome, the sad and the grim. This is epitomized in the rendering of the 'Man of Sorrows', a devotional image in which the broken body of Christ is supported by one or two angels.[22] The gruesomely realistic portrayal of the tortures of St. George should be seen in this context.

Accuracy of observation is also the keynote of the battle scene (fig. 4). The armour is depicted with sufficient realism to make it a factor to be considered in the dating of the picture. The Christians are arrayed in fully developed plate armour, complete with pauldrons, or shoulder guards, and protective discs at the chest and elbow, though some still wear the mail aventail. The Moors are recognizable as the bodyguard of the Cordovan Caliphs – negroes recruited in North Africa.[23] They wear flowing robes and no armour, and carry *adargas*, the heart-shaped Arab shields, of which two are charged with devices of a scorpion and a turtle. The Moorish king in the foreground wears a typical Hispano-Moresque sword. As in the torture scenes, the viewer is spared none of the pain suffered in the battle. St. George's own sword pierces the agonized face of his opponent from one cheek to the other, and at the top a Moor thrusts his dagger into the mouth of a Crusader, while he himself has been wounded three times.

All this is not to suggest that the retable is lacking in the elegance and love of surface decoration typical of the International style. The scene on the upper left, for example, showing St. George armed by the Virgin and angels, has all the charm one would expect from a work of this period (fig. 6). The king's daughter is very fashionably dressed in a high-waisted *hopa*, or cassock, with long sleeves reaching nearly to the

7. St. George retable: *The people of Silene before the king.* (After cleaning)

ground (figs. 3, 8). The most prominent figures are dressed in sumptuous brocades. These consist of floral designs on a gold ground intricately punched with dots; the remainder of the surface is painted red, leaving the floral pattern reserved in gold (plate 3). This technique of punching the gold with a myriad of dots to achieve the rich effect of brocade is typical of Valencian painting of this period. The other draperies, solidly modelled with highlights of graded tones, are mainly magenta, crimson and deep blue. Most of the outlines are incised.

The realism of the faces on the retable is, therefore, tempered by a distinct elegance of dress and posture. This mixture of realism and elegance finds a parallel in certain aspects of Franco-Flemish book illumination of the opening years of the 15th century, for example in the additions made in *c.*1405 to the Duc de Berry's 'Très Belles Heures de Notre-Dame'.[24] This degree of facial naturalism first emerged in the Netherlands and became more widespread when the employment of Flemish illuminators in Paris brought strong elements of naturalism to the elegance of French court art of the period.[25] We have seen that the facial types of the retable are linked first and foremost with what Post called the 'ill-favoured physiognomies' of the somewhat earlier *Incredulity of St. Thomas* panel in Valencia cathedral (fig. 17). Yet the mixture of realism and elegance discernible in the figures of the retable suggests that the influence of early 15th century Franco-Flemish painting may also be inferred (compare fig. 24).

The background of the picture is predominantly gold. Of nineteen scenes, only five are effectively without gold background; in most of the others it covers about a third of the composition. The gold is patterned both on the haloes and at the outer edge of each compartment. This dominance of gold goes hand in hand with a relatively undeveloped use of landscape and interiors, compared to the advanced painting of Italy and France of the time. Interior space is achieved by the usual tiled floors and coffered ceilings. Their patterns run in parallel lines and show no sign of converging. In the last scene, lower right, the lines of the throne actually draw further apart as they recede, instead of converging (fig. 15). However, this is unusual, and in some scenes – notably the two on the right in the upper register (figs. 7, 8) – a distant view of turreted buildings, coloured red and pink, is successfully shown. In general, the depiction of landscapes and interiors belongs to types which, with Italy as the source, had spread throughout Western Europe in the second half of the 14th century. Only in his deployment of the rows of fighting soldiers in the central scene does the artist achieve a more advanced and independent rendering of space.

Most scholars who have dealt with the retable speak of it as the work of several hands. Pedro Nicolau, the principal associate of Marzal de Sas, Gonzalo Perez[26] and Miguel Alcañiz[27] have all been suggested as collaborators in this work. Indeed, it is not unreasonable to suppose that several artists worked on a painting of this size. Yet a close examination of the retable during cleaning does not support this theory, but reveals an underlying unity of style. The master may well have had assistance with the draperies and accessories, but the main parts of the retable appear to be the work of one painter who has left his stamp on every face and gesture.

The question remains: can his identity be firmly established? Post's identification with Marzal de Sas was based on the comparison with the *Incredulity of St. Thomas* in Valencia Cathedral (fig. 17). He compared the unusual facial types, which he described as 'gaunt, hard-featured, Teutonic', with the prophets in the frames of the retable.[28] In particular, the long-nosed apostle on the upper right hand corner of the *Incredulity* is very similar in facial type to St. George himself,

8. St. George retable: *The dragon tied with the princess's girdle*; above: *St. Matthew.* (After cleaning)

particularly in the scenes of the poisoned cup (fig. 10) and the falling idols (fig. 13). More generally, the draperies in both paintings are bulky and heavy, the cloth often lying in folds independent of the body beneath. The pattern on the floor is similar to that in the Baptism and the scenes of the cross and of the

9. St. George retable: *St. George before Dacian*; *the King baptized*; *St. George in prison*; *St. George tortured on the table*. (Before cleaning; panels in wrong order)

10. St. George retable:
St. George drinks the poison; the enchanter is executed. (After cleaning)

wheel in the retable (plate 3 & fig. 11). Yet the draperies and floor patterns are part of the general stylistic features of the time, and the attribution remains based on the comparison of the facial types. The similarities are indeed striking and, allowing for the fact that the retable is a later work, it is certainly possible that the two paintings are by the same artist. But it remains a sad fact that the only reasonably documented work by Marzal de Sas, while demonstrating the nature of his influence on subsequent Valencian painting, provides insufficient evidence to allow a firm attribution of the St. George retable. Post was the first to stress this point and his own attribution was never more than tentative.[29] To this caveat must be added the fact of the deplorable condition of the *Incredulity of St. Thomas.* The one documented work of this major artist is hidden by such an impenetrable layer of dirt that any close comparison of details and of colour is at present out of the question. It is fortunate that there is a good pre-War photograph.

Post, followed by the Valencian art historian Leandro de Saralegui, went on to attribute several other paintings to Marzal de Sas. First of these are two small panels of the Nativity of Christ and the Death of the Virgin in the Philadelphia Museum (fig. 19).[30] These are certainly very close to the St. George retable, with the same bearded figures with their prominent, almost bulbous noses, but they are more cursory in treatment. The apostles in the *Death of the Virgin* all have essentially the same faces repeated with only minor variations, which contrasts strongly with the individualization in the retable. They are closely related but probably not by the same hand. Another of Post's attributions, parts of an altar-piece with scenes of St. Vincent, is similar to the retable but not closely comparable in either style or quality (fig. 20).[31] These panels are usually classified as 'Workshop of Marzal de Sas'.

More similar to the retable is a group of paintings attributed by Post to Marzal and his followers but

subsequently ascribed to Miguel Alcañiz, a Majorcan artist recorded in Valencia from 1421–32 – though apparently active there from about 1410 – and from 1434 in Majorca. The attribution was based on Saralegui's identification of an altar-piece of St. Michael in the Museum at Lyons with the one commissioned by the church at Jerica from Alcañiz in a document of 1421.[32] On the basis of this identification Saralegui gave to Alcañiz the Holy Cross retable from S. Domingo, Valencia (Valencia Museum) (figs. 21–23) and a Crucifixion[33], as well as the retable of SS. Giles and Vincent from the Priory of St. John of Jerusalem, Valencia[34], and various other works.[35]

Alcañiz has been suggested as a collaborator on the St. George retable and there is no doubt that his style is similar. In particular the Holy Cross retable – which Post attributed to Marzal himself – has a strong resemblance to the retable. The compartments crowded with lively, gesticulating figures and containing scenes of battle and single combat, the long-nosed facial

types and the treatment of the reddish, turreted buildings, all link it with the style of the St. George retable. Yet Alcañiz's figures, elegantly dressed and at times almost prancing, are essentially closer to the idealized, courtly tendencies of the International style. Comparing the scene of Heraclius killing Chosroes II on the Holy Cross retable (fig. 22) with those of the King of Silene (fig. 7) or St. George before Dacian (fig. 9), it becomes clear that despite their close relationship, Alcañiz does not aspire to the strongly individualized and solidly modelled figures of the St. George retable. Even more than his men and women, Alcañiz's horses are unreal, ethereal creatures (figs. 23) compared with the solid, monumental and accurately observed horses of the retable (figs. 3, 4).

This discussion of related works produced in Valencia in the first quarter of the 15th century has not produced a firm answer to the question of who painted the St. George retable and when. Nor are the documents any more conclusive. The recorded paintings of

12. St. George retable:
The Saint sawn asunder.
(After cleaning)

Marzal de Sas cover the period 1393 to 1405. In 1407 he apprenticed his son Enrique to a silversmith. The last known record concerning him appears in the minutes of the Valencian city council of April 26, 1410:

'The Council, knowing how Master Marçal the painter was suffering from grave poverty and illness, and in great praise of his work and for the instruction given to many persons of his art, grants him for the length of time that it pleases the Council and no longer the said Master Marçal should have his estate and habitation in the top room above the flour store in the said city.'[36]

We have no means of knowing whether Marzal ever recovered from his 'grave poverty and illness' sufficiently to continue his professional work. Recently a document has been found recording the marriage, on April 24, 1430, of Marzal's daughter Ursula.[37] Marzal himself, we learn, was no longer living on that occasion, but his widow Margaret was still alive. Girls

tended to marry at about 15–18, which would place Ursula's birth in about 1412–15. This is not evidence that Marzal was painting pictures at that date, but it does indicate that he was still active in the second decade of the century.

To judge from the style and costume, the retable should be dated *c*.1410–20. The costume, in particular the *hopa* of the princess, has been dated *c*.1410 in a monograph on Spanish dress.[38] The predominance of the gold background, particularly the lack of landscape in the scene of George fighting the dragon, suggests a date not later than *c*.1420. The realism in the modelling and expressions of the faces would seem to indicate a date after 1410, though it is well to remember that the *Incredulity of St. Thomas*, which has similar faces, is dated 1400. The fully developed plate-armour depicted in the battle scene has been dated *c*.1420 by one specialist[39]; others prefer to place it *c*.1420–30.[40] The armour of King James may be compared, for example, with that of the St. George carved by Pere Johan on

13. St. George retable: *The Saint prays and the idols fall*; *the torture in the cauldron of lead*. (Before cleaning; panels in wrong order)

the doorway of the Palace of the *Diputacio* in Barcelona, which is dated 1418.[41] This also has the developed pauldron and protective discs, which are not found regularly before the 1420's.

Clearly, therefore, if the documents are interpreted to mean that Marzal de Sas was principally active in the period 1393–1405 and that he ceased to paint before 1410 when he had fallen on evil times, then he must be ruled out as the possible author of the retable, which appears to post-date 1410 and which may well be as late as 1420. On the other hand, his daughter's marriage in 1430 suggests that Marzal was still active in the second decade of the century and lack of extant documents does not prove that he received no commissions at this period. The evidence remains inconclusive. Some thirty painters are recorded in Valencia in this decade and the work of less than half a dozen of these is identified. It is possible that the author of the retable – without doubt one of the major European artists of his time – remains to be identified. Yet the link with Marzal remains indissoluble and as long as the problematic nature of the

evidence is recognized, it is reasonable to attribute the retable to Marzal de Sas (?) and to date it *c.*1410–*c.*1420.

III. ST. GEORGE

(a) The sequence of the story

At the Council of Rome in 494, Pope Gelasius, in the presence of seventy bishops, sought to separate the authentic books of the Church from those he considered apocryphal. He included the lives of the saints in his survey, and among those which he considered to be the work of heretics and sectarians was the Life of St. George.[42]

This Life is known to us from two 9th century Latin texts, which were doubtless derived from a Greek original. It described the martyrdom of the Saint in gruesome detail and included some twelve separate scenes of torture and seven miracles. On four occasions during the tortures the Saint died, and three times his resurrection was brought about by divine intervention. Such a story, it was felt by Pope Gelasius and his bishops, clearly overstrained credence and

14. St. George retable: *St. George drawn through the city.*
(After cleaning)

forthwith it was pruned of its excesses. Briefly, the scenes of torture were reduced to five, the miracles to three and the resurrections totally omitted. The original Life has been called by scholars the 'apocryphal version' and the expurgated text the 'canonical version'; both were in circulation throughout the Middle Ages and there are various recensions half-way between the two. The apocryphal version appears in Syriac, Arabic and Coptic texts. Western medieval texts show some dependence on the apocryphal version, but contain fewer tortures and omit much of the supernatural of the original story, in accordance with the censure of Pope Gelasius. The popularity of the Saint is underlined by the fact that there are very many Western MS versions in Latin and vernacular languages dating from the 12th to the 15th centuries. Of these, the one contained in the very popular and influential *Golden Legend* of Jacobus de Voragine (d.1298) was one of the shorter versions.

These Western medieval texts all contain the story of St. George and the dragon. This, it might be thought, goes without saying, but the battle with the dragon is not in fact an original part of the St. George legend, and it does not appear in the early medieval versions. Indeed, the legend had existed for over six centuries before the dragon was added to it in the 12th century. It was probably taken over from the life of another saint, perhaps St. Theodore – like St. George a warrior saint – who was known as a dragon-killer from the 9th century.[43] There is of course a long literary tradition of heroes fighting serpents or dragons, going back to Perseus – who saved Andromeda by slaying the monster – and beyond that to the Egyptian god Horus. This has led to the suggestion that St. George was the direct inheritor of the Perseus-Horus myth,[44] but it can be shown that the story had been adapted for several Christian saints before St. George.[45] The story of the dragon was

15. St. George retable: *Execution of St. George, fire from heaven kills Dacian.* (After cleaning)

added to the St. George legend in the early 12th century when he became popular in the West as the protector of the Crusading armies. Of the many episodes of the Saint's life known to us, discussion here will be limited to those depicted on the Museum's altar-piece.

It became apparent, from an examination of the various versions of the Life of St. George, that the scenes on the retable were no longer in the correct sequence. Accordingly, when the picture was dismantled for cleaning last year and its structure could be examined, a reconstruction was attempted, rearranging the panels to fit the sequence of the story (compare figs. 1 and 2). For structural reasons the panels on each side could not be moved across to the other side. In some cases the compartments could not be separated because a single wooden panel had been used for two scenes painted one below the other,

which further limited the extent of possible permutations. But apart from these structural factors, it is quite easy to see how the sequence of scenes could have been upset by a few mistakes made when the altar-piece was re-erected in 1864, or perhaps before. In the reconstruction proposed here, the order of the scenes follows the text with only one exception.

Reading across the painting from left to right (fig. 2) the first scene, showing St. George armed by the Virgin and angels, does not occur in the Lives. The story proper begins in the second panel. The setting is Silene in Libya. By the city there was a pond, in which lived a dragon threatening the whole country. To pacify this dragon the people of Silene were forced to give up to it a man or child and a sheep every day, and this sacrifice is shown in detail on the retable (scene 2, fig. 6). After many children and young people had been devoured by the dragon, the

lot fell upon the king's daughter. The king objected and offered gold and silver if he could keep his daughter, whereupon his people replied – to quote the Caxton translation of the *Golden Legend* –
'How sir! ye have made and ordained the law, and our children be now dead, and ye would do the contrary. Your daughter shall be given or we shall burn your house.'[46] (scene 3, fig. 7).
The king was forced to agree to give up his daughter and, after a respite of eight days, dressed as for her wedding, she was led to the place where the dragon was. It happened that at this time St. George, a knight of Cappadocian descent, living in Palestine, was passing by. On seeing the princess and discovering why she was there, he drew his sword and then rode against the dragon and pierced it with his spear (lower central panel). After the fight St. George asked the princess for her girdle, and when he had tied it round the dragon's neck the beast followed him meekly (scene 4, fig. 8). On returning to the city, St. George killed the dragon and cut off its head. So impressed were the inhabitants of Silene that the king, queen and princess and fifteen thousand men, not to mention the women and children, were baptized by Bishop Alexander (scene 5, fig. 9).
So much for the story of the dragon; the remaining scenes illustrate St. George's martyrdom which, as we have seen, was described in the early Christian Life of the Saint.
At this time, in the reign of Diocletian (284–305), there was a great persecution of the Christians and many forsook God and sacrificed to the idols. On hearing of this, St. George gave up his knight's habit, sold all his possessions to give the money to the poor and took the habit of a Christian. He then went before the local ruler Dacian and denounced the pagan gods as devils (scene 6, fig. 9). Unable to make the Saint sacrifice to Apollo, Dacian at once ordered him to be tortured. First he was tied to a cross and his flesh scraped with iron combs (scene 7, & plate 3). Then he was placed on a table, nailed to it and tied to it with chains (scene 8, fig. 9). After this he was put in prison, where Christ and the angels came to him in the night to give him comfort (scene 9, fig. 9). Seeing himself unable to overcome the Saint, Dacian called his enchanter, who promised to deal with the matter. He mixed a strong poison with some wine and gave it to St. George to drink. St. George took it, made the sign of the cross on it and drank it without

16. St. George retable: *St. James the Greater* in the *guardapolvos*. (Before cleaning)

coming to any harm. The process was repeated a second time and, when he saw his magic overcome by a power stronger than his own, the enchanter knelt at the feet of St. George and prayed to him to make him a Christian. Thereupon Dacian had him executed on the spot (scene 10, fig. 10). This is the only scene now out of place in the sequence of the story; it cannot be moved as it is on the same panel as the scene below. It is possible that the artist's source differed in this instance.

Dacian now ordered St. George to be placed between

18. Bohemian School, c.1380. *The Agony in the Garden* (detail) from the Třebŏn retable. National Gallery, Prague.

two wheels with sharp points (scene 11, fig. 11), but the Lord intervened and the wheels were broken. Then Dacian ordered him to be tied to two posts and sawn asunder with a large saw (scene 12, fig. 12). During this torture he gave up his spirit to the Lord. He was then placed in a cauldron of molten lead, but, with the Lord's protection, he seemed well at ease as though in a bath (scene 13, fig. 13).

These tortures having proved of no avail, Dacian now cunningly flattered St. George, who pretended to agree to worship the idols. Before a large audience in the temple, the Saint prayed to the Lord to destroy the temple so that the people might be converted. 'And anon the fire descended from heaven and burnt the temple and the idols and their priests . . . ' (scene 14, fig. 13). On the following morning Dacian ordered St. George to be drawn naked through the city (scene 15, fig. 14) and then to be beheaded. When this had been done, fire fell down from heaven and burnt Dacian and all his servants (scene 16, fig. 15).

Most of the scenes illustrated in the retable can be found in the *Golden Legend*, but there are several indications that this was not the artist's source. Two of the scenes – St. George nailed to the table (scene 8) and sawn asunder (scene 12) – do not appear in the *Golden Legend*. The torture of the saw, arguably the most horrible of the whole gruesome series, occurs in the early apocryphal Life but was one of the scenes expurgated for the canonical version. It was, never-

17. Marzal de Sas, *The Incredulity of St. Thomas*, fragment from an altar-piece; 1400. Valencia Cathedral.

theless, retained in some Western medieval texts, including the version in the Catalan language which is known to us from the two late 14th century manuscripts.[47] The scene of the Saint nailed to the table also occurs in the Catalan version, and there are several points of detail in which the retable agrees with the Catalan text rather than with the *Golden Legend*. In the first torture, for instance, the Catalan version describes the cross and the iron combs, whereas the *Golden Legend* has the Saint raised on a gibbet and beaten. In the penultimate scene the Catalan version describes St. George drawn through the city naked, but there is no mention of his nakedness in the *Golden Legend*. The retable shows Dacian as a king, as he appears in the Catalan version, whereas the *Golden Legend* describes him as only a provost. The inclusion of two entire scenes omitted in the *Golden Legend*, as well as these differences in detail, suggest that the artist was using a manuscript close to the Catalan text, rather than relying on the most popular Western version.

The central panel of the retable represents the battle of Puig (1237), when James the Conqueror, King of Aragon, won a victory over the Moors through the appearance of St. George amid the Christian host (fig. 4). King James is shown in the centre, his horse draped in the colours of Aragon – red and gold; St. George is next to him. The knight behind the king on the left may be identified as Don Guillén de Aguilo, whose arms contained the crowned eagle that figures so prominently on his tabard. He was a close confidant of the King and one of the commanders in the battle.[48]

The story of St. George helping the Christian armies against the forces of Islam originated in the First Crusade. Several 12th-century historians, including William of Malmesbury, tell the story of St. George appearing in the Christian host at the siege of Antioch in 1098.[49] St. George had long been honoured as a military saint in Byzantium, but it was only with the arrival of the Crusaders in the East that he was adopted as the principal protector of the Christian armies. The legends concerning St. George developed in the course of the 12th century, and at the third Crusade in 1189–92 the knights of Richard I proclaimed him their special guardian.[50] It is to his connection with the Crusades that St. George owes his popularity in medieval Western Europe.

The *Golden Legend* popularized the Saint's part in the

19. Follower of Marzal de Sas, *The Death of the Virgin*. Philadelphia Museum of Art.

20. Follower of Marzal de Sas, *The Death of St. Vincent.* Catalan Museum, Barcelona.

siege of Jerusalem in 1099, but meanwhile the story had been taken up by the Spaniards. St. George appears in accounts of every Christian victory over the Moors of Spain from the battle of Alcoraz (1096) onwards,[51] and it was through his part in these wars that he became the patron saint of Aragon and Catalonia. Among the many battles in which his intervention carried the Christian forces forward to victory was that of Puig in 1237. This victory was depicted on the retable as it led directly to the reconquest of Valencia, completed in 1238.

(b) The iconography
Our discussion of the literary sources of the retable have led to the conclusion that the cycle illustrated a local version of the legend similar to the Catalan text known to us. However, it should be borne in mind that artists tended to use pictorial models wherever these were available, and in the case of St. George there existed a pictorial tradition to which an artist working shortly after 1400 could readily turn.

In particular, the scene of St. George and the dragon had become widely popular by that date. We have seen that this legend first appeared in literary sources in the early 12th century and it was illustrated at about the same time. The earliest known depiction is on a Greek coin of Roger of Antioch (1112–19)[52] and this, like other 12th and 13th century examples in Byzantium and the West, shows the Saint alone, on horseback, spearing the dragon. The well known relief on the tympanum of Ferrara Cathedral (c.1135) is exceptional in showing St. George fighting the dragon with a sword; this was not to be the usual form until the time of Raphael. In the earliest examples, the dragon is depicted as a snake.

This composition is derived from an ancient pictorial tradition especially popular in Roman art in which the Hero, Victor or Emperor is seen on horseback driving a lance into a beast or snake or a defeated enemy. There are examples on late Roman coins and reliefs which could well have provided the pictorial models for the early illustration of St. George and the dragon.[53] Conversely, the St. George on the coin of Roger of Antioch, for example, would be indistinguishable from the Emperors and Victors of these Roman scenes, were it not for the inscription bearing his name.

This was the usual form of the scene in the 12th and 13th centuries, but from the 14th century it was elaborated to include the princess[54] and a landscape background. By about 1400, therefore, when the subject, as an embodiment of the knightly ideal,

21. Miguel Alcañiz, *Retable of the Holy Cross*; c.1410. Museo de Bellas Artes, Valencia.

became widely popular, the iconography of St. George and the dragon had become fairly standardized. A splendid example very similar to the retable appears in the Hours of the Maréchal Boucicaut (Paris, Musée Jacquemart-André MS2) recently dated c.1405–8 (fig. 24).[55] The Saint rides across the scene thrusting his spear downwards into the dragon, which is in the shape of a reptile with four legs and a tail. The king's daughter is standing in the middle distance with the sheep which was to be her companion in the sacrifice. Although it has no landscape background, the Valencian retable conforms closely to this type (fig. 3), though St. George is shown grasping the lance with both hands as he thrusts it into the dragon.[56]

The central scene, St. George coming to the aid of the Crusading armies, never became as widely popular as his exploit against the dragon, but it also was depicted, particularly in France, from the 12th century.[57] The earliest known representation, a wall painting in the church of S. Pierre-de-Chevillé near Poncé (Sarthe), shows two unidentified military saints on horseback fighting the Saracens. In another 12th-century wall painting at S. Jacques-des-Guérets, St. George is depicted leading the Crusading knights as they ride into battle, and another of c.1300 in the Cathedral at Clermont-Ferrand has the Saint in the midst of the fight. However, although one can point to these examples showing St. George himself, this representation of the battle of Puig must be set in

22. Miguel Alcañiz, *Retable of the Holy Cross*; detail: *Heraclius Killing Chosroes II*.

23. Miguel Alcañiz, *Retable of the Holy Cross*; detail: *Combat between Heraclius and Chosrces.*

the context of such battle scenes, with two clashing armies of mounted knights in armour, so common in Western art from the 12th century. In Spain there was a tradition of painting battle scenes of Christian knights fighting Moslems of which the artist of the retable could hardly have been unaware. Close parallels can be found in the manuscripts of the *Cantigas* of Alfonso X (d.1284) (fig. 25), and although the scene in the St. George retable is painted in a more naturalistic manner, it clearly belongs to this compositional tradition.[58]

Of the other scenes of the life of St. George, only two – the binding of the dragon and the torture on the wheel – were sometimes depicted independently. The princess leading the dragon 'as it had been a meek beast and debonair' was occasionally included with the dragon slaying scene. It appears, for example, on a 14th-century wall painting in Santa Chiara, Assisi, and on an English, late 14th-century carved panel from an oak chest in this Museum.[59] A simplified version of St. George on the wheel appears as representation of his martyrdom in French and German Psalters and Passionels (Lives of Saints) from the 12th century onwards, but these usually show the saint twisted within the wheel and are not similar to the composition on the retable.[60]

The search for possible pictorial models of the retable's martyrdom scenes leads, naturally enough, to the earlier illustrative cycles of the life of St. George. These are rare before the 15th century, but at least four such cycles, covering the period c.1280–1400, still exist. The earliest of these appears on the windows of a chapel formerly dedicated to St. George in the Cathedral of Clermont-Ferrand (1283–87).[61] Clermont was on the main route through France of the Crusaders, which helps to explain the dedication to St. George and the extensive description of his story in 36 roundels in four windows. Unfortunately, too many of the original roundels were replaced in the 19th century to allow for a close comparison with the retable, but in the scenes where such comparison is possible, the compositions are not very similar. At Clermont there are also four frescoes of c.1300 dedicated to St. George, but of these only the scene of St. George fighting the Saracens provides a close parallel to the retable.[62]

Equally far removed from the retable is the St. George cycle in the hall of Hradec Castle in Czechoslovakia, dated by inscription 1338.[62] The story is told in two registers originally covering all four walls, but of this extensive cycle only six scenes coincide with the eighteen of the retable and even these are not very close in detail.

Artistically, the most splendid cycle is that painted by Altichiero and Avanzo in the Oratorio di S. Giorgio in Padua (1378–84).[63] This consists of six frescoes, each with an elaborate architectural setting

89

24. Hours of the Maréchal de Boucicaut, *St. George and the Dragon*, c.1405–08. Musée Jacquemart André, Paris, MS 2, fol. 23.

are close in detail, but there is sufficient overall similarity to make it plausible that such a manuscript of Saints' Lives provided a pictorial source for the retable (compare figs. 13 and 26).

In Spain itself there is only one cycle of St. George – and that consisting of a mere five scenes – which may safely be dated earlier than the Valencian retable. This is on an altar-piece by Luis Borrassá (active 1383–1425) in the Convent of Vilafranca del Panadés, near Barcelona, in which St. George shares the available space with scenes from the life of the Virgin (fig. 27).[66] This painting, tentatively placed in c.1392–1400, only just predates the Museum's retable, and contains only five scenes. Two of these – the Saint tortured on the cross and drawn through the city – show striking similarities, which suggest that at least some of the retable's models could be found in contemporary Spain.

This supposition is borne out by the similarity of some of the scenes with those of the martyrdom of certain other saints popular in Spain. The torture on St. Andrew's cross (plate I) is very similar to the treatment meted out to St. Vincent (who was martyred at Valencia in 304 A.D.) in, for example, a mid-14th century Catalan altar frontal (fig. 28)[67] and the

25. Battle scene from *Las Cantigas* of Alfonso the Wise of Castile, c.1260–80. Escorial, MS T.I.1

and a multitude of figures. Each of these scenes reappears on the retable but they are not very similar in detail and three out of the six are quite different.

These monuments demonstrate the existence of large illustrative cycles of St. George in the late 13th and 14th centuries,[64] but they do not significantly add to our knowledge of the sources of the Valencian retable. There exist, however, two cycles which are more relevant to our enquiry. The first is contained in a 14th century *Passional* of Hungarian origin, but Italian in style and character (Vat. Lat. 8541; fols. 54v, 55, 56v),[65] consisting of ten scenes, nine of which are paralleled in the retable (fig. 26). Not all of these same composition was also used for St. Eulalia.[68] Even the scene of St. George sawn asunder which, as we have seen, does not occur outside Spain, is paralleled by St. Quiricus, who is seen suffering the same torture on a Catalan painting of about 1300 in the Barcelona Museum.[69] Once a composition of this kind was well known, it could be readily adapted to any other saint suffering the same martyrdom.

There are other details also that point to the artist's use of Spanish models. The execution of the enchanter, for example, is depicted in an oriental manner (fig. 10). His throat is slit from behind, a form that occurs frequently in Islamic and particularly Persian painting (fig. 29),[70] whereas in Byzantine and Western art outside Spain beheading is the method usually shown. This may be taken as an example of Islamic influence on Christian iconography in medieval Spain. It was probably derived from a pictorial source, whereas the Moors' armour in the battle scene may well have been due to the artist's own observation from life.

However, when all these possible sources have been discussed, it remains true that several scenes on the retable (1, 2, 3, 9) find no parallel in earlier St. George cycles nor in those of other well-known saints. We have seen that we are dealing with a major artist

and the search for iconographic prototypes should not blind us to the possibility, indeed the likelihood, that some of these illustrations represent his own interpretation of the text and others a free adaptation of his pictorial models. There were St. George cycles upon which he could draw, but for the detailed and graphic description of the excruciating story of the martyrdom, the retable is a landmark in the development of realism in 15th-century narrative illustration.

IV. THE ORIGINAL HOME OF THE ALTAR-PIECE

Among all the uncertainties concerning the great altar-piece, one fact stands out clearly: it was painted for a confraternity of civic militia called the 'Centenar de la Ploma' whose insignia it bears. At the top of the painting, in the upper *guardapolvos*, is the cross-bow – the Centenar was a company of archers – and the cross of St. George, the Confraternity's patron saint (fig. 30). The crossbow is repeated on the extreme left and right corners just below. The other spaces between the figures on the *guardapolvos* have been filled with 19th-century replacements, but the four plaques at the top form an integral part of the original structure.

26. Passional (lives of Saints), *St. George in the cauldron of lead; the Saint prays and the idols fall*. Italo-Hungarian, *c*.1340–50. Vatican Library, MS Vat. Lat. 8541, fol. 55 (compare fig. 13)

The insignia were first identified in 1923 by Elias Tormo, who pointed out that the retable must have been painted for the Centenar de la Ploma.[71] In 1930 Chandler Post enlarged on Tormo's discovery in suggesting that the retable was originally in the chapel of the Centenar de la Ploma in the church of San Jorge (St. George), Valencia, which was demolished in the 19th century.[72] Five years later Post (VI, p. 583) supported this hypothesis with a reference to a well known 18th-century guide to Valencia, Orellana's *Valencia Antigua y Moderna*, in which there is a brief description of an altar-piece in the chapel of the Centenar de la Ploma in the church of San Jorge. At the same time Saralegui also identified this altar-piece with the one in the Victoria and Albert Museum,[73] and this identification has been widely accepted ever since. However, we shall see that, although the retable's connection with the Centenar de la Ploma is beyond dispute, the question 'where was its original home?' must be reconsidered in the light of new evidence.

The Centenar de la Ploma, traditionally said to have been founded by James the Conqueror in the 13th century, in fact owed its origin to King Pedro IV.[74] The foundation was a result of the war of 1356–65 between Pedro the Cruel of Castile and Pedro IV of Aragon. The kingdom of Valencia had been subject to the Aragonese crown ever since James the Conqueror, King of Aragon, drove out the Moslems in 1237–38, but this did not automatically commit Valencian forces to Aragonese wars. In this case, the decision to come to the aid of Pedro IV was reached by the Valencian city council in November 1364. Consequently a company of Valencian archers fought in 1365 at the battle of Morvedre, in which the Castilians were finally defeated. It was in recognition of their part in this battle that, on June 3 1365, Pedro IV created the 'Compania de Ballesters' and bestowed upon it all the privileges of such a royal foundation. Apart from natural gratitude, Pedro's action may be set in the tradition of medieval kings granting privileges to civic institutions to counterbalance the power of the feudal nobility.

The newly-formed company was a troop of municipal militia consisting of 100 archers (*ballesters*) – hence the name 'Centenar'; 'de la Ploma' was added because of the feather the archers wore in their helmets. The privileged status of the Centenar in Valencian affairs is indicated by the fact that it served as the custodian of the city banner. This banner, which still exists in the Historical Museum of Valencia, was carried by the Centenar de la Ploma in peace – on several processions each year – and in war. The company's patron saint was St. George; not surprisingly, for he was the most popular of military saints and his popularity had grown with the success of the wars against the Moslems in which, as we have seen, he had taken such an active part. Over their breast-plates, the members of the Centenar wore a white silk shirt with the red cross of St. George on the front and the back[75] rather as St. George himself is shown on the retable.

The royal foundation of 1365 referred only to a military company and it was not until 1371 that this company in turn founded a confraternity, the 'Cofradia del Centenar de la Ploma'. Pedro IV granted privileges to the Confraternity on July 10 of that year and, on this occasion, the purpose and rules of the foundation and the duties of its members were clearly set out[76]:

(1) to bury the company's dead

(2) to attend the funerals of members' wives and children

(3) to tend sick members and their families

(4) to honour St. George on his feast day

(5) candles bearing the Cross of St. George to be carried at funerals

(6) the membership fee to be fixed at ten sous

(7) rules for admission in exceptional cases to be drawn up

(8) members' wives and children to have privileges

(9) three chapter meetings to be held each year

(10) prayers to be said for the dead

(11) an annual banquet to be held on St. George's day

(12) number of members to be fixed at 100 men and 150 women

(13) the Confraternity to have the right to make new ordinances for its internal regulation.

The Confraternity's privileges were confirmed by John I in 1393, when membership was extended to include 500 men and 600 women. At the same time the Centenar was confirmed in the unhindered enjoyment of its possessions, including pictures, precious stones and ornaments of gold and silver.

It will be apparent that by the time the retable was commissioned in about 1410–20, the Confraternity of the Centenar de la Ploma was a large and wealthy institution with a considerable status in civic affairs. The very size and quality of the retable itself provides supporting evidence for this.

The Centenar was still active as a military company in the 15th century – it helped the king's forces in the rebellion of James of Aragon in 1464 – but in succeeding centuries its military significance declined

28. Catalan school, mid-14th century, retable of St. Vincent, detail: *St. Vincent tortured on the cross*. Catalan Museum, Barcelona

27. Luis Borrassá (active 1383–1425), *Scenes of St. George* from a retable in Vilafranca del Panadés, near Barcelona, *c*.1400.

and its civic activities were limited to taking part in processions. The Confraternity continued to exist as a privileged civic institution until the early 18th century, when Philip V abrogated the local laws, institutions and privileges of the kingdom and city of Valencia. The Centenar de la Ploma, founded as a Company in 1365 and as a Confraternity in 1371, was formally abolished in 1711.

From about 1400 the Confraternity had both a chapel in the church of San Jorge and also a meeting-house

nearby. The church was on the Plaza San Jorge, now Plaza Rodrigo Botet, and the house in the adjacent street, which is still called the Calle de Ballesters. The house was demolished in 1807 to make way for the civic theatre, which was completed in 1832[77]; the church was demolished in the middle of the 19th century.[78]

The church of San Jorge was founded in 1324 as the collegiate church of the Orders of Montesa and St. George of Alfama, but from the beginning it was subject to the authority of the rector of St. Andrew's, the local parish church.[79] Owing to disagreement between the Orders and St. Andrew's, the church of San Jorge was consecrated only in 1401. Before that date the Centenar de la Ploma, also dedicated to St. George, had been permitted, by agreement with the Order of St. George of Alfama, to take over one chapel in the church. It was dedicated to Our Lady of Victory in memory of the Christian reconquest.

This was the chapel which, according to Post and subsequent authorities, housed the Museum's retable. Post cited Orellana, who described the chapel as showing the insignia of the Centenar, the crossbow and the Cross of St. George on the lamps: 'and the same insignia may be seen on the pedestal of the retable of Our Lady of Victory, an appropriate invocation in this church of St. George, for this saint gained the miraculous and renowned Victory of Puig

29. Persian, (Herat), *c.*1440. The Shāhnāma: *Hūmān killed by Bizhan*. Royal Asiatic Society MS Morley 239. (Compare fig. 10)

de Enesa . . . '.[80] This description could be taken as applying to the St. George retable – even though there is no mention of St. George – for it does contain an image of the Virgin and Child at the top. However, there is a more detailed description of the altar-piece of Our Lady of Victory which firmly excludes this identification. This description appears in a book by Joseph Vicente Orti, published in 1740, and also in the more famous guide-book *Antiguedades de Valencia* by Josef Teixidor, written in about 1767:

'Still revered in it is a picture of Our Lady, some five palms high, with the Infant Christ on her left arm, with a scroll at the foot of the throne inscribed *Nra. S.a. de la Vitoria*, which is in the chapel on the right on entering the church at the main door. And on the pedestal of this retable the insignia of the Confraternity are visible, that is the cross and the crossbow.'[81]

This is a precise description and quite clearly it cannot refer to the St. George retable. Even were it argued that the presence of St. George is simply omitted, the retable's Virgin and Child panel contains no scroll at the foot of the throne, and the size 'some

five palms high' (about 3 ft. 6 in.) must exclude once and for all the identification of the St. George retable with the altar-piece in the Confraternity's chapel in the Church of San Jorge. The possibility that it was on the main altar of the church cannot be affirmed or excluded for lack of evidence. Yet it is unlikely that the main altar-piece would bear the insignia of the Centenar de la Ploma, when the church itself belonged to the Orders of Montesa and St. George of Alfama. Historians of the Order of Montesa mention an ancient crucifix in this church, but no retable of St. George.[82]

In the Calle de Ballesters, adjacent to the church of San Jorge, on a site now occupied by the city's principal theatre, stood the meeting-house of the Centenar de la Ploma. This house contained a large chapel and, as it is relevant to the history of our retable, it is worth quoting J. V. Orti's description published in 1740:

'On the ground floor of the house there was a chapel which was some 40 palms wide, some 60 palms high and about 120 palms long, with a vault – as the eye can see there was once – and at the foot of the spring of each arch there are still circular shields, those on the Gospel side with the Cross of St. George and a crossbow in those on the Epistle side. Of the altar, there now remain only traces, for there is no retable, but an arch of plaster, painted black, with a scroll inscribed IN TE DOMINE SPERAVI, NON CONFUNDAR, and above this arch at the right corner there is a Cross of St. George and at the opposite corner a crossbow, and above this arch on the flat part of the cornice, this inscription: MISERERE MEI DEUS SECUN-DUM, and all this ornamentation (*which was for the retable of the altar in the empty space which still remains in the middle*) [my italics] terminated in a triangle of plaster.'[83]

30. St. George retable; the insignia of the Centenar de la Ploma: the crossbow and the Cross of St. George.

Final proof is lacking, but this description strongly suggests that the Museum's retable of St. George may be identified with 'the retable of the altar in the empty space which still remains in the middle'. The chapel was large and very high: 60 palms are about 40 feet, sufficient to accommodate the 22 ft. high retable and leave ample space above it for the plaster arch and inscriptions. Indeed, it could be argued that such a large 'empty space' required a large picture to fill it.

Having excluded the Confraternity's chapel in the church, the chapel in the meeting-house becomes the likeliest place and we now know that this chapel contained a large retable. It was probably sold when the Centenar was abolished in 1711, so that by 1740 only the remnants of the altar remained. We know from the royal confirmation of the Centenar in the unhindered enjoyment of its possession that it had 'pictures, crowns, precious stones . . . banners' in 'the house of the church of St. George in Valencia',[84] and it is at least likely that the retable was for three centuries in the chapel of this house, filling the space so precisely described by Orti in 1740.

N. S. BROMMELLE AND H. H. ROGERS

Appendix: *Conservation treatment of the Valencian altar-piece*

Restoration work on the Valencian altar-piece had to be done because some of the panels had shown signs of splitting and warping. This deterioration was very slow, but methods of arresting conditions of this kind are well known and can be applied with confidence. The removal of the varnish (probably 19th century) has been a rewarding but subsidiary task.

The Valencian altar-piece occupies a prominent and important position at the east end of the Gothic gallery, and removal from exhibition for any length of time might be undesirable. Consequently, when the decision was made to carry out conservation treatment, it was decided that the altar-piece should be only partially dismantled at one time, and the sections replaced as conservation treatment to a particular panel was completed. In this way students and visitors to the Museum would also have the opportunity to compare the cleaned and uncleaned areas as the work progressed. This can only be a preliminary and comparatively brief report on the work now being carried out, and various different problems and conditions may arise when further panels are removed and examined.

The altar-piece (apart from the border pieces and predella) is composed of 15 separate panels – 3 large centre panels, and 6 panels in either wing. The panels so far examined are of soft wood, a resinous type of pitch or yellow pine, the wing panels being made from a single plank of timber approximately 22 inches in width, the centre panels from two similar pieces of timber, butt jointed. The pilasters are separate members and attached to one side of each of the wing panels, and on either side of the large centre panels, with spiked metal dowels.

The gold relief work on the pilasters has mainly been carved from the timber support, whereas on the main panels the gold tracery, moulding, and relief work is an over-lay, glued and secured to the face of the panels with large iron nails.

The panels are strengthened on the reverse with several heavy pieces of timber, and cross battens which have also been secured by nails driven through from the front of the panels. This method of support employing fixed members across the grain of the panels causes constraint by restricting the natural movement of the panels as the wood absorbs and gives up moisture from the atmosphere. As a result, over the years many have suffered serious fissures and cracks.

In order to stabilize the panels, it has been decided to remove all the fixed supporting members from the reverse, and replace the reinforcement by covering the back completely with two sections of balsa-wood attached with a wax-resin adhesive (a mixture of beeswax and gum damar). Balsa is particularly suitable for this type of work, giving adequate support without causing constraint and the wax mixture also acts as an excellent moisture barrier to stabilize and prevent any further undue dimensional change. Sections of square aluminium channel are being attached to the back, which will serve as a housing for retaining tenons as the panels are replaced.

A panel during treatment showing cleaned areas

areas and features to be prepared with red bolus and gilded. The very fine gold tooling would also be carried out at this stage.

Microscopic samples of the various pigments have been taken, and are being analysed for us by Miss J. Plesters at the National Gallery laboratory. It is interesting to mention that Miss Plesters has in some samples identified the blue pigment smalt, which shows the characteristic patchy grey discolouration sometimes associated with its use in oil media; this could be an indication that the work was not painted exclusively in a tempera medium, although further investigation will of course be necessary before arriving at a firm conclusion.[1]

There is no detailed record of previous treatment, but the altar-piece had been varnished at some time and the surface probably rubbed over from time to time with some type of oil mixture, which was common practice in the 19th century. Cleaning tests showed that, although the discoloured oil-resin was very hard, it could be removed quite safely with the usual solvents. Below the varnish, however, was an underlying film of ingrained dirt and grime, which had been allowed to accumulate for many years before application of a varnish. This proved to be very resistant to normal solvents, until further tests showed that the remaining discolouration could be removed successfully with a very dilute reactive solution and wax mixture.

Cleaning has shown the work to be in remarkably fine condition, revealing the brilliance of tone and colour which had previously appeared flat and dull under the discolouration. There are of course small areas of damage, loss and wear, which one must expect in an altarpiece of this period; fortunately they occur in relatively unimportant parts, and have so far not presented any major restoration problems. The traditional water gilding is also seen to be in exceptionally fine condition.

After cleaning and restoration the panels are being re-varnished with a protective film of synthetic resin and microcrystalline wax.

Construction of the panels closely followed the traditional method of the period. After attachment of the tracery and relief work, the panels were covered with a fine canvas before the heavy gesso ground was applied. It is rather unlikely that the gilding was carried out by the artist himself; it would probably have been undertaken by a specialist craftsman under supervision. The incised lines in the gesso, which may be seen in many areas of the work, are in all probability the preliminary drawing made by the artist, which would also serve as a guide to indicate the various

1. J. Plesters, 'A preliminary note on the incidence of discolouration of smalt in oil media', *Studies in Conservation*, 14 (1969), pp. 62–74

PLATE 3. St. George Retable: *St. George raised on a cross and scraped with combs.* (After cleaning)

Notes

1. J. C. Robinson, *Reports* (MS), 1864, ii, p. 160.

2. *Ibid*, p. 175.

3. The part played by the Virgin in achieving this victory over the infidels was recognized on the battlefield and recorded by chroniclers: see P. A. Beuter, *Primera Parte de la Coronica general de toda España y especialmente del Reyno de Valencia*, Valencia 1604, cap. 32, p. 182ff for a full description of the battle.
The theme of the Virgin and Child crowned by angels is of early medieval origin (cf. Gospel Book of Bernward of Hildesheim, early 11th cent., Hildesheim Cathedral, see G. Cames, *Byzance et la Peinture Romane de Germanie*, 1966, p. 193, fig. 278) but it did not become popular until the 15th century. Only rarely is this subject combined with that of the nursing Madonna (cf. Turin, Museo Civico, Heures de Milan, fol. 120, *c.*1405; M. Meiss, *French Painting in the time of Jean de Berry. The late 14th century*, 1967, p. 128, pl. 50). For the history of the nursing Madonna in Spanish art of the 13th–15th centuries see Post, ii, p. 231ff, figs. 151, 168f, 201, 216; M. Trens, *Maria: Iconografia de la Virgen en el Arte Español*, Madrid, 1946, p. 461ff, fig. 277).

4. Many of them carry scrolls inscribed with their names. Flanking the Virgin and Child: Jeremiah and an unnamed prophet. In the four main registers (revised order, see fig. 2) reading from left to right:
Top register: Isaiah; Simeon; Jeremiah; Isaiah; Obadiah; a prophet.
Second register: Amos; a prophet (inscription illegible); Jonah; a prophet; Zephaniah; a prophet.
Third register: David; Amos; a prophet; a prophet; Hosea; a prophet.
Bottom register: David; Elisha; Ezechiel; Daniel; a prophet.

5. Left side, reading upwards: St. Simon(?) with sword and book.
St. John the Evangelist, with palm branch and book.
St. Andrew with cross and book.
St. Bartholomew, with sword and book.
Top from left to right: St. Thomas(?) with spear and book.
St. Matthew(?) with book.
St. Peter, with key and book.
St. Jude, with halberd and book.
Right side, reading downwards: St. James the Less with fuller's club and book.
St. Philip(?), with spear.
St. James the Greater with palmer's hat, staff and wallet.
St. Paul, with sword and book.

6. On Spanish retables see C. R. Post, *A History of Spanish Painting*, ii, 1930, p. 191f; Joseph Braun, *Der Christliche Altar*, 1924, ii, p. 329, pls. 252–4.

7. For reproductions of comparable Valencian frames of the early 15th century see Post, iii, figs. 253, 264, 265, 273–5.

8. A. L. Mayer, *Geschichte der Spanischen Malerei*, Leipzig, 1913, i, p. 57; 1922 ed. p. 35ff (repr.).
J. R. Van Stuwe, *Oude Spaansche Kunst*, 1914, frontispiece.

V. Von Loga, *Die Malerei in Spanien*, 1923, p. 18f, fig. 15.
H. Isherwood Kay in R. R. Tatlock (ed.), *Spanish Art*, 1927, p. 30.
G. Rouchès, *La Peinture Espagnole de Moyen Age*, 1930, p. 73f.
Post, iii, 1930, p. 58ff, figs. 269–71.
Leandro de Saralegui, *Archivo de Arte Valenciano*, 19, 1933, p. 36ff, fig. 1; *Ibid*, 22, 1936, pp. 32–39, fig. 40f.
Juan de Contreras, Marques de Lozoya, *Historia de Arte Hispanico*, ii, Barcelona 1934, p. 331f, figs. 348–52.
Maria Elena Gomez-Moreno, *Mil Joyas del Arte Español*, 1, 1947, p. 277f, pl. 450.
E. Lafuente Ferrari, *Breve historia de la pintura española*, 4 ed. Madrid, 1953, p. 89.
José Gudiol-Ricart, *Ars Hispaniae*, ix: *Pintura Gotica*, Madrid 1955, p. 143f, fig. 109f.
F. Jimenez-Placer, *Historia del Arte Español*, Barcelona-Madrid, 1955, p. 437f, fig. 830.
J. A. Gaya Nuño, *La Pintura Española fuera de España*, Madrid 1958, p. 301, Cat. No. 2619, pls. 33f.

9. A. Igual Ubeda, *Historiografia del Arte Valenciano*, Valencia 1956, p. 33.
F. Almela y Vives, *Destrucción y Dispersión del Tesoro Artistico Valenciano*, Valencia 1958, p. 12.

10. E. Dominguez Gonzalez, *Guide du Musée National de Ceramique*, 4e ed., Valencia 1965, p. 36 (repr.).

11. J. Vicens Vives, *Manuale di historia economica de España*, 3rd ed., Barcelona, 1964, pp. 165, 267.

12. The history of the Catalan School in the 14th century is conveniently summarized by Post, ii, 1930, pt. 4 and more recently by Gudiol, *op. cit.*, pp. 53–105. See also M. Meiss, 'Italian style in Catalonia', *Journal of the Walters Art Gallery*, IV, 1941, pp. 45–87.

13. This attribution, originally made by Juan Ainaud, has been accepted by Gudiol, *op. cit.*, pp. 79ff, and esp. 132ff. See also Post, iii, figs. 249, 299.

14. Post, iii, p. 14f, fig. 253.
Italian influence on Spanish painting of this period is the theme of A. de Bosque, *Artistes Italiens en Espagne du XIV siècle aux Roix Catholiques*, 1965.

15. Many of these are published by J. Sanchis y Sivera, *Pintores Medievales en Valencia*, 1930, pp. 48–52; the remainder by L. Cervero y Gomis, *Pintores Valentinos; su cronologia y documentatión* (Separata de Anales del Centro de Cultura Valenciana), Valencia 1964, p. 121ff, and *Ibid*, *Archivo de Arte Valenciano*, 27, 1956, p. 107.

16. J. Sanchis, *La Catedral de Valencia*, Valencia 1909, p. 517, pl. 64.

17. Post, iii, 1930, p. 57f, fig. 268.

18. *Les Primitifs de Bohême*, exhibition catalogue, Brussels-Rotterdam 1966, Nos. 35–37 (repr.).

19. See note 8.

20. British Museum MS Cotton, Nero C. iv, E. Kitzinger, *Early Medieval Art in the British Museum*, pl. 46.
For a discussion of the development of this tradition in the 14th century see M. Meiss, *French Painting in the time of Jean de Berry. The late 14th century*, 1967, p. 162.

21. See especially O. Pächt, 'Early Italian nature studies and early calendar landscape', *Journal of the Warburg and Courtauld Institutes*, 13, 1950, p. 13.

22. For an illuminating discussion of this aspect of the International style see E. Panofsky, *Early Netherlandish Painting*, 1953, p. 71ff. For the iconography of the Man of Sorrows, see Meiss, *op. cit.*, p. 122f. An early French example showing Christ's body still lacerated from the Flagellation is in the Très Belles Heures de Notre-Dame of Jean de Berry (Paris, Bibl. Nat., nouv. acq. lat. 3093), *c.*1382; see Meiss, fig. 15.

23. F. Buttin, 'Les Adargues de Fès', *Hesperis Tamuda*, 1, 1960, p. 442ff. On the armour, see also James G. Mann, 'Notes on the armour worn in Spain . . . ', *Archaeologia*, 83, 1933, p. 293, pl. 83; Marti de Riquer, *L'Arnès del Cavaller. Armes i armadures Catalanes, medievals*, Barcelona 1968, p. 112, figs. 162, 165; and the section on 'Espadas Hispano-Arabes' in J. Gil Dorregaray, ed., *Museo Español de Antiguedades*, 1, Madrid 1872, p. 573ff, pl. 44. For these references and for information concerning the armour I am indebted to Mr. Claude Blair.

24. The miniatures referred to are in the so-called Turin Hours (destroyed in 1904) see Meiss, *op. cit.*, figs. 30–35, pp. 250ff, 337f.

25. Meiss, *op. cit.*, p. 250. For a discussion of Netherlandish naturalism at this period see Panofsky, *op. cit.*, cap. iv, esp. p. 95ff. Two manuscripts of *c.*1400 with naturalistic, individualized facial types are the Astrological MS in New York (Morgan Library M.785) and the Apocalypse in Paris (Bibl. Nat. MS Néerl. 3) see Panofsky, figs. 135–7; 150–2.

26. Saralegui, *Archivo de Arte Valenciano*, 22, 1936, p. 34.

27. Gudiol, *loc. cit.* (see note 8).

28. Post, iii, p. 63f.

29. *Ibid.*, p. 58.

30. *Ibid.*, p. 66ff, fig. 272; Saralegui, *Archivo de Arte Valenciano*, 23, 1952, p. 6, figs. 42–43.

31. Three panels remain: St. Vincent on the gridiron (Perpignan Museum); St. Vincent tortured on the cross (formerly Tiocca collection, Paris); and the Death of St. Vincent (Barcelona Museum). See Post, iii, p. 72, fig. 274; vi, (2), 1935, p. 56off, fig. 246; Saralegui, *op. cit.*, 1952, p. 3of, fig. 47; A. L. Mayer, *Apollo*, 28, 1938, p. 86 (Tiocca coll. panel); Exhibition catalogue, *Trésors de la peinture Espagnole*, Paris, Musée des Arts Décoratifs, 1963, No. 31 (repr.).

32. L. de Saralegui, 'Miguel Alcañiz, Es el Maestro de Gil y Poujades?', *Archivo Español de Arte*, 26, 1953, p. 237ff; *ibid*, *El Museo provincial de Bellas Artes de San Carlos*, Valencia 1954, p. 113ff; *ibid*, *Archivo de Arte Valenciano*, 27, 1956, pp. 3–41. Saralegui's attribution was accepted by Gudiol, *op. cit.* (see note 8) p. 149ff. The hypothetical connection between Alcañiz and the Maestro del Bambino Vispo is discussed by Bosque, *op. cit.* (see note 14). The documents concerning him are published by Sanchis and by Cervero (see note 15). In a document of 1420 recently published by Cervero, *Archivo de Arte Valenciano*, 36, 1965, p. 22, Alcañiz is described as a native of Majorca. For the Holy Cross retable see F. M. Garin Ortiz de Taranco, *Catalogo-Guia del Museo Provincial de Bellas Artes de San Carlos*, Valencia 1955, p. 79, No. 254, pl. iv.

33. Formerly Jackson Higgs collection, New York; sold at Christies, June 21 1968, lot 103. Originally published by Post, iv, (2), fig. 237 as school of Marzal; most recently by Saralegui, *Arch. Art. Val.* 27, 1956, p. 25, fig. 60, as by Alcañiz.

34. Divided between the Metropolitan Museum and the Hispanic Society of America. C. B. Andrews, *Connoisseur*, lix, 1921, p. 146; Post, iii, p. 83f, fig. 280; more recently Saralegui, *Arch. Art. Val.*, 27, 1956, p. 3off, figs. 61–64.

35. See note 32.

36. Sanchiz y Sivera, *Pintores . . .*, p. 52.

37. Cervero, *Pintores Valentinos* (see note 15), p. 123.

38. C. Bernis Madrazo, *Indumentaria Medieval Española*, Madrid 1955, p. 72f, fig. 115, see also p. 48ff.

39. Sir James Mann (see note 23).

40. This is the view of Mr. A. V. B. Norman, for whose opinion I am very grateful.

41. Riquier *op. cit.* (see note 23), figs. 161, 198.

42. J. E. Matzke, 'Contributions to the history of the legend of St. George . . . ', *Publications of the Modern Language Association of America*, Baltimore, 17, 1902, p. 464ff.

43. J. B. Aufhauser, 'Das Drachenwunder des hl. Georg in der griechischen und lateinischen Ueberlieferung', *Byzantinisches Archiv*, Leipzig, v, 1911, p. 231ff, esp. p. 240.

44. A view represented by M. E. Williams, 'Whence came St. George?', *Notes and Queries*, 168, 1935, pp. 21ff, 38ff, 56ff.

45. Aufhauser, *op. cit.*, p. 242ff.

46. *The Golden Legend . . . as Englished by William Caxton*, ed. F. S. Ellis, Temple Classics, 1900, iii, p. 127.

47. R. d'Alos-Moner, *Sant Jordi, Patró de Catalunya*, Barcelona 1926. The text is published on pp. 16–61; the MSS (889, Catalan Library, Barcelona; 2.F.i. Bibl. Real., Madrid) are discussed on p. 15f.

48. Saralegui, *Arch. Art. Val.*, 1936, p. 36. According to Beuter, *op. cit.* (see note 3), p. 184, it was Aguilo's lieutenant who carried the banner of St. George at the battle of Puig.

49. Matzke, *op. cit.*, 18, 1903, p. 152; P. Deschamps, 'La Legende de S. Georges et les Combats des Croisés dans les Peintures Murales du Moyen Age', *Fondation Piot, Monuments et Mémoires*, 44, 1950, pp. 109–123, esp. p. 113ff.

50. St. George's day was proclaimed a public holiday in England at the Council of Oxford in 1222, but it was not until the foundation of the Order of the Garter by Edward III in 1347–48 that St. George formally became the patron saint of England. See G. J. Marcus, *St. George of England*, 1929, p. 54ff.

51. Deschamps, *op. cit.*, p. 113f.

52. J. Roosval, *Nya Sankt Görans Studier*, Stockholm 1924 (with an English Summary), pl. 6, fig. 1.

53. O. von Taube von der Issen, *Die Darstellung des Heiligen Georg in der Italienischen Kunst*, Halle, 1910, p. 24; *ibid*, *Münchner Jahrbuch der Bildenden Kunst*, vi, 1911, p. 186ff, pl. 1. For Thracian rider reliefs see D. Tudor, *Corpus Monumentorum Religionis equitum Divinorum*, I *The Monuments*, Leiden/Brill, 1969.

54. She does appear on some earlier depictions, for example on the 12th century wall painting at Cressac; Deschamps, *op. cit.*, pl. xii.

55. M. Meiss, *French Painting in the time of Jean de Berry: the Boucicaut Master*, 1968, p. 131f; other historians have suggested a date *c*.1410–15: J. Porcher, *French Miniatures from Illuminated Manuscripts*, 1960, p. 69.

56. Roosval, *op. cit.*, p. 194, pls. 4–5, reproduces other examples of this type.

57. The examples mentioned here are all discussed and reproduced by Deschamps, *op. cit.*, esp. fig. 2 and pl. XIV. For Clermont-Ferrand see Y. Bonnefoy, *Peintures Murales de la France Gothique*, 1954, fig. 6. One of the few English examples is on the tympanum of Fordington Church, 12th century.

58. J. Guerrero Lovillo, *Las Cantigas*, Madrid 1948, esp. pl. 70, cf. also pls. 7 and 198. For a discussion of the depiction of Moorish soldiers by Spanish artists see the article by Buttin cited in note 23.
A scene of combat between Christian and Moslem was depicted on the ceiling of the Sala de los Reyes in the Alhambra, Granada, by an Italianate artist in *c*.1400 (repr. Gudiol, *op. cit.* fig. 33), compare also the Moorish horsemen on a cassone in Altenburg (Bosque, *Artistes Italiens en Espagne*, pp. 59, 75, repr.), and on Alcañiz' Holy Cross Retable in the Valencia Museum (see above, p. 78).

59. No. 82–1893. A. Marguillier, *Saint Georges* (L'Art et les Saints) n.d., p. 11 (repr.). For the Italian compositions in the 14th century see Taube, *Darstellung*, p. 48ff.

60. For example in Chartres Bibl. Com. MS 500, f.73v, 12th cent.; a Cistercian Psalter, *c*.1260, Besançon, MS 54, and a Legendary from Regensburg, after 1271, Keble College, Oxford, see H. Swarzenski, *Die Lateinischen Illuminierten HSS des XIII. Jahrh. in den Ländern am Rhein, Main und Donau*, 1936, p. 112, n.6, figs. 355, 559, with further examples; the St. Blasien Psalter, *c*.1230, see H. Bober, *The St. Blasien Psalter*, New York 1963, p. 48f.
The same composition appears on a window from Chartres now in Princeton, see *Princeton University Museum of Historic Art, Record*, 13, 1954, cover illustration. Other scenes of St. George's martyrdom are occasionally illustrated in Passionals. See for example A. Boeckler, *Das Stuttgarter Passionale*, Augsburg 1923, fig. 38; see also above, pp. 83–85.

61. H. du Ranquet, *Les Vitraux de la Cathédrale de Clermont-Ferrand*, 1932, p. 16ff, figs. 15–25, 27–31, 35, 38.

62. V. Dvořáková, J. Kraśa, A. Merhautová, K. Stejskal, *Gothic Mural Painting in Bohemia and Moravia, 1300–78*, Oxford 1964, p. 132f, pls. 29–32.

63. G. L. Mellini, *Altichiero e Jacopo Avanzi*, Milano 1965, figs. 164, 166, 172–77; H. W. Kruft, *Altichiero und Avanzo*, Diss., Bonn 1966, p. 78ff.

64. From the sparse evidence available, Byzantine cycles appear to have been limited to relatively few scenes and bore little resemblance to the Western cycles under discussion: for example the wall painting in the church of Staro Nagoricino, see *Yugoslav frescoes*, Arts Council exhibition 1953, Nos. 42–43.
A later painters' guide recommends eight scenes for a St. George cycle: *Malerhandbuch des Malermönches Dionysios vom Berge Athos*, München 1960, Section 429.

65. Meta Harrsen, *The Neckcsei-Lipócz Bible*, Washington 1949, pp. 4–6, 53–66; the St. George cycle is described on p. 59.

66. J. Gudiol Ricart, *Borrassá*, Barcelona 1953, p. 45ff, figs. 18, 27–28. Of the Spanish cycles immediately following the Museum's retable, the one attributed to Gonzalo Perez II in the church at Jerica (Gudiol, *Ars Hisp.*, IX, p. 156, fig. 119; Post, VI, (2), p. 582f) is clearly based on the latter; the four panels by Bernardo Martorell in the Louvre, on the other hand, show little resemblance, see J. Gudiol Ricart, *Bernardo Martorell*, 1959, pls. 4–9; *Peinture Espagnole . . .* , exh. Paris 1963, nos. 27–30.

67. From Estimariu, in Barcelona Museum, G. Richert, *Mittelalterliche Malerei in Spanien*, Berlin 1925, fig. 50.

68. Post, II, p. 240 fig. 155.

69. Richert, *op. cit.*, fig. 22: W. W. S. Cook, *La Pintura Romanica sobre tabla en Cataluña*, Madrid 1960, p. 16, pl. 6.

70. For example in MSS of the Shāhnāma, such as the one in the Royal Asiatic Society (Morley 239), see esp. B. W. Robinson, *Apollo Miscellany*, 1951, p. 20, fig. V. On this MS see also J. V. S. Wilkinson and L. Binyon, *The Shāhnāmah of Firdausi*, 1931, and B. W. Robinson, *Persian Miniature Painting from collections in the British Isles*, Victoria and Albert Museum 1967, No. 19, for a complete biography. This MS is dated *c*.1440 but the tradition goes back to the 14th century.
For other examples of this composition in Persian MSS, see Wilkinson and Binyon, *op. cit.*, pl. XVI; and I. Stchoukine, *Les Peintures des Manuscripts Tîmûrids*, 1954, pl. IX. It appears in Spanish art occasionally from the 13th century, see Gudiol, *Pintura Gotica*, fig. 2. See also Saralegiu, *Arch. Art. Val.*, 1933, p. 39 and G. Bazin, *Gazette des Beaux-Arts*, 1929 (1), p. 47.

71. Elias Tormo, *Levante* (Guias Calpe), Madrid 1923, p. cxxxiiif.

72. Post, III, p. 58ff.

73. Saralegui, *Arch. Art. Val.*, 22, 1936, p. 34.

74. F. Sevillano Colom, *El 'Centenar de la Ploma' de la Ciutat de Valencia (1365–1711)*, (Episodiis de la Historia), Barcelona 1966, pp. 9, 20ff. Colom effectively disposes of the evidence adduced by L. Querol y Roso, *Las Milicias Valencianas desde el siglo XIII al XV*, 1935, p. 69, and others, claiming that the Centenar was founded by James the Conqueror.

75. Teodoro Llorente, *Valencia*, II, 1889, p. 110ff.

76. Colom, *op. cit.*, pp. 60–69 for the account that follows.

77. Marcos Antonio de Orellana, *Valencia Antigua y Moderna*, ed. C. Corbí y de Orellana, Valencia 1923, p. 146; Vicente Boix, *Historia de la Ciudad y Reino de Valencia*, I, 1845, p. 418.

78. After Boix, it is no longer described in Valencian guide books.

79. F. H. de Samper, *Montesa Illustrada*, Valencia 1669, II, p. 794ff.

80. Orellana, *op. cit.*, p. 152f.

81. J. V. Orti y Mayor, *Fiestas Centenarias . . . de Valencia celebro en el dia 9 de Octubre de 1738 La Quinta Centuria de su Christiana Conquista*, Valencia, 1740, p. 51, whose text was copied almost verbatim by J. Teixidor, *Antiguedades de Valencia*, II, Valencia 1895, p. 98.
I am much indebted to Mr. R. W. Lightbown for help in interpreting these Spanish texts.

82. Samper, *op. cit.*, p. 795.

83. 'En la habitacion baxa de la Casa avia una Capilla, que tenia de ancho unos quarenta palmos, de alto unos sesenta, y de largo unos ciento y veinte palmos, con una boveda que se conoce avia, y al pie de cada arrancamiento de arco aun extan unos Escudos à forma de circulos, en que esta la Cruz de San Jorge en los de la parte de el Evangelio, y una Ballesta en los de la Epistola. De el Altar quedan aora solamente los vestigios, porque no ay Retablo, sino un arco de yesso pintado de negro con su rotulo que dice: IN TE DOMINE SPERAVI, NON CONFUNDAR; y sobre este arco, al angulo de la derecha se vè la Cruz de San Jorge, y al angulo opuesto una Ballesta; y encima de dicho arco en el plano de la cornisa esta inscripcion MISERERE MEI DEUS SECUNDUM, y todo este adorno (que lo era para el Retablo de el Altar, en el vacío que aora queda en medio) se remata con una Peschina de yesso.'
Orti, *op. cit.*, p. 52; copied with minor emendations by Teixidor, *op. cit.*, II, p. 99.

84. Colom, *op. cit.*, (see note 74), p. 69.

DAVID OWSLEY AND WILLIAM RIEDER

The glass drawing room from Northumberland House

INTRODUCTION

IT is largely an academic question whether Robert Adam was more a decorator than an architect, but it cannot be denied that he lavished a great deal of attention on interiors. In his first ten years of practice, Adam built only one new country house: Mersham-Le-Hatch, and in the few subsequent examples, facades clearly received minor consideration. He built far fewer buildings than he decorated, for the wave of country house construction in the previous half century was largely ended by the late 1750's, and the private palace gave way to the smaller-scale villa. At this propitious moment, Adam appeared on the scene with a programme of decoration derived from classical 'grotesques', his immediate source being their Renaissance interpretation in the Villa Madama and in the Vatican Loggie. A scheme which both coincided with and helped to foster a new interest in classicism, it immediately became the modish Establishment style and provided a formula for ornament which was intermittently copied and re-interpreted for the next century and a half.

In his external architecture, Adam made use of massing in a manner closely following that of Burlington and Kent, but his study of antique *thermae* (popularized by Burlington's 1730 publication of Palladio's drawings, *Fabbriche Antiche*) and the use of the columnar screen produced a variety of spatial permutations in his interiors – circular, elliptical, octagonal – which contrasted markedly with the regular repetition of rooms favoured by the earlier tradition. Because of an eye which saw primarily in flat, linear, two-dimensional terms, Adam's talent and main interest lay in decoration. His designs became flatter, thinner and more elongated as his style developed, making it gradually more effete.

The Glass Drawing Room at Northumberland House, midway in his career and certainly Adam's most daring design, was also one of the most important, both as a reflection of his artistic theories and as an example of their brilliant execution. Half hall of mirrors, half elegant drawing room, it helped at the same time to create, to reflect, and to parody the Northumberlands' fashionableness. Like all the newest fads, it risked being thought absurd, but was no less successful for that. The idea – an extension and elaboration of the late baroque room surrounded by pier glasses, the 'spiegel-kabinett' – was not new with

Adam. He would have been familiar with its eighteenth-century Italian prototypes, such as Juvarra's rooms in the Royal Palace at Turin, the gallery of the Palazzo Doria in Rome or the chinoiserie porcelain room of the Portici Palace in Naples, this last completed during the architect's Italian tour.

Though his style was often derivative, there are several innovations inherent within these designs which make him the most *avant-garde* English architect of the century. He once repeated some of the Northumberland scheme in a watered-down version; however the room remained a unique conception. Neither Adam nor anyone else tried to duplicate it, which only suggests that it failed to have the anticipated popular impact. In its use of colour and light and in the integration of walls, ceiling and floor, it is a reflection of his intellectual and stylistic subtlety and is the most dramatic English interpretation of the baroque mirror room, a monument in the history of interior design.

THE HOUSE

Northumberland House was one of the most splendid of the seven great Tudor and Stuart private palaces[1] which once studded the Thames side of London's Strand. Constructed on the site of the old convent of St. Mary of Rouncivalle[2] as a four-towered square block around a central courtyard by Bernard Jansen and Gerard Christmas for Henry Howard, Earl of Northampton, it was completed between 1605 and 1609.[3] On Howard's death in 1614 it passed to his nephew, the Earl of Suffolk, hence its early name, Suffolk House (fig. 1). Algernon Percy, tenth Earl of Northumberland, married Suffolk's daughter in 1642 and bought the house for £15,000, £5,000 having been deducted from its full value by way of the marriage.[4] Thereafter it was known as Northumberland House. The Proud Duke's grand-daughter, Elizabeth, married Charles Seymour, sixth Duke of Somerset, and their son Algernon made extensive changes to the house in 1749, simplifying the Strand facade (fig. 2) 'to make it look less like a prison . . . '.[5]

At the same time was begun 'a new wing on the right-hand side of the garden, which will contain a library, bed chamber and a waiting-room'[6] – the west wing, which extended towards the Thames off the garden front. This south side originally held the 'halle' and 'cloyster' but the first Percy occupant had moved the private apartments there from the noisy Strand front a century before.[7] It was here that

Robert Adam created the brilliant Glass Drawing Room for Algernon Seymour's daughter, Elizabeth, and her husband, Sir Hugh Smithson, a Yorkshire baronet.[8] In 1750 Smithson, through his wife,[9] became Earl of Northumberland and took the name of Percy. He extended the new garden wing[10] and built an enormous two-storey picture gallery, 106 ft. × 26 ft., whose pretentious size and style, as well as questionable art were noted by both Walpole and Count Kielmansegge.[11]

THE PERCYS

The new Lord and Lady Northumberland were one of London's gayest couples. Wealthy in his own right from his great-grandfather's haberdashery fortune,[12] richer still by his marriage to Elizabeth, he was 'one of the handsomest men of his generation, tall, well-made . . . superior in natural intelligence'.[13] His wife became heiress to the vast Percy estates on her brother's death in 1744[14] and succeeded in remaining heiress despite the efforts of her grandfather, the old Duke of Somerset, to have his Wyndham heirs named in her place.[15]

Under the Earl's able administration, annual Percy rentals jumped from £8,607 per annum in 1749 to £50,000 in 1778;[16] the Northumberland coal mines were responsible for most of the increase, though he did much to improve the farmlands there as well. A fashionable host, he was lavish but businesslike (save for an equally fashionable weakness for gambling) in all his activities,[17] especially in the building and decorating programmes at his three principal residences: Alnwick Castle,[18] Syon House,[19] and Northumberland House. After a series of important political and cultural posts, he was created Duke of Northumberland in 1766.[20] From 1760 until his death in 1786, he was one of Robert Adam's most important clients.

2. Northumberland House as engraved in 1753 by T. Bowles after the painting by Canaletto.

3. The Glass Drawing Room shortly before the 1874 demolition of Northumberland House.

Walpole describes the Duchess as 'a jovial lump of contradictions, familiar with the mob whilst stifled with diamonds . . . attentive to the most minute privileges of her rank, whilst shaking hands with a cobbler'.[21] Her enterprising spirit with the Charing Cross and Covent Garden street mobs helped win her son's[22] campaign for M.P. to Westminster against Wilkes.[23] Walpole, with typical malice, points out that the Duchess's private retinue outnumbered that of Queen Charlotte,[24] to whom she was a formidable Lady-of-the-Bedchamber, 1761–70. She was an inveterate and intelligent note-taker, evaluating the social customs and artistic trends of the day, and she chronicled her extensive travels in a chatty journal,[25] which reflects her catholic interests and critical eye and is one of the most valuable documents of the period. In it she comments on architecture in a manner both serious and charmingly personal, noting dimensions, charts, decorative details, and commenting on draughty hallways and miscellaneous gossip about architects. At Northumberland House she catalogued all the pictures, sculpture and silver. Over a period of two decades she and the Duke furnished their three

houses in a series of styles, from mid-Georgian through Chippendale to Adam, always in the vanguard of fashion. As a woman much concerned with architecture and decoration, she was no doubt an exacting client and closely followed every stage of the new drawing room designs.

THE ROOM

Adam's sparkling Glass Drawing Room (fig. 3) was inspired by, and was intended to reflect, the rich and elegant lives of the Duke and Duchess of Northumberland. With its eight large pier glasses and walls sheathed with red and green spangled glass panels overlaid with the gilt metal paraphernalia of Neo-Classicism, the whole lit by candelabra on chimney-piece and side tables and a large central chandelier, it was a splendid chamber for the 'parade of life'. Representing Robert Adam in his most elaborate and garish style, it was a creation suited to the Duke's expensive taste[26] and to the glittering entertainments for which Northumberland House was famous.[27] Unfortunately the death of the Duchess in 1776, a year after its completion, prevented her from enjoying it.[28]

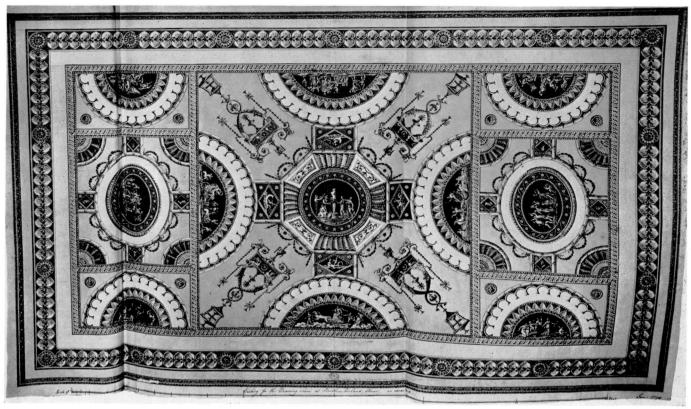

4. Adam's 'as executed' ceiling design, June 1770. Sir John Soane's Museum.

The architect's detailed bill for designs for every part of the new drawing room survive at Alnwick Castle[29] as well as a few suppliers' and workmen's bills.[30] Together with the important group of designs at Sir John Soane's Museum and the 1786 inventory of Northumberland House taken at the Duke's death,[31] they provide the foundations upon which an appraisal of the room's eighteenth-century appearance can be formed. Its somewhat sad progress through the subsequent century can be detailed by a later architect's plans, bills for refitting, and photographs taken prior to its demolition. Fortunately some fragments were saved and have been installed in the Museum[32] but they can only begin to suggest the brilliance of the original effect.

In any given project, Adam's first designs were frequently for ceilings,[33] as he considered them a key to the total ensemble. The 'as executed' ceiling design (fig. 4)[34] at the Soane Museum with its central octagon cross, grotesques and cameo-like lozenges, was ultimately inspired by the Udine-Peruzzi loggia ceiling at the Villa Madama,[35] which Adam had visited in 1756 while living in Rome. It bears the date June 1770, which marks the beginning of the Northumberland House scheme. An entry in the accounts[36] for March of that year, 'Paid Mr. Halfpenny for copying the rough draft of the Plan of Northumberland House' confirms this early date and refers either to the old plan originally supplied to Adam or a working drawing.

The same ceiling sketch was resubmitted by the architect on June 9, 1773. No other designs for the room predate 1773, which suggests that the project was only just begun in 1770 when it was discontinued for three years. The earliest record of work under way occurs in the accounts under July 1, 1773, 'Paid the Plasterers and Carpenters' Men at Northumberland House . . . '.[37]

The design indicates a ceiling 36 ft. × 22 ft., the exact dimensions of the room, and it would thus have been placed directly above the cornice, the usual practice with Adam ceilings. However, its close relationship with the wall elevations makes it an atypical design. The tripartite end-sections repeated the same divisions of the walls while the arched pier glasses were echoed above in large semicircular lunettes. With a carpet repeating the same forms below, the result was a tight geometrical box where decorative motifs repeated and varied on all six sides were added to reflecting walls and mirrors to create a *tour de force* of neo-classical design. The effect was considerably weakened in the nineteenth century when the room was widened, a cove introduced,[38] and the ceiling altered to fit the new dimensions (fig. 5).

As an X-plan central square balanced by related rectangular ends, it is a design entirely typical of Adam's work at this time (cf. ceiling designs for Lord Lansdowne, Lord Eglinton, and the Duke of Chandos[39]). The tints of the drawing indicate that

5. A watercolour of the drawing room, c.1870. Syon House.

6. An alternate ceiling design 'not executed'. Pen and ink. Sir John Soane's Museum.

against a pale green background, motifs were picked out in bright shades of red, blue and gold. Two sketches for the ceiling (fig. 6)[40] show an alternate plan which was not adopted.

The relationship between Adam's carpet and ceiling designs varies from one in which the lower repeats the pattern of the upper with only small changes in motifs such as the Osterley drawing room and Harewood music room, to one in which they do not relate at all, as in the Syon Red Drawing Room. The proposed carpet for the Glass Drawing Room (fig. 7)[41] restates the tripartite plan of the ceiling and some of

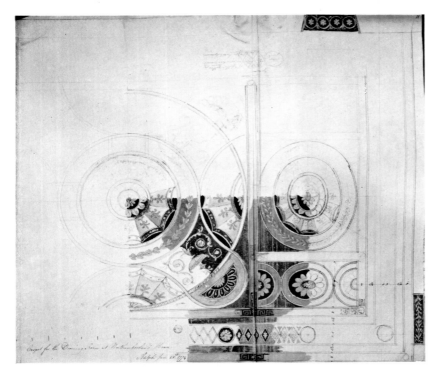

7. 'Carpet for the Drawing Room at Northumberland House, Adelphi, June 25, 1774.' Watercolour, pen and ink, pencil. Sir John Soane's Museum.

its larger forms but relates them in a rhythmically freer, more unified way. The carpet sketch, which is listed in Adam's bill,[42] traces areas pencilled 'brown, purple, green, yellow' to complement rather than repeat the colours of the ceiling. The 1786 inventory notes 'A large Carpet to cover the Room 36 f by 22 . . . ' which would have covered it entirely. The scale of the drawing indicates a length two feet shorter, but it was evidently never executed as no bill or fragment remains.

The most valuable documents for the study of this most extraordinary of Adam's interiors are the three wall elevations (figs. 8–10)[43] dated June 9, 1773, which reveal a room completely surrounded by mirrors and red glass panels. Six of the eight mirrors are tripartite designs divided by female terms and baluster forms with raised arched centres which reflect a distant relationship to the Palladian window. They reveal Adam's idea of the breakdown of architectural function. No longer is the wall a place for lining up separate and coherent unities – door, pier glass, window – with space between so that each

8. 'Section of the Drawing Room at Northumberland House, London, June 9, 1773.' Watercolour, pen and ink, pencil. Sir John Soane Museum.

9. Adam's elevation for the north wall. Watercolour, pen and ink, pencil. Sir John Soane's Museum.

10. 'Section of the Drawing Room, Northumberland House, London.' Design for end wall. Watercolour, pen and ink, pencil. Sir John Soane's Museum.

reads as an individual entity. Rather, by this stage of development, the vertical plane has become a continuous field for the even spread of decorative detail, and thus the mirror merges into wall and window with the whole effect one dazzling, dancing vibration of light and tone. The 1874 views (figs. 3, 11, and 12) show this unique room where mirrors reflect walls which in turn reflect mirrors. The combination of small-scale ornament, refracting foil behind the glass panels, and vast areas of mirror, creates an interior where walls cease to exist as solid architectural boundaries. This is Adam's boldest step into such interior theatricality, and, as such, one of his most important designs.

Theatricality is very much the operative idea. He used a similar decoration in only one other place: Drury Lane, altered in 1775. The interior view from *The Works*,[44] showing square piers supporting two levels of boxes, gives no hint, without the following contemporary newspaper description, that the architect has repeated the Glass Drawing Room scheme in simplified form. 'Small pilasters, the height of which is conformed to the different tiers of boxes, support and adorn them. They are made more light and more gay by inserting in Front of each a Panel of Plate Glass, which in the lower Order is placed over a Foil or Varnish of spangled Crimson, which looks both rich and brilliant. The Capitals are gilt and are what our Artists call the Grecian Ionick. The glass of the second Order is placed over a green spangled Foil or Varnish, and has an Effect no less beautiful than the former.'[45] Most critics applauded the new decoration, but at least one was displeased. 'The general plan of the interior of this theatre is very convenient, but the ornament of the galleries and boxes are frippery and unmeaning. Slender columns of glass may strike the vulgar as very fine, but the judicious would wish to see propriety consulted, as well as the rage of gaudy decoration.'[46]

David Garrick, a friend of Robert Adam, lived in the central house of the architect's recently completed Adelphi Terrace, and leased the Drury Lane Theatre.

11. The Glass Drawing Room, c.1873.

12. The drawing room looking west. The north door of each end wall was false.

In 1773 he had invested £12,000 into the newly established Company of British Cast-Plate Glass Manufacturers, Ravenhead, St. Helen's, Lancashire,[47] into which Northumberland had also invested an unknown sum. The company began production in 1776,[48] and hence the eight pier mirrors from the Glass Drawing Room could not have originated there, as has been claimed.[49] Nevertheless, it is a curious coincidence that Adam's first design for a room surrounded with glass was made in the year that Garrick and Northumberland invested in a large glass company, and the suggestion that the Northumberland House scheme was created in the hope that it would launch a taste for glass-panelled rooms – a fashion which could only increase the prestige of the client, lead to further commissions for the architect, and aid the financial situation of two friends – does not seem extreme. Its repetition in the theatre, however stylistically apt, was evidently to little avail as the idea did not spread.[50]
The drawing room mirrors, cast in St. Gobain, Picardy, were ordered from Peter Reilly, 'Upholster, Dealer, Chapman' of Gerrard Street, Soho.[51] A memorandum from him in the Alnwick accounts, dated June 29

1773,[52] gives the dimensions for all the mirrors and shows that the chimney and overmantel were the last parts of the design to be established.[53] After some haggling over the price (finally settled at £1,465), Reilly smuggled them via the diplomatic bag of the Venetian Resident, Baron Berlindis, a ruse which proved as unsuccessful as it had on previous occasion.[54] They were stopped at the customs, and Northumberland was forced to pay the usual seventy-five per cent duty.
The mirror glass and wall panels were drilled at Northumberland House. Bills from Richard Ledgley[55] and Charles Dologal[56] survive to tell us who performed at least part of this work. Thomas Thomas's bill for 65 yards of 'Bays'[57] indicates that the mirrors or wall glass, or both, were backed with baize. New window glass was provided by Richard Christmas in December 1773.[58]
Adam's drawing room is a delicate and small scale *Gallerie des Glaces* in mock porphyry. A French metaphor is in fact much to the point and can be extended to cover parallel developments. Just as Berain and Lepautre earlier in the century had gradually invaded

the wall panel with proliferating acanthus scrolls, so Robert Adam saw the mirror as a place for progressively more flamboyant displays of overlaid neoclassical ornament, from the early entrance of the urn into the Combe Bank mirror and cabinet design of 1767,[59] through the intermediate decoration of the Luton group of 1772,[60] to the late Northumberland example, where the panoply of classical motifs threatens to eclipse the mirror altogether.

On the window wall the girandoles sprout directly from the mirrors, which are a continuation of the pier tables below – the divisions within the central pier glass are continued in the legs of the table. This represents an overall unification of design which simultaneously tends to reduce the three-dimensional into two. These mirrors represent the culmination of a development started ten years before, when Adam was still thinking in Kentian terms.

Flanking the giant mirrors were wood-frame, lead and copper inset pilasters topped with Corinthian gilt wood capitals. The central portion of each was covered with clear glass painted moss-green on the reverse, flecked with shredded, confetti-like gilt copper and backed with varnished cloth, the whole simulating highly polished green granite or porphyry. The glass was overlaid with 'filigrane toy work'[61] of gilt stamped copper palmettes, from whose volutes depended strings of four husks. This delicate gilt tracery and the gilt lead overlays of the red panels gave the room that light and playful aspect characteristic of Adam's later work.

The walls above the mirrors and doors and between the pilasters were covered with large panels similarly foiled but in a deep crimson colour, suggesting red Egyptian porphyry. Over the glass, these sections were completed with gilt cast lead oval and round mouldings framing the oil paintings on paper[62] and the usual motifs from Adam's classical repertory.

Each overdoor painting is surrounded by four roundels, connected by a square chain of husks, which is the alternate design faintly sketched in on the right side of the original elevation (fig. 10), rather than the round chain proposed on the left, a form less firmly related to the door and pilasters and one which conflicts with the nearby ovals. In the same process of simplifying and regularizing the end walls, single mirrors were installed in favour of the proposed tripartite ones.

In the Glass Drawing Room classical motifs are repeated in various media: for example, the tripod and anthemion which are painted on the ceiling, stuccoed on the frieze, overlaid in copper and lead on the glass panels, are finally inlaid with scagliola into the chimney-piece and marble table slabs, an attempt to bring all parts of the room into a unified decorative whole.

All but one of the oval paintings on paper have been lost, and three of the Minervas now displayed in the Victoria and Albert Museum are photocopies. The one original Minerva, the small overmantel and four overdoor paintings (of which only two are included in the reconstruction) are in the general style of G. B. Cipriani[63] or possibly Antonio Zucchi.

The vertical lead insets of the pilasters[64] and door frames[65] and some of the lead overlays on the glass walls can be traced to their founder, G. Collett, who also provided the cast lead frames to the overdoor roundels[66]. Four gilding bills remain from Dominique Jean, the iron founder and ormolu worker later employed at Carlton House.[67] Dominique Jean's bill of February 25, 1775, for 'Gilding 16 Branch and nozal and pan . . . £1. 12. 0.' referring to the chandelier indicates that work continued at least until that date.

In the Victoria and Albert rendition, the long frieze of blue-green and gold urns and honeysuckle was copied in paint from an eighteenth-century fragment, with compensation for its discoloration. The similar door friezes are, however, original. The original six-panelled doors (fig. 10)[68] were probably painted apple-green, as indicated by Adam in a watercolour sketch, to match that same bright colour in the cornice, friezes, door surround insets and dado. The drawing shows that Adam also intended gilt applied tracery for the panels (for which an alternate sketch exists – fig. 13), as well as rosette and fluted border surrounds, and a vertical beading down the centre of each door. In Room 125, where the fragments have been assembled, the left mahogany door is eighteenth-century and in the Adam taste; the other was made to match in the Museum workshops. The red foiled glass was also restored in the Museum to replace lost or broken areas.[69]

Adam's three elevation drawings indicate two-branch gilt girandoles around the room, on the window side extending from relief urns applied to the mirrors and on the other three walls to the glass panels. Together with a pair of three-branch gilt candelabra on the

13. Preliminary sketch of door panels for Northumberland House, Adelphi, February 22, 1775. Pen and ink. Sir John Soane's Museum.

14. Marble and composition chimney-piece from the Glass Drawing Room, now in the Green Drawing Room, Syon House.

chimney-piece they achieve an even distribution of light. Beginning in the mid-sixties with separate mirrors and pier tables with echoing motifs as in the Croome Court set,[70] Adam gradually extended the mirror down until it joined the pier table and the two became one element, a unification which in French furniture had been effected in the early rococo. The same cohering process is seen in the Northumberland mirrors, now built directly into the wall as a continuation of the pier tables, as well as the lights, formerly embodied as candelabra set before mirrors (and still in that form in the Glass Drawing Room chimney-piece) which have now climbed up the wall and emerge as girandoles directly from the glass. In its quiet and elegant way, it was a revolutionary design, which was, however, probably never executed, for no record of the wall lights survives, and the 1768 inventory lists only 'A Chandelier in the middle of the Room . . .'. The 'three immense lustre chandeliers' which illuminate an earlier author's description of the room[71] apparently never existed. The dolphin-topped chandelier in the 1874 photographs appears to date from the refitting of 1821 and now hangs in the Green Drawing Room at Syon

House. It is not unlike the great cascades of drops produced by Parker and Perry for Carlton House earlier in the century.[72]

Also in the Green Drawing Room is the original chimney-piece from Northumberland House (fig. 14), composed of a classical scagliola frieze with centre oval plaque of Diana flanked by two inset painted panels of dancing nymphs; the frieze is supported by inset Ionic columns. It is considerably more delicate than the rather ponderous Kentian chimney-piece design shown in the wall elevation, and with its inset columns more architectural than the alternate proposal, dated 1773 (fig. 15).[73] In fact it is a reworking of the 1761 chimney-piece for Shardeloes and closely related to the contemporary (*c.*1775) example in the Tapestry Room at Osterley, with its three-part frieze and Ionic panel pilasters.[74]

THE FURNITURE

Though not unskilled in perspective rendering, Adam conceived of most furniture and all ornament in primarily two-dimensional terms. It has frequently been noted that his was not a particularly sculptural art, and much of his free-standing furniture attests to that shortcoming. As far as this is concerned, the architectural pieces, such as the pier tables, are not immune.[75] Adam quite sensibly reasoned that as long as chairs, settees and tables were intended to stand against a wall, they should be designed in context with that wall. It was not a new idea: the French had been doing it for half a century, but Adam was its chief English proponent.

His three sectional elevations for the Glass Drawing Room and a design for a semi-circular pier table slab (fig. 16) are the only surviving indications of what was intended for furniture. The 1786 inventory lists the room's contents eleven years after its completion and a description of its eighteenth century appearance must be limited to the furnishings mentioned there.

'A pair of circular Marble pier Tables done in Skioll [sic.] with brass mouldings round the Edge on carved and gilt frame' refers to the two flanking tables on the window wall, today in the Red Drawing Room at Syon House (fig. 17). It is these tables which have scagliola and marble tops executed to the design (fig. 16) dated May 6, 1774.[76] Although the tops closely resemble those in the salon at Nostell Priory made to Adam's designs by Richter and Bartoli in 1777, the frames, aside from a similar honeysuckle frieze motif,

15. 'Chimney Piece for the Drawing room at Northumberland House, Adelphi, 1773'. An alternate design. Watercolour, pen and ink. Sir John Soane's Museum.

have little in common. They are more in the spirit of the documented Adam pier table at Saltram executed in 1772 by Joseph Perfetti.[77] The ormolu border around the upper grooved edge of the slabs is an enrichment not found among related tables designed by Adam. The two pier tables originally proposed in the 1773 elevation (fig. 8) are among the most atypical and curious pieces in Adam's oeuvre: midway between pier tables and commodes, their cupid's bow fronts, awkward relief caryatids and squat proportions were wisely left unexecuted. The architect presented them in the drawing with slight variation, a choice of Kentian scroll legs or fluted columns (just as Chippendale showed chairs half gothic, half rococo) as alternate possibilities.

112

PLATE 4. A section from the Northumberland House Glass Dra
Room installed in the Museum. Room 125. The door is not or

16. 'Slab for the Duke of Northumberland, Adelphi, May 6, 1774.' Design for top of pier table. Watercolour, pen and ink. Sir John Soane's Museum.

17. One of a pair of semicircular pier tables from the Glass Drawing Room. Syon House.

A rectangular pier table with an antique mosaic top (fig. 18) which stood beneath the central mirror of the window wall, now also in the Red Drawing Room at Syon, was designed *en suite* with the flanking semicircular tables. Entered in the inventory as 'A Square pier Table Mosaic Marble on a carved and gilt frame' at £30, it shows the relative expense of mosaic vs. scagliola, the other two tables being listed at £35 the pair. It has lost its delicate apron swags which the other two retain, intended as a variation on the festoons and drops beneath the dado rail. The arrangement of forward legs, in two pairs spaced at the sides, which here echo the division of the mirror above, is a common one in Adam pier tables, whereas the curved stretchers are extremely unusual and reflect a strained attempt to interrelate the set. As with the semi-circular tables, here too the finished product represents a simplified design in contrast to that proposed in the elevation, which called for a bow front pier table, a design which Adam was not to repeat.

A pair of confidantes[78] was executed to stand beneath the pier mirrors on either side of the chimney-piece (fig. 19). Later re-covered in rosetted silk[79] and now in the Print Room at Syon, they can give little idea of the colour harmony achieved with the original 'three coloured Damask' mentioned in the inventory. Although they bear a close resemblance to the settee provided for Sir Abraham Hume in 1780,[80] the considerable differences between the proposed version and those executed suggest that they are not to an Adam design. That in the elevation appears with a scrolled crest rail and four forward legs and it bears little resemblance to the eight-legged example with smooth curvilinear crest rail now at Syon. Whereas

Adam shows a confidante with two flanking chairs *en suite*, the actual version is about one-third longer than that indicated in the elevation (10 ft. 8 in. vs. 7 ft. 6 in.) so that the matching chairs (fig. 20) (2 ft. 5 in. wide) would not have room to fit in their position against the wall. In comparison with Adam's scale, the confidantes appear, in the nineteenth-century photographs, overly large beneath the wall mirrors. But there are other reasons, stylistic as well as documentary, to suggest that Adam was not involved in the seat furniture.

The complete set consisted of two confidantes, two settees (fig. 21) and four armchairs. Listed in the inventory in two groups, they were all covered in the same three-coloured damask. The architect, in designing chairs and settees *en suite*, usually placed the rails at the same height. In the executed set, the chairs look large and out of scale to both confidantes and settees, primarily because their seat rails are two inches higher. This represents an inopportune design if the chairs had been intended to sit adjacent to either of the large pieces. However, there was not room for them to do so, either on the long or end walls (each settee is 8 ft. long vs. the elevation's proposed 5 ft. 3 in.), which suggests only one other place for them to rest: the window bays. They would thus be proportionately larger to better fill the bays. Adam's frequent plan for furnishing a room is to balance each settee with two chairs, leaving one for each window bay, but the designer of this set evidently preferred to leave the larger pieces standing alone.

One of the armchairs is signed 'J. Cullen' (fig. 22). James Cullen, who is recorded at 56 Greek Street, Soho, from 1765–79, was an important 'Upholder and

Cabinet-maker' who numbered among his clients the Duke of Atholl, the Earl of Waldegrave, the Duke of Abercorn, and the Earl of Hopetoun[81] at Hopetoun House, which he began furnishing two years after Robert Adam had completed work begun there by his father, William. There are, however, no records of Cullen having followed designs by Adam. Cullen was particularly current with new styles, as shown in his supplying a mirror in the neo-classical manner to

19. Confidante and two arm-chairs *en suite* by James Cullen. Syon House.

Hopetoun as early as 1766.[82] That he was in the mid-seventies providing furniture in the newly fashionable French style to Northumberland House underlines this. There seems no reason to question that the entire set of eight pieces is by Cullen. Although his extra-ordinary attention to detail at Hopetoun might suggest that he could have taken similar control at North-umberland House and supplied the additional furniture and hangings as well, some mention of his name would in this case be expected in the remarkably complete records at Alnwick, and it does not occur.

Although Cullen was involved with Reilly, Cobb, and Baron Berlindis in importing French furniture, his role appears to have been merely as owner of the warehouse where the goods were stored.[83] In fact he considered it an insult not to be asked to 'finish' (i.e. assemble and upholster) the furniture. Nevertheless Cullen's connections with this group allow the possi-bility that he merely labelled a suite of imported furniture and sold it to Northumberland. But the pronounced rake of the back legs (fig. 20) is typical of English chairs in the French style at this time and the proportions of the confidantes in particular combine to suggest English manufacture.

The inventory includes one additional group of furni-ture for the Glass Drawing Room: '12 Cabriole Chairs in carved and gilt frames, covered with Needle Work . . . .'.[84] Unless they were considerably smaller than the Cullen chairs, there would not have been room for them to flank the settees, nor would they normally have done so unless designed *en suite*, which the inventory makes clear they were not. This leaves no space for them, except standing in the middle of the room – an unusual practice in England in the eighteenth-century when chairs were lined up against the wall. Possibly they constituted an 'extra' set of chairs, brought into the room as the occasion required – a party or musical evening – and otherwise left in storage. This

20. One of four chairs which stood in the window bays of the drawing room.

21. One of two settees designed for the end walls.

was not an uncommon practice at the time and such sets were usually lined up in a nearby hall when not in use, in this case probably in the vestibule or 'Waiting Hall' directly behind the Glass Drawing Room. Nevertheless, to the current studies of the placing of eighteenth-century furniture they present a problem: the room is too crowded with them, and too empty without. An alternate arrangement would have been to align them in secondary rows before the settees, as was done with *chaises courantes* in France, for example in the Salon of the Hôtel Nivernais, Paris,[85] although this was not a common English practice. No traces of the set remain.

At present in the private dining room at Syon House is a tripod-supported tea urn with three looped candle branches (fig. 23) traditionally from Northumberland House. The inventory mentions 'A Tripod Vase and Lamp with three Branches gilt'. The classical tripod had been reinterpreted by James Stuart in the late 1750's and was taken up by Adam a few years later both for small urns such as this – there is another in the dining room at Kedleston[86] – and large pedestals. The use of looped branches is unusual for Adam and since Matthew Boulton specialized in ormolu tripod

candelabra both to Adam designs and style, it is a feature which may represent the work of this brass-founder. A bill at Alnwick records that Boulton was providing work for Northumberland at this time.[87] Currently displayed on the chimney-piece from the Glass Drawing Room is a handsome pair of covered bronze vases with ormolu oval plaques of classical figures (fig. 24). The pair may belong to the garniture listed in 1786, '7 Ornaml Vases and 2 standing Branches on the Chimney piece . . . " One of the vases appears in that place in the 1874 watercolour (fig. 5).

LATER ALTERATIONS TO THE GLASS DRAWING ROOM

Northumberland House passed through a succession of dukes within the half-century after Adam's decoration and each one commissioned changes to the south front, but owing to indecision and short life-spans, nothing was finally altered until 1821. After the first Duke's death in 1786, the second asked James Wyatt to redesign the first floor apartments on the river side, but his finely finished design of 1790[88] remained unexecuted. The third Duke, upon taking possession

22. Signature of James Cullen on back seat rail of chair in fig. 20.

in 1817, commissioned Thomas Hardwick, whose father had worked at Syon, to remodel the interior. His plans,[89] awkwardly showing the difficulty of changing the upper storey rectangular rooms to elliptical ones, were wisely shelved for further thought. Hardwick's more important contribution was, in this instance, merely to record the south front elevation as it existed in 1819 (fig. 25),[90] confirming that the drawing room at that time still had four window bays. The succession of rooms in the 1786 inventory indicates that the drawing room was located on the ground floor, west of the main entrance and the 'Waiting Hall'. The same document proves that it was built to Adam's plan with four bays, as it was furnished with eight pier glasses (three on each long wall and one at each end) and four 'three col^d Silk Damask festoon Window Curtains and gilt Cornices'. But in 1819 it was decided that Adam's alterations, however visually pleasing, had weakened the building.[91] The exterior wall was now dangerously out of plumb and so another architect, Thomas Cundy,[92] was

24. One of the pair of bronze and ormolu vases from the drawing room, listed in the 1786 inventory as being on the chimney-piece. Syon House.

called in to design an entirely new south facade, as well as to change the apartments on that side and provide two new grand staircases, one inside and one out (fig. 26).[93] The two windows each in the Tapestry Room and Small Dining Room (located in the projecting flanks of the Hardwick elevation) were combined into two wide tripartite ones, and the facade in between was reduced from nine bays to seven, thus the drawing room was given three windows rather than four. A comparison with the ground floor plan drawn about seventy years earlier (fig. 27),[94] before the Adam decoration, shows the nature and extent of Cundy's changes. In rebuilding the south wall, each window was widened from $3\frac{1}{2}$ ft. to 5 ft. with proportionate increases in the

23. A three-tap tea urn traditionally from the Glass Drawing Room, possibly by Matthew Boulton. Syon House.

25. 'Drawing from the River Front of Northumberland House in its present state, May, 1819.' By Thomas Hardwick. Muniment Room, Syon House.

intervening piers. Adam had designed this wall in the drawing room with three pier glasses, the central one slightly wider. To accommodate the new arrangement, Cundy removed one of the narrow piers and duplicated the wide central tripartite one to form the second pier,[95] retaining as much of the original Adam decoration as possible, while necessarily sacrificing some of the subtlety of spacing. The nineteenth-century photographs and watercolour show the resulting disparity of scale between the window and chimney walls[96] and the dislocation with the ceiling. The new garden facade was placed about 5 ft. south of the old, adding considerable space to the state apartments. In order to save the drawing room ceiling, it was raised and a decidedly un-Adam-like cove introduced. The double anthemion band framing the ceiling was removed from the ends, and also the plain bands from the sides to adapt it to the altered proportions.[97] This left the end walls to be widened. A comparison of the original elevation (fig. 10) with one of the walls as it appeared after the change (fig. 12) shows that it was disassembled, shifted slightly south and rebuilt with an added panel at each end. The lightly shaded areas of the Cundy plan (fig. 26) confirm that structural changes were made in three of the drawing room walls. During the renovation, one of the overdoor roundels was damaged and replaced, as one of those displayed at the Museum bears an 1818 watermark. Shortly after the new construction, the firm of Morel and Hughes refitted all the rooms of the south wing.[98] In the Glass Drawing Room they upholstered the settees and chairs with 'green ground rosette silke'[99]

and in so doing rearranged the furniture grouping. The four cartouche back chairs with leafage at the crest rail centre, carved *en suite* with the two confidantes and two settees were covered with this material, as were eight chairs of closely related form from the adjacent Tapestry Room. The two cabriole sofas *en suite* with this latter set of eight had been polychromed and covered with tapestry in 1810 and are now in the Long Gallery at Syon. The twelve cabriole chairs covered with needlework mentioned in the inventory were evidently removed from the room at this time and were probably sold in the auction of 1874, as their present whereabouts is unknown. After the refitting, several pieces of undistinguished Victorian furniture were added and the once vibrant Glass Drawing Room rode out on its melancholy path towards disassembly.

DECLINE AND FALL

During the Great Exhibition of 1851, the seventh Duke of Northumberland, at the request of Prince Albert, opened his house to the public. The guide book[100] published for the occasion provides a pretentious and fascinating Victorian evaluation. The Glass Drawing Room, the *dernier cri* of 1775, is now old-fashioned, fussy, and of considerably less interest to the writer than Thomas Cundy's 'Magnificent Staircase' of 1821: a 'gorgeous production . . . without exception, the most splendid feature of the building'.[101] The drawing room is thought passé, 'a very antique and seemingly old looking chamber . . . It is of the

26. 'The Plan of the Parlour Story at Northumberland House, Thomas Cundy, Arch^t - Pimlico, April, 1821.' Muniment Room, Syon House.

most magnificent description, though the ornaments are quaint, and, in many respects overdone . . . The gilding and carving are of the most profuse order – perhaps carried to excess, wall and roof being literally one mass of intricate and involved workmanship, the numerous details of which, however perfect and beautiful individually, detract from the harmony of the whole . . . The effect . . . though elaborate in the highest degree, is perhaps too intricate and discordant; wanting that simplicity and harmony of arrangement which are necessary for the production of great designs'.[102] While at first the criteria of simplicity and harmony hardly seem representative of interior design

in 1851, the writer has astutely understood the *avant-garde* aesthetic of Paxton's Crystal Palace, and that an Adam type of uniform decorativeness was no longer acceptable.

The eighth Duke resisted pressure to sell Northumberland House and its property towards the Thames, but was compelled[103] to do so in 1873 to the Metropolitan Board of Works, the price approximating £500,000.[104] Most of the furniture, the best chimneypieces,[105] important Soho tapestries,[106] carpets and other fittings were removed to other Percy residences in London, Syon and Alnwick. The proud lead Percy lion, which had crowned the Strand front for 122

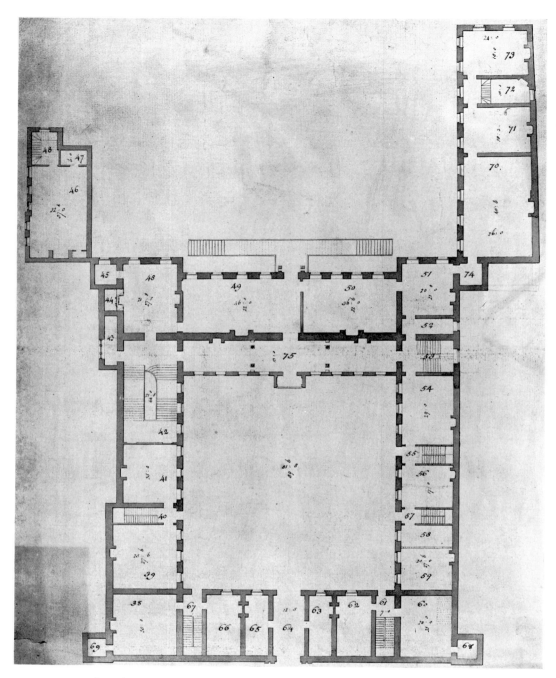

27. 'Plan of the Ground Floor', Northumberland House, c.1750. Muniment Room, Syon House.

years, was placed atop the Thames facade at Syon House as a companion to the stone one above Adam's gateway. The Glass Drawing Room was dismantled, crated, and stored in the riding school at Syon. What remained of the furnishings and fittings was sold at public auction in 1874. Writing in 1912, E. Beresford Chancellor lamented the demolition of the historic house: 'In 1874 the last remains of this great house, commenced by a Howard, continued by a Percy and completed by a Seymour . . . were sold at auction and in its stead a large thoroughfare formed, on the sides of which immense hotels jostle each other . . .'.[107]

After World War II, the present Duke sold the crated sections of the room, including the ceiling, to Mr. Bert Crowther of Syon Lodge, after which they were unfortunately rented as decor for a post-war debutante ball. Not surprisingly, some of the panels were damaged during this period and some were sold to a French collector.[108] In 1955, H. D. Molesworth, then Keeper of the Department of Woodwork at the Victoria and Albert Museum, spotted the forlorn remains at Syon Lodge. Through the generosity of the late Dr. W. L. Hildburgh, F.S.A., the Museum was able to acquire these last traces of Robert Adam's most elaborate late style, and, thanks to the painstaking restoration by the Department of Conservation, they sparkle once again as precious remnants of the unique and glittering Glass Drawing Room (fig. 28).

Notes

We would like to thank Peter Thornton and Desmond Fitz-Gerald of this Museum, Miss Dorothy Stroud of Sir John Soane Museum, John Harris and John Cornforth for their help in preparing this article. And especially the Duke of Northumberland, for the many courtesies extended, both at Syon and Alnwick.

* * *

1. Essex, Arundel, Worcester, Salisbury, Durham, York, and Northumberland Houses. E. Beresford Chancellor, *Private Palaces of London*, London, 1908, p. 27.

2. *Ibid.*, pp. 50–51.

3. L.C.C., *Survey of London*, xviii, The Strand, London, 1937, p. 12.

4. Ian Dunlop, 'Northumberland House, London', *Country Life*, cxiv, July 30, 1953, p. 340.

5. L.C.C., *Survey of London*, *op. cit.*, p. 13. Extract from letter from Duchess of Somerset to Lady Luxborough, June, 1749.

6. *Ibid.*

7. This new wing begun by Algernon was not finished until *c.*1757–58.

8. Gerald Brenan, *A History of the House of Percy*, London, 1902, vol. ii, pp. 428–30. The Smithson's in the sixteenth century were tenant farmers at Stanwick Manor, Yorkshire. Hugh Smithson (d.1677) amassed a fortune as successor to Ralph and William Robinson, haberdashers of London: he then purchased the Manor of Stanwick and a baronetcy in 1660. His grandson, also a Sir Hugh Smithson, died in 1729, the baronetcy going to his grandson, the Hugh Smithson who married Elizabeth Seymour.

9. *The Complete Peerage*, ed. H. A. Doubleday and Lord Howard De Walden, vol. ix, 1936, p. 742: 'Algernon Seymour, Duke of Somerset, Earl of Hertford, son of Elizabeth, daughter of Joceline Percy, Earl of Northumberland. On the death of his mother in 1722 he succeeded to the vast Percy estates. In consequence of his maternal descent he was created on 2 October 1749 Earl of Northumberland with special remainder (failing heirs male of his body) to his son-in-law Sir Hugh Smithson, Bart., and the heirs male of his body by Lady Elizabeth, his wife (only surviving child of the grantee . . .). Algernon died 7 February 1750.'

10. Arthur T. Bolton, *The Architecture of Robert and James Adam*, London, 1922, p. 39. Bolton refers to 'one of the wings which Robert Mylne had . . . built'. However, Mylne's work at Northumberland House has not been proved and his diary makes no mention of having been employed there.

11. *Letters of Horace Walpole*, ed. Mrs. Paget Toynbee, Oxford, 1903–05, vol. iv, pp. 52–53. Walpole to Sir Horace Mann, May 5, 1757: 'Lord Northumberland's great gallery is finished and opened: it is a sumptuous chamber, but might have been in a better taste.' However displeasing to Walpole's eye, the room contained fine plaster work, probably by one of the Francini brothers. Count Kielmansegge in his *Diary of a Journey to England in the Years 1761–1762*, London, 1902, pp.

146–47, gives the most complete description of the proportions and decorations and suggests the occasionally superheated nature of his hosts' elegance. 'Four large crystal chandeliers, each with twenty-five candles, light up the room even more brilliantly than is necessary, and I certainly think that it would not be easy to imagine a more splendid sight than this gallery presents when filled with people, all vieing with one another in the beauty of their dress.'

12. Brennan, *op. cit.*, p. 428. He possessed over £4,000 a year, practically unencumbered, and was heir to another property worth £3,000 annually.

13. *Ibid.*, p. 425.

14. He was George Seymour, Lord Beauchamp.

15. Brenan, *op. cit.*, pp. 438–42.

16. *Ibid.*, p. 446.

17. Francis Bickley, ed., Historic Manuscripts Commission 'Report on the Manuscripts of the Late Reginald Rawdon Hastings, Esq.', vol. iii, 1934, pp. 149–50. Letter dated September 4, 1770, from the Reverend Theophilus Lindsey to Francis, Tenth Earl of Huntingdon, regarding work at Alnwick Castle, ' . . . £10,000 was expended the year before last. You know that the Duke of Northumberland is so good a calculator and contractor as to have always work done for his money. There are still betwixt one and two hundred hands daily employed in widening the river and finishing a new-made chapel, etc.'.

18. Alnwick Castle, Alnwick, Northumberland.

19. Syon House, Brentford, Middlesex.

20. Northumberland was Lord of the Bedchamber to George II and George III, 1753–63; Lord Lieutenant of Ireland, 1763–65; Vice-Admiral of North America, 1764; Trustee of the British Museum from its foundation in 1753 to his death in 1786; and Master of the Horse, 1778–80. He fought Grenville's Stamp Tax and joined Lord Chatham in opposing the American War. As Duke of Northumberland, he was First Duke of the Third Creation. *Complete Peerage*, *op. cit.*, p. 743, lists him as Eighteenth Earl and Third Duke.

21. Horace Walpole, *Memoirs of George Third*, 1894, i, pp. 333–34. We wish to thank Wilmarth S. Lewis for locating this quotation.

22. Hugh (Smithson) Percy, b.1742. Tory MP Westminster, 1763–76. *Complete Peerage*, *op. cit.*, p. 744. He became Second Duke of Northumberland on his father's death in 1786. The First Duke's natural son was James Smithson, b.1765, who founded the Smithsonian Institution, Washington, D.C.

23. Toynbee, *op. cit.*, ix, p. 74. Walpole writes October 22, 1774, 'Wilkes has met with a heroine to stem the tide of his conquests, her Grace of Northumberland, who has carried the mob of Westminster from him; sitting daily in the midst of Covent Garden; and will elect her son'. Three days later Walpole refers to the lady as 'Duchess of Charing Cross' in a letter to Lady Ossory, October 27, 1774, *Walpole Correspondence*, xxxii, p. 211.

24. Toynbee, *op. cit.*, xiv, p. 87.

25. James Greig, *Diaries of a Duchess*, London, 1926. The diaries are now at Alnwick.

26. 'Indeed *price* is no article, or rather *is* a reason for my Lord Northumberland's liking anything.' Walpole to Horace Mann, October 28, 1752. Toynbee, *op. cit.*, III, p. 128.

27. Count Kielmansegge commented on a party for 600 on November 6, 1761, 'The house is well adapted for so large a party and is rightly considered one of the best houses in London, particularly on account of its large saloon and gallery.' *Diary of a Journey to England in the Years 1761–1762, op. cit.*, p. 145.

28. This unhappy event may account for the apparent lack of contemporary descriptions of the entertainments at Northumberland House during the period immediately following the room's completion in 1775.

29. Alnwick MS, U. I. 46.

30. Alnwick MS, U. III. 6, nos. 1–4 (packet 1), nos. 1–14 (packet 2).

31. Soane MS, H. VI. 2. d., pp. 60–61.

32. Victoria and Albert Museum, W.3–1955. Room 125.

33. Damie Stillman, *The Decorative Work of Robert Adam*, London 1966, p. 25.

34. Soane Museum, II, no. 33.

35. John Fleming, *Robert Adam and his Circle*, London 1962, p. 203.

36. Alnwick MS, U. I. 44. Receipts and Disbursements by Thos. Butler from June 16, 1766 through February 22, 1777.

37. *Ibid.*

38. The cove is an infrequent element in the architecture of Neoclassicism. One of its rare Adam appearances is in the Red Drawing Room at Syon.

39. Stillman, *op. cit.*, figs. 134, 135, 136, 138.

40. Soane Museum, II, nos. 32, 102.

41. *Ibid.*, XVII, no. 173.

42. Alnwick MS, U. I. 46.

43. Soane Museum, XXXIX, nos. 5, 6, 7.

44. Robert and James Adam, *The Works in Architecture*, London, 1778, II, section 5, pl. 7. 'Inside View of the Theatre-Royal in Drury Lane as it appears from the Stage. Altered and decorated in the year 1775.'

45. *Public Advertiser*, September 30, 1775. We are indebted to Mr. Walter Ison for this information. Quoted in Greater London Council *Survey of London*, XXXV, *The Theatre Royal, Drury Lane and The Royal Opera House, Covent Garden*, London, 1970, p. 46.

46. James Ralph, *A Critical Review of the Public Buildings . . . in and about London and Westminster*, 1783, p. 76. Quoted in *Ibid.*, p. 48.

47. G. Bernard Hughes, 'A Drawing Room in Glass', *Country Life*, CXIX, May 24, 1956, p. 1126. For a history of the formation of this company, see William Henry Bowles, *History of the Vauxhall and Ratcliff Glass Houses and their Owners, 1670–1800*, London, 1926. For a summary of 'Parliamentary Proceedings Relating to the Cast Glass Company', see Geoffrey Wills, *English Looking Glasses*, London, 1965, Appendix I.

48. T. C. Barket, *Pilkington Brothers and the Glass Industry*, London, 1960, p. 47.

49. Hughes, *loc. cit.*

50. Charles Cameron's rooms at Tsarskoe Selo (now Pushkin Palace), near Leningrad, particularly the Blue Room and Cabinet of Mirrors in the First Apartment, 1780–82, with walls of milky glass overlaid with eagles and sphinxes in bronze, show the influence of Clérisseau (whom Cameron knew in Rome in the 60s) and a general awareness of Adam's work of the 70s. Though they contain numerous mirrors which heighten the contrast of polychrome materials (agate and jasper), they do not appear to be specific reinterpretations of the Glass Drawing Room. See Georges Loukomski, *Charles Cameron*, London, 1943, pp. 49, 85.

51. For the history of Reilly's importing activities, including the documents concerning the mirrors, see William Rieder, 'Furniture-Smuggling for a Duke,' *Apollo*, September, 1970, pp. 206–209. This information was uncovered at Alnwick by Mr. Colin Streeter of the Metropolitan Museum, New York, and Mrs. Tessa Craib-Cox, Winterthur, Delaware, to whom we are particularly grateful.

52. Alnwick MS, U. I. 42.

53. 'Four Glasses each full 97 French Inches in Heighth (at this time a French and English inch are approximately equal) and full 56 such Inches in Breadth.' These became the flanking mirrors of the chimney and window walls. 'Two Glasses each full 97 French Inches and full 43 such Inches in Breadth': for the end walls. 'One Glass full 97 French Inches in Heighth and full 30 such Inches in Breadth': the centre glass of the window wall, the dimensions of which are corrected in a subsequent note. 'And one Chimney Glass 78 French Inches in Heighth and 59 such Inches in Breadth, but as the exact Size of the said Chimney Glass cannot yet be ascertained it is hereby agreed that in Case it shall be found necessary to vary from the Dimensions above mentioned the Addition to or Diminution of the Size thereof shall be allowed or paid for in Proportion to such Variation . . .'

54. A large consignment of furniture imported the same way the previous year and divided between the shops of Reilly, James Cullen, and John Cobb, was seized by the Customs. See Geoffrey Wills, 'Furniture-Smuggling in Eighteenth-century London', *Apollo*, August, 1965, pp. 112–17.

55. Alnwick MS, U. III. 6 no. 1 (packet 2), dated August 5 (1775).

56. Two bills: Alnwick MS, U. III. 6. nos. 4, 7 (packet 2) dated December 7, 1774 and January 10, 1775. Dologal's name is spelled Delagall in the 'Abstract of Tradesmen's Bills for Work done for the Drawing Room at Northumberland House . . .' which provides a list of all such surviving bills and precedes the two packets designated U. III. 6.

57. *Ibid.*, no. 2 (packet 2). Dated November 1, 1774, for '13½ yds @ 14d', the rest 'narrower' @ 12d 'for putting behind the glass in the draughing-Room'.

58. Alnwick MS, U. III. 6. no. 3 (packet 1). Dated December 17, 1773, for '132 feet of fine Crown Glass in the new Windows for the Room under alteration . . . £8. 16. 0d.'.

59. Eileen Harris, *The Furniture of Robert Adam*, London 1963, fig. 57.

60. *Ibid.*, fig. 62.

61. Sir William Chambers's phrase 'filigrane toy work' is quoted by Geoffrey Webb, *Georgian Art*, Burlington Magazine Monograph III, London, 1929, p. 24.

62. The paintings original to the room would not have been executed by Matthew Boulton's 'mechanical process' which did not come into use before 1776; see Eric Robinson and Keith R. Thompson, 'Matthew Boulton's Mechanical Paintings,' *The Burlington Magazine*, August, 1970, pp. 497–507.

63. Dunlop, *op. cit.*, attributes the paintings to Cipriani. Giovanni Battiste Cipriani (1727–1785) painted mythological scenes for several Adam interiors: Lansdowne House, London, 1762 and 1771; 19 Arlington Street, London, 1763–66; Audley End, 1770.

64. Bill signed 'G. Collett' of Jack and Collett. Entry dated November 12, 1773, for lengths 1 ft. 2 in. corresponds with the brown and gold painted lead sections set into the pilaster borders. They have a raised design of beaded circles enclosing a three-petal flower.

65. Lengths 1 ft. 1¼ in. correspond with lengths in the green and gold painted lead sections in the door surrounds. These have a similar series of raised beaded circles, though their centres alternate two different floral designs.

66. Entry dated April 23, 1774, lists '16 Large Patres with Mask Faces and Husks at 18s-od-Sett £3 12. 0.'. The 'Mask Faces' refer to the Apollo faces in the round gilt lead ornaments. Collett's bill shows that he was supplying Syon House at the same time, and it is likely that he was responsible for the gilt lead overlays on the window embrasures and on the ivory pilaster plaques in the Red Drawing Room there.

67. See Dorothy Stroud, *Henry Holland*, London, 1966, p. 82, where he is given as Jean Dominique. In the royal accounts and Northumberland bills, he is consistently referred to as Dominique Jean and signs himself as such. Although French craftsmen in the eighteenth century sometimes gave their surname first, the occasional abbreviated mention of Domk Jean and D. Jean suggests that his surname was in fact Jean.

68. Soane Museum, xxxix, no 7. That Adam's six-panel doors were executed is clear from the 1874 watercolour and photographs.

69. The gilt copper was scraped from panels not used in the reconstruction, cleaned, and applied to newly painted glass. The different shades of red do not reflect original and new areas, but rather the unstable pigment used in the reapplication and vagaries of uneven light exposure.

70. Harris, *op. cit.*, fig. 11.

71. Hughes, *loc. cit.*

72. Ralph Edwards, *The Shorter Dictionary of English Furniture*, London, 1964, p. 182. The collection of drawings for lighting fixtures by Perry & Co. in the Department of Prints and Drawings at the Victoria and Albert Museum (95.C.83–85) is largely of the late 19th and 20th century. The Syon chandelier is closely related to that in the Music Room at Buckingham Palace (John Harris, G. de Bellaigue, O. Millar, *Buckingham Palace*, London, 1968, p. 62) and reveals a similar handling of the motif as the dolphin furniture at the Brighton Pavilion (Clifford Musgrave, *Regency Furniture*, London, 1961, pl. 11).

73. Soane Museum, xx, no. 17.

74. The Adamesque marble chimney-piece with its centre relief plaque of a plump Minerva, substituted by the Victoria and Albert Museum, came from the museum stores without provenance and is evidently late 19th century. Unfortunately it is a bit bold for the delicacy of the room and too narrow to visually support the mirror above.

75. Many of Adam's pier tables (e.g. Croome Court), when viewed from the side, have the tendency to visually cant forward, as their legs taper on only three sides.

76. The tables in their present state reflect the 1823 restoration by the firm of Morel & Hughes. 'To thoroughly repairing and strengthening the frames of two semi-circular pier tables, and making good the deficiencies, also bleaching and polishing the statuary marble tops inlaid with scagliola and repairing and water gilding the ormolu mouldings, the additional carving by Mr. Ponsonby: £7–14–0.' Alnwick MS, U. I. 64, vol. 2, p. 38.

77. Harris, *op. cit.*, fig. 21.

78. A form introduced into England from France in the early 1770's, it became quite popular within the decade. In the 1788 edition of *The Cabinet-Maker and Upholsterer's Guide*, Hepplewhite wrote, 'This piece of furniture is of French origin and is in pretty general request for large and spacious suits of apartments. An elegant drawing-room, with modern furniture, is scarce complete without a confidante: the extent of which may be about 9 feet . . .'.

79. Morel & Hughes, 1823: 'To thoroughly repairing the frames of two confidantes, ripping the stuffed parts, opening the horse hair, and restuffing the backs and ends with the old materials and an addition of new, making two squabs for the seats, four cushions for the ends, and four new down pillows in white jean cases. £32–10–0. To covering the above confidantes with [green ground rosette] silk, and making cases for the squabs, and cushions, and pillows, lined and finished in every respect as sofas, £14–6–0.'

80. Harris, *op. cit.*, fig. 124.

81. Coleridge, *op. cit.*, p. 161. Cullen's extensive work in furnishing and fitting Hopetoun from 1755–66 is thoroughly chronicled, pp. 161–69.

82. *Ibid.*, fig. 411.

83. *Geoffrey Wills*, *op. cit.*, p. 115.

84. 'Cabriole' in inventories at this time indicates a concave back and does not refer to the shape of legs.

85. F. J. B. Watson, *Louis XVI Furniture*, 1960, p. 35.

86. Clifford Musgrave, *Adam and Hepplewhite and other Neo-Classical Furniture*, London, 1966, fig. 2.

87. Alnwick MS, U. I. 42. '13 Dec. 1774. Paid Dᵗ by Messrs Boulton & Fothergill of Birmingham on his Grace p. order 51-8-0.'

88. Syon MS, Class B. Div. XV. 2. e. 'Design for an alteration to the apartments in the south front of Northumberland House on the one pair of stairs.'

89. Syon MS, Class B. Div. XV. 2. f. (3), (4).

90. *Ibid.* (1).

91. In a letter dated May 2, 1819 (Percy Family Letters, xciv), C. R. Cockerell comments to the third Duke that Adam in

changing the south wall from its earlier plan of 2-5-2 bays had weakened the structure.

92. The first record of Cundy's work at Northumberland House is a receipt for designs, dated November 10, 1820. Alnwick MS, U. III. 8. a.

93. Syon MS, Class B, Div. XV. 2. g.

94. *Ibid.*, k. 2.

95. This explains the presence of some gilt wood framing motives among the fragments in the Museum, as Cundy would have found it easier to have the few extra pieces carved rather than recast. It is the discarded pier glass which is referred to in a drawing of a mirror at Alnwick (library): 'Memo: there is also one old plate 78 × 40 sided plate in hand from old Glass Drawing Room'.

96. In 1853 Charles Barry made elevation drawings of the Glass Drawing Room (now in the record tower at Alnwick) which show the same contrast.

97. In 1821 Robert Jones repainted the cove and ceiling to match, though it is not known how closely he followed the Adam scheme. Jones's expensive bill for work in the several rooms affected by the alterations was £1,893. Alnwick MS, U. I. 83.

98. Their bill in 1823 for the Glass Drawing Room was £1,898 15. 10 and for the entire project a staggering £34,111. 9. 7. Alnwick MS, U. I. 64. Two entries reflect the architectural changes in the drawing room. 'To four pieces of cornice of corresponding members with the cornice of room, to fill up the spaces left unfinished in the piers between the windows and at the ends of do. £3.18.0.' 'To 19 yards of superfine Axminster carpet to surround Your Grace's large carpet. £44.13.0.'

99. Fourteen extra yards of this silk were supplied at the time of the 1823 refitting. The last of this material was used in 1966.

100. *Northumberland House: Its Saloons and Picture Gallery, with a Description of Its Magnificent Staircase*, London, 1851.

101. *Ibid.*, p. 11.

102. *Ibid.*, p. 8.

103. Henry B. Wheatley, *London Past and Present*, 1891, p. 605, 'Northumberland House was sold . . . under the compulsory clause of An Act of Parliament, to the Metropolitan Board of Works in 1873'.

104. Hughes, *loc. cit.*

105. One of the chimney-pieces from the first Duke's great picture gallery is now in the billiards room at Syon House. Its mate and overmantel, the former gift of the late Dr. W. L. Hildburgh, F.S.A., the latter a gift of Mr. Bert Crowther, are displayed in the Victoria and Albert Museum, Room 63, Museum No. A.60–1951.

106. Three of these panels are at Alnwick Castle, the rest at Albury Park.

107. E. Beresford Chancellor, *Annals of the Strand*, London, 1912, p. 270.

108. Verbal information from Mr. Derek Crowther.

JOHN PHYSICK

Five monuments from Eastwell

I

'EASTWELL lies towards the middle of Kent, towards the *South-East* part of it, by a little Brook which runs into the greater Stoure, about Two miles to the *South-Westward* from Wye; in the Bailliewick of *Chart* and *Longbridge*, Hundred of *Wye*, Lath of *Scray*, East Division of the County, and Division of Justices in the Lath of *Shipway*. 'Tis in the Deanery of *Charing* and the Diocese of *Canterbury*; and the Church is dedicated to the Blessed Virgin; it is small but hath a good old Tower. In the *south* Chancel is a Noble Monument of the *Finches* Family, with Two Figures lying in White Marble; the Dome of the Monument is supported by Eight Pillars of black Marble, and round the Tomb are the Names of Twelve of the Noble Family buried here, Eight Men, and Four Women. There is also another Tomb of an Earl of *Winchelsey*, and on it I saw the Arms of *Kemp* and *Moyle*. Another of Sir *Henry Finch*, and one of his Lady, whose name was Bell.' Thus, somewhat inaccurately, wrote John Harris[1] at the beginning of the 18th century, in one of the earliest printed references to Eastwell Church and its monuments. By the end of the same century, the historian Edward Hasted[2] recorded: 'On the south side of the Chancel is the tomb of sir *Thomas Moyle*. In the *south* chancel is a sumptuous tomb on which lie the figure of a man and a woman in white marble, at full length; it had till within these few years, a beautiful dome or canopy over them, supported by eight pillars of black marble, the fragments of which now lie scattered about the chancel. It was erected for *sir Moyle Finch, knt.* and *bart.* who died in 1614, and Elizabeth his wife . . . They had eight sons and four daughters, whose names are round the sides of the tomb. And there is another monument for *sir Heneage Finch*, knt., Sergeant-at-Law, and Recorder of *London*, who died in 1631, and of his first wife *Frances*, daughter of *sir Edward* (sic) *Bell*, who died in 1627. At the upper end of the south isle is a vault, for the Finch family, in which are 38 coffins, the Hon. Edward Finch-Hatton, father of the present *Mr. Hatton*, of Eastwell, being the last who was buried in it.'

The monuments at Eastwell, like many in Kent, were strangely disregarded during the next century and a half, and seem only rarely to have been illustrated, although there are the occasional references to them in books about the county. The writer first saw them in 1936 when, as a boy, he was taken to Eastwell by an uncle, then vicar of the nearby parish of Throwley. Thirty years passed before he visited this lonely church again, but by then disaster had befallen it.

The park of Eastwell, in which the church stands, had been occupied by the army during the Second World War. As a result, the church became utterly neglected, for no maintenance work was carried out during that time. Architecturally somewhat dull, its main interest lay in some early stained glass[3], and in the monuments. Within a radius of about two miles were other churches whose claims to conservation were stronger than that of Eastwell – to the east is the splendid building of Boughton Aluph; to the west, Westwell with its unusual tripartite chancel arch; and in Eastwell Park, on the north side, Challock[4]. By the end of the war the structure of Eastwell Church had badly deteriorated and no-one should have been surprised when, during a gale

1. Eastwell Church, Kent, looking south-west, July 1965. (National Monuments Record.)

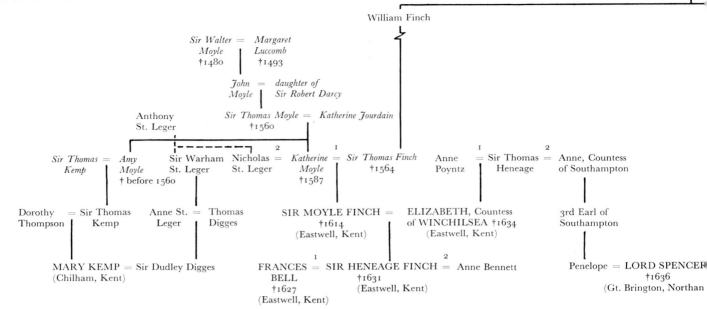

in 1951, the roof of the nave collapsed. Owing to its isolated position and its few parishioners it was not thought pastorally necessary to rebuild the ruined church.

In 1966 only the west tower, the south porch, which had become a small chapel with a monument during the 19th century, and a modern brick building, were about all there was to see (fig. 1). The once delightful church, standing on the banks of a large lake, presented a dismal spectacle of overgrowth and damp neglect. However, the parish and its friends, realizing the importance of the sculptures, had erected the brick shelter on the site of part of the chancel, and south chapel; it was stark and absolutely utilitarian, but it provided protection for the monuments, not only from the effects of weather, but also from vandals, whose activities in the area were only too apparent.

During the next few years, every effort was made to find a home for the monuments, but without success. One reason was financial; it would have taken a lot of money to dismantle them properly, and no local organization would have been able to raise sufficient funds. Another reason was that no neighbouring church was really willing to have them, indeed none, except Challock and Boughton Aluph, would have been large enough. When it appeared that the monuments could not be adequately housed in the neighbourhood, the Council for the Care of Churches enquired whether the Museum would accept them. This was agreed and the Museum undertook to pay for their removal and re-erection. The rector was able to obtain the necessary faculty from the Canterbury Diocese, and during 1967/68, the sculptures were brought to London. They have been placed in Room 50 (West), which is being re-arranged as a gallery of English sculpture of the 17th, 18th and 19th centuries. No bodies or other remains of any sort were found within the tomb-chests when they were dismantled. The shelter has now been demolished, and an incorrect commemorative plaque marks the site[5]. The photographs chosen to illustrate this article show the monuments either in the church, or in the shelter.

Eastwell had six monuments of interest – five of artistic value, which are those in the Museum, and another of no sculptural merit which is still in Kent. It is reasonable that this should have remained on the site of the church, as attached to it is a romantic local legend. In form, the monument consists of an altar tomb, with an indent for a brass, formerly on the north side of the chancel, and it probably commemorates Sir Walter Moyle (died 1480). However, certainly since the early 18th century, it has been pointed out as the tomb of an illegitimate son of Richard III, who was, as an old man, cared for by Sir Thomas Moyle. Whatever the truth behind the tradition, the parish registers record that 'Rychard Plantagenet was buried the xxij day of December, anno ut supra [1550].' Philip Parsons noted on August 31, 1790,[6] that 'there was also, about thirty years ago, the ruins of a building in Eastwell Park, which, they say, was his house; and a well (now filled up) called Plantagenet's well.'

II. THE FAMILIES OF MOYLE AND FINCH

The family of Moyle came from Cornwall to Kent during the 15th century, and settled in the pleasant Stour valley, to the north of Ashford, in the region of Eastwell and Boughton Aluph, and Sir Thomas Moyle's grandfather, Sir Walter Moyle, was living in the parish of Eastwell in 1459. He and his wife Margaret (Luccomb) both asked in their wills to be buried on the north side of the chancel of the church[7]. Other members

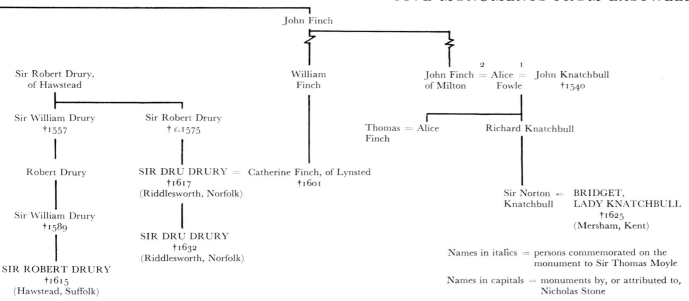

John Finch

Sir Robert Drury, of Hawstead

William Finch

John Finch of Milton = Alice Fowle = John Knatchbull †1540

Sir William Drury †1557 — Sir Robert Drury † c.1575

Thomas Finch = Alice — Richard Knatchbull

Robert Drury

SIR DRU DRURY †1617 (Riddlesworth, Norfolk) = Catherine Finch, of Lynsted †1601

Sir William Drury †1589

SIR DRU DRURY †1632 (Riddlesworth, Norfolk)

Sir Norton Knatchbull = BRIDGET, LADY KNATCHBULL †1625 (Mersham, Kent)

SIR ROBERT DRURY †1615 (Hawstead, Suffolk)

Names in italics = persons commemorated on the monument to Sir Thomas Moyle

Names in capitals = monuments by, or attributed to, Nicholas Stone

of the family lived at Buckwell in Boughton Aluph, in which parish the name remains in Buckwell Farm. The Moyles married into such local families as the Kemps of Olantigh, near Wye (kinsmen of the Cardinal Archbishop of Canterbury), the Finches, and the St. Legers of Ulcombe, and Leeds Castle. The first person with whose monument we are concerned is Sir Thomas Moyle. In 1537 he became a member (and eventually Chancellor) of the Court of Augmentations, which administered the monastic property seized by Henry VIII, and was knighted on October 18 of that year. Two years later he was sent to Glastonbury Abbey to look for treasure supposedly buried there, and to collect evidence for use against the Abbot. Sir Thomas was elected a Member of Parliament in 1542, and became Speaker of the House of Commons. Although apparently in favour with Henry VIII, he seems to have been careful not to antagonize Mary Tudor. Opposing Wyatt's rebellion against the Queen,[8] he was zealous in hunting down Protestant heretics. For instance, in 1554, he tried John Bland, vicar of Adisham, and imprisoned him at Maidstone; Bland was later burned at Canterbury.

Sir Thomas Moyle purchased the estate of Eastwell from the three daughters and co-heiresses of Sir Christopher Hales, Henry VIII's Attorney-General, and rebuilt the house. At his death in 1560, he likewise left no sons, but only two daughters, Katherine and Amy (or Anne).[9] Katherine married Sir Thomas Finch, who died at the beginning of 1564 when shipwrecked off Rye en route for France; his widow was remarried to Nicholas St. Leger. The other daughter was married to Sir Thomas Kemp, and died before her father.

Lady Finch (later Mrs. St. Leger) lived at Eastwell, and on her death in 1587, the estate was inherited by her elder son, Moyle Finch (fig. 6).[10] He obtained a licence from Queen Elizabeth in June 1589 to enclose 1,000 acres of parkland, and to embattle the house. Finch, born in 1551, was admitted to Gray's Inn in 1568, and from 1575 entered the House of Commons, as member first for Weymouth, then for Kent, and later for Winchelsea. Knighted on May 7, 1584, at Greenwich, he was also Sheriff of Kent, and was subsequently created one of the first Baronets by James I, on June 29, 1611. He married Elizabeth (fig. 8), daughter of Sir Thomas Heneage, Chancellor of the Duchy of Lancaster, and Vice-Chamberlain to the Household, a favourite of Elizabeth I's, who made him many grants of land, particularly in Essex. Heneage married as his second wife Anne, widow of the 2nd Earl of Southampton; he died in 1595 and was buried in St. Paul's Cathedral.[11]

When Sir Moyle Finch died in 1614, his widow was one of the wealthiest women in England. Just before his death it had been suggested that he was about to be created a peer,[12] and Lady Finch was doubtless dismayed that his untimely death had prevented her advancement. However, she had inherited Copped Hall[13] from her father and was in possession of an estate that was especially coveted by others, ultimately to the advantage of herself and her son Heneage.

From about 1618 it was suggested that Elizabeth Finch was using her estate in order to bargain with those who could win her a peerage.[14] An influential lady, enormously rich, but wanting more money and land, was Frances Howard, wife of the king's kinsman, the Duke of Lennox and Richmond; she was negotiating with Lady Finch in 1623, and in that year it was noted that 'the Recorder [Heneage Finch] is to be one of the sergeants and knighted, and his mother made Viscountess Maidstone, for exchanging her fair house at Copt-hall, Essex, with the Duke and Duchess of Richmond for Cobham in Kent.'[15]

Although the Finches did not receive the Cobham estate, Lady Finch was elevated to the peerage, and Heneage knighted, both paying for their honours, as can be seen from an agreement dated February 1623/24 'Whereas William Lord Gray, Baron of Warke,[16] Elizabeth, Viscountess Maydestone, and Sir Heneage Finch Kt recorder of London are become bound to me Esme, then Earle of March, now Duke of Lenox in the some of 4,000 *l.* condiconed for the payment of 2,000 *l.* on the 28th of May next ensuing the date hereof know yee that I the said Duke of Lenox do declare and promise that Sr Edward Conway his Maties Secretary shall and may receive 1,000 *l.* wch shalbe due and payable as aforesaid to his own proper use.'[17]

Lady Maidstone was once more raised in dignity five years later, by Charles I, who created her Countess of Winchilsea. Lionel, Earl of Middlesex, received a letter in which it was caustically noted that 'Your Lordship's shee neighbour must needs have a fair large house, for her ordinary one cannot contain the honour; she is now Countess of Winchelsey, and Sir John Finch drinks 5,000 *l.* by the bargain for his service to the late Parliament.'[18]

The fourth son of Sir Moyle Finch and Lady Winchilsea, Heneage Finch (fig. 14), was called to the Bar in 1606, and like many of his relatives, entered Parliament. Appointed Recorder of London in 1621, two years later he was knighted and became Sergeant-at-Law, and in 1626 he was elected Speaker of the House of Commons. His first wife was Frances, daughter of Sir Edmund Bell of Beaupré Hall at Outwell in Norfolk (another casualty of wartime neglect). She died in 1627, and in April 1629 he married Elizabeth, the wealthy widow of Alderman Richard Bennett, for whose hand Sir Edward Dering, a cousin by marriage of Heneage Finch,[19] had also been a suitor. At the beginning of 1631, Finch was appointed one of the Commissioners for the repair of St. Paul's, but he died in December of the same year. His eldest son, also named Heneage, became Lord Keeper, and was created Earl of Nottingham. He is commemorated by a magnificent four-poster monument, probably the work of William Stanton,[20] at Ravenstone in Buckinghamshire. The eldest son of the Earl of Nottingham, Daniel, succeeded his father in 1683, and his kinsman John as the 7th Earl of Win-

chilsea in 1729; the two earldoms have remained merged since then.

The last of the personages commemorated in the Eastwell monuments is Emily Georgiana (died 1848), second wife of George Finch-Hatton, 10th Earl of Winchilsea and 5th Earl of Nottingham. She was the daughter of Sir Charles Bagot, G.C.B. (the younger son of the 1st Lord Bagot), whose wife Mary was the daughter of William, 3rd Earl of Mornington. Brothers of the latter were the Marquess of Wellesley and Arthur, Duke of Wellington, who were thus great-uncles of Lady Winchilsea.

III. DESCRIPTION OF THE MONUMENTS

1. A.187–1969 (figs. 2, 3).
Monument commemorating Sir Thomas Moyle (died 1560) and his wife Katherine. Also named on the tomb-chest are Moyle's father and mother, John Moyle and his wife, a daughter of Sir Robert Darcy;

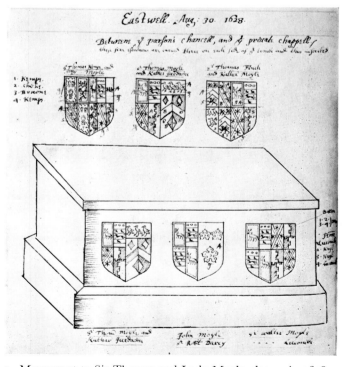

2. Monument to Sir Thomas and Lady Moyle, drawn in 1628. (Society of Antiquaries of London.)

his grandfather and grandmother, Sir Walter Moyle (died 1480) and Margaret (Luccomb) (died 1493); and his two daughters and co-heiresses and their husbands, Amy and Sir Thomas Kemp, and Katherine (died 1587) and Sir Thomas Finch (died 1564).

In its original position in Eastwell Church, the tomb-chest, of Caen-stone, stood between the chancel and the south chapel, with its eastern end against the wall. The two longer sides of the monument are each divided by four fluted pilasters into five compartments;

3. Monument of Sir Thomas and Lady Moyle, at Eastwell, July, 1965. A.187–1969. (National Monuments Record.)

at either end is a round-headed niche, between which are three round-headed panels, each with a shield of arms. These shields are carved, and the colours are not painted (as was common), but consist of small pieces of inlaid composition, the natural stone being left to represent silver. In some cases, neither the charges, nor the colours, are indicated correctly.[21] The stone of which the monument is constructed must have been formerly used in a building, as inside the tomb-chest there are some quatrefoil decoration, arch-mouldings and part of a window-transom.

4. Detail of a coat of arms on the Moyle monument. A.187–1969.

Reading round the monument from the former north-east shield, the heraldry is:

1. *Lettered* SYR THOMAS KEMP   AMYE MOYLE
Kemp. Quarterly 1 and 4: *Gules, three garbs or, within a border engrailed of the last* (for Kemp); 2. *Azure, three lions rampant argent, within a border of the last* (for Chiche); 3. *Sable, in bend between two cotises, three lions passant argent, in sinister chief an eagle's (?) head*[22] *of the last* (for Browne). Impaling Moyle: Quarterly, 1. *Gules, a mule passant within a border argent, a mullet for difference of the last* (for Moyle); 2. *Gules, a greyhound courant or between two bars argent, charged with three martlets sable, in chief as many plates* (for Mooles); 3. *Gules, three martlets argent in fess* (false coat of arms); 4. *Per pale or and azure, a chevron between three lozenges, all counterchanged* (and omitted from this particular shield *on a chief gules as many martlets argent*) (for Jourdain); 5. *Argent, a saltire sable between four estoiles gules* (for Luccomb); 6. *Quarterly embattled argent and sable* (for Keyle).

The heraldry is not entirely that emblazoned in the Visitation of Kent by Robert Cooke in 1574 for either the Kemp or the Moyle families. In the quarterings of the Moyle shields on the tomb, the three martlets have feet, and look rather like crows. In the third quartering of the sinister shield, what is given as a separate coat of arms, should really be the chief which is missing from the fourth quartering; this is rectified on the other shields on the tomb in which the quartering appears. There is also uncertainty about the Christian name of Sir Thomas Moyle's daughter, who married Sir Thomas Kemp. She appears as Anne in the pedigree

5. Monument to Frances, Lady Finch (died 1627), 1951.
A.185–1969. (National Monuments Record.)

of Moyle[23] in the 1574 Visitation, but in that for
Kemp she is given as Amye[24], and this pedigree is
countersigned by her husband. She also appears as
'Amye' or 'Amie' on two monuments[25], and in his
will[26] her father refers to 'Amye my other daughter
deceased'. However, in the transcription of the Eastwell
parish registers she is referred to as 'Anne'[27].

2. *Lettered*   SYR THOMAS MOYLE   KATIERYN IVRDAYN
Quarterly, 1. Moyle, 2. Mooles, 3. Luccomb, 4. Keyle. Impaling
Jourdain, *a mullet for difference.*

3. *Lettered*   SYR THOMAS FFYNCHE   KATHERYN MOYLE
Quarterly 1 and 4, *Argent, a chevron between three griffins passant sable*
(for Finch); 2. *Azure, three eaglets displayed in bend between two
cotises argent* (for Belknap); 3. *Sable, three shovellers[28] argent* (for
Peplesham). Impaling Moyle (Quarterly, 1. Moyle, 2. Mooles,
3. Luccomb, 4. Keyle), *a mullet or for difference.*

4. *Lettered*   SYR THOMAS MOYLE   KATHERYN IVRDAYN
The same shield as No. 2.

5. *Lettered*   SYR THOMAS MOYLE   (fig. 4)
Quarterly, 1. Moyle, 2. Mooles, 3. Luccomb, 4. Keyle, *a mullet
or for difference.*

6. *Lettered*   SYR THOMAS MOYLE   KATHERYN IVRDAYN
The same shield as No. 2.

7. *Lettered*   IOHN MOYLE   SYR ROBERT DARCY[29]
Moyle (Quarterly, 1. Moyle, 2. Mooles, 3. Luccomb, 4. Keyle),
impaling *Argent, three cinquefoils gules* (for Darcy).

8. *Lettered*   SYR WALTER MOYLE   LVCOMBE[30]
Quarterly, 1 and 4 Moyle, 2 and 3 Mooles; impaling Quarterly,
1 and 4 Luccomb, 2 and 3 Keyle.

2. A.185–1969 (fig. 5).

Mural monument in white Carrara marble to Frances,
Lady Finch (died 1627), and her husband Sir Heneage
Finch, consisting of a tablet flanked by Ionic columns
supporting an entablature and a broken pediment
enclosing an armorial cartouche. The capitals are
decorated with swags (one missing on the left) and
two swags with ribbons are attached to the bottom of
the tablet.

Lettered (*in capitals*):[31]

CONJUGI SUAE
PLUSQUAM DESIDERATISSIMAE
FRANCISCAE
EDMUNDI BELL DE BEUPREEHALL EQUITIS AURATI FILIAE,
CONJUGUM, MATRUM, FAEMINARUM OPTIMARUM, OPTIMAE,
SECULO HUIC NON INEPTAE, CUJUS MORES TOLERAVIT,
VITA VERO RETULIT ANTIQUI, POSTERISQUE RELIQUIT
SINGULARIS EXEMPLI SUI FRUCTUM, DOLOREM BREVIS,
HENEAGIUS FINCH
EQUES AURATUS, SERVIENS AD LEGEM AC RECORDATOR
CIV. LOND. POST UNDECIM LIBEROS, vii SCILICET FILIOS ET
iv FILIAS PLACIDISSIMO QUATUORDECIM PLUS ANNORUM
CONJUGIO SUSCEPTOS, E QUIBUS FILIJ iii AC FILIA i
QUIBUS ADSIS O DEUS
SUPERSUNT
HIC AD PARENTUM HUJUS SEPULCHRUM
POSUIT
SIBIQUE, QUOD ET IPSA DESIDERAVIT DESTINAT
OBIJT ILLA. xi DIE APRIL.
MDCXXVII
ILLE

Heraldry. The cartouche in the pediment has the arms
of Finch:

Quarterly; 1 and 4, *Argent, a chevron between three griffins passant
sable.* 2 and 3, *Gules, three lions rampant or* (for Herbert), *a mullet
sable for difference*[32] impaling Bell (*sable, a fess ermine between three
bells argent.*

Lady Finch was the daughter of Sir Edmund Bell
and the grand-daughter of Sir Robert Bell, who was
elected Speaker of the House of Commons on May 10,
1572.

That this monument was erected by her widowed
husband, Sir Heneage, both for her and for himself, is
confirmed by two facts. One is that the epitaph ends
abruptly at the word 'Ille' and was obviously meant
eventually to record Sir Heneage's death; and the
other is to be found in his will, dated April 16, 1631,
in which he said, 'I earnestly desire to be buried in
Eastwell church in the vault where my most noble
father and my dearly beloved wife together with the

first pledge of our love our first sonne lye all interred and where a poore monument in remembrance of my wife and myself is already erected.'[33]

Beneath the inscription is a socket into which a decorative feature was once fixed. It may have been a cartouche of arms, but it seems more likely to have been a winged cherub-head.

3. A.186–1969 (figs. 7, 9, 10, 11, 12).

Monument to Sir Moyle Finch (died 1614) and his wife Elizabeth, Countess of Winchilsea (died 1634).[34]

The memorial consists of an alabaster tomb-chest standing on a wide pavement of touch and white marble (with two semi-circular lobes on the longer sides), in which can be seen the sockets for a wooden railing which once surrounded the tomb. On top is a bier supporting two recumbent effigies in white Carrara marble. The male effigy is in armour, with a sword (part missing) at his left. He has a square-cut beard, his eyes are closed, and his hands rest on his stomach. The female effigy, with open eyes, wears a coif, with a veil, a falling ruff, and a gown over a simple dress. The bodice has a row of buttons and tabs at the waist. The head of each effigy rests on a cushion. The tomb-chest is decorated with panels of serpentine which have badly deteriorated (not due to exposure after the collapse of the church roof), and on its top, surrounding the effigies, are the bases of eight columns, which formerly supported a canopy.

The monument is now only a fragment of what it once was. The canopy with the eight marble columns was taken down in 1756, as it was thought to be unsafe and that the effigies, among the most outstanding in Kent, might be damaged if it collapsed. As Hasted noted[35], fragments of the canopy and columns still littered the chancel of Eastwell at the end of the 18th century, but they were probably discarded when the church was restored in the mid-19th century. Fortunately, we know, to some extent, the original

6. (*left*) Sir Moyle Finch (died 1614). (Private collection.)
7. (*below*) Effigy of Sir Moyle Finch, after the fall of the nave roof, 1951. A.186–1969. (National Monuments Record.)

8. (*left*) Elizabeth, Lady Finch, afterwards Countess of Winchilsea (died 1634). (Private collection.)

9. (*above*) Effigy of Elizabeth, Countess of Winchilsea, after the fall of the nave roof, 1951. A.186–1969. (National Monuments Record.)

appearance of the monument, from a drawing of about 1628 which belonged to an ancestor of the writer, Sir Edward Dering. The drawing (fig. 10) which has been attributed to John Philipot the herald, is contained in a volume devoted to Kentish monuments and stained glass compiled between 1628 and 1634, now in the Library of the Society of Antiquaries.[36]

The sketch shows the north side of the monument, and it permits us to see the now destroyed canopy, on top of which is a strange and unusual construction. In a lunette at the centre of the side is the heraldic achievement of Lady Winchilsea, beneath an inscription tablet, and on either side is a pilaster. At the visible end (the east) is a curious curved tablet with lettering and a shell top – presumably the west end was similar. In front of these alcoves are seated a putto holding an inverted torch, and a putto with a spade. On the summit is an enormous griffin (one of the supporters of the Finch arms) holding a lozenge on which are the arms of Heneage (*Or, a greyhound courant sable, between three leopards faces azure, all within a border engrailed gules*). As this, like the other achievement shown in the drawing, makes no heraldic allusion to Sir Moyle Finch, one must suppose that he was similarly commemorated on the south side of the monument, which is not shown. Under the canopy, over the effigies, is strapwork decoration, and in the centre is suspended a flying putto.

This drawing, although it allows us to appreciate that the monument was indeed splendid, poses a number of questions. Was it drawn very hurriedly in the church, or later from notes? Was it copied from a design? Was the monument complete at the time? Comparison with the monument shows many differences. The proportions in the drawing are not accurate; the columns are rectangular; the effigies are not raised on the low bier above the tomb-chest; Sir Moyle Finch is not wearing his very conspicuous padded breeches; neither effigy has its head on a cushion. Lady Winchilsea is depicted wearing a countess's coronet; and here the drawing points out a feature not previously observed, as the effigy's head has holes and indentations in which the coronet, presumably of metal, was once placed.

There can, however, be no doubt that the Dering drawing represents the Eastwell monument, for it is captioned 'In ye private chapell this monument for Sr Moyle Finch Knt and Baronett and his Lady Elizabeth Countess of Winchelsey', and on the previous page is the date 'Aug: 30. 1628'. Although the construction on top of the canopy may be somewhat out of scale in the drawing, it is not surprising that there were soon doubts as to its stability; the general appearance is clumsy and the effigies look like the work of a conventional carver rather than the very distinguished sculptures that they are.

The Dering drawing records inscriptions which were on the canopy as follows:

'These are ye two severall inscriptions upon ye two severall sides of the last monument.

Moilo Finch equitis aurati et Baronetto, filio Thome Finch equitis aurati ex Catharina filia et cohaerede Thome Moyle paru dignitate, viro animi corporis et fortunae totibus ornatissimo marito charissimo et desideratissimo Amantissima coniux quacu numerosa prole ex ea ortus coniunctissime vixit Elizabetha Thome Heneage equestri dignitate viri et Elizabethe Regine à sacris consilijs et procamerarij filia et haeres stircomnum vidua in honorem vicecometissa de Maydeston sibi et haeredib. masculis de corpore suo euecta, in coniugalis fidei et amoris testimonū hoc monumentū qd sibi destinavit gemens posuit.'

And:

'Illustri prognatus stirpe ipse illustrior, magnanimj veritatis amantissimus, Justitae cultor, pacti servantissimus. In magnis opibus mundi spretor maximus virtutis arma non voluptatis ratus. moribus incorruptis, vitae integerrimus. qd dictaret Ratio et mens recti conscia sequi paratus: Impterritus minis, Pius et egenis ferre opem promptissimus. Assertor verae fidei constantissimus. In Sacrosanctis scriptis versatissimus, cuius Cor peritus Christi amor possederat. Terrae huic cadaver diuidens animan polo, ad Christum migravit 18. decembr. Anno. 1614.'[37]

10. Monument to Sir Moyle Finch, and his wife Elizabeth, Countess of Winchilsea, drawn *c.*1628. (Society of Antiquaries of London.)

11. Monument to Sir Moyle Finch and the Countess of Winchilsea, in the south chapel of Eastwell Church, after the collapse of the nave roof in 1951. A.186–1969. (National Monuments Record.)

12. In the protective brick building, 1965.

Lettered in capitals around the bier on panels of touch are the names of twelve children:

Theophilvs Finch [(1573–*c.*1619), second Baronet, estranged from his mother, and married to Agnes, daughter of Sir Christopher Heydon].

Heneage Finch [born 1576, died young].

Thomas Finch [(1578–1639), knight, 3rd Baronet, 2nd Earl of Winchilsea, married to Cecilie, daughter of John Wentworth].

John Finch [born 1579, married to Anne, daughter of Thomas Walker, of Westminster].

Heneage Finch [(1580–1631), see Monument 4].

Frauncis Finch [(born 1587), married to Anne, the only daughter of Michael Barker, of Bilston, Suffolk].

William Finch [born 1591].

Robert Finch [?].

Elizabeth Finch [born 1583, died young].

Elizabeth Finch [born 1589].

Katherine Finch [born 1583, wife of Sir John Wentworth].

Ann Finch [born 1575, wife of Sir William Twisden, Bart.].

The list of these names given on the Dering drawing

13. Head of the effigy of Lady Carey, Stowe-Nine-Churches, Northamptonshire, by Nicholas Stone. (Mr. Bruce Bailey.)

14. (*below*) Sir Heneage Finch (died 1631) (formerly in the collection of the Kent Archaeological Society; photograph, National Portrait Gallery).

15. Monument by Nicholas Stone to Sir Heneage Finch (died 1631), 1951. A.184–1969. (National Monuments Record.)

differs inasmuch as it gives the name of the second son as 'Henry'.

4. A.184–1969 (fig. 15)[38].

Monument to Sir Heneage Finch (1589–1631), Recorder of London, Serjeant-at-Arms, and Speaker of the House of Commons between 1626 and 1628. By Nicholas Stone. The mural monument of touch and white Carrara marble, consists of a high base containing the inscription tablet flanked by plain pilasters. Above this is the half-length effigy of Finch in legal dress, with his hands folded. Higher up, on the wall, are two cartouches, with traces of gilding on the frames; these bear the arms of Sir Heneage impaling those of his two wives.

Lettered:[39]

HENEAGIO FINCH
Equiti aurato, Servienti ad Legem Recordatori
per decennium Londinensi:
Ac Parlamentario, in secundis Sereniss: Caroli Regis
Ordinum Comitijs Proloquutori:

MOILI FINCH ET ELIZABETHAE

(quae viro superstes vicecometissae Maidston et
Comitissae de Winchilsey dignitatibus aucta)

FILIO,
OPTIMO, PATRONO, MARITO, AMICO VIRO

Ex Elizabetha coniuge secunda,
Antiquo Cradocorum genere orta, binis susceptis filiabus;
ac peracto iusti coniugij biennio   M.VII.D.XX.
Spiritum in manus Salvatoris sui, cui constrantissime in=
servivit. placidissime (dum hydrope corripitur) resolvit
V Die Dec. Ao. CHRISTI M.D.C.XXXI.
Vixit Annos L   Men: XI   Di: V.
Franciscus frater natu non affect minimus (una cum Tho:
Twisden consobrino) ex testamenta haeres modicum hoc
ingentis Desiderij et Doloris
Monumentum P.

Habes (ô nunquam moriture) heu cito nimium
Quem ipse in vivis dictitasti tumulum:
Mori nempe negavit
Virtus inclyta, intemerata fides,
Assiduitas invicta, alma Iustitia.
Inter Primos qui pie Literatus,
Nulli Bonitate Secundus extitisti.
Abrepto in coelis A Dno quid invidemus
Cui parem in terris posteri vix videbunt.

Heraldry:

The lower cartouche contains the arms of Finch quarterly with Herbert, impaling Bell, for his first wife, Frances; above is a smaller cartouche with Finch impaling Cradock, *Argent, on a chevron azure, three garbs or*, for his widow.

The monument is referred to by Nicholas Stone in his account-book:

'October 1632   Agreed with Mr Frances (*sic*) Finch Esquyer for 50£ agreed for the tombe of Ser Hanegs Finch Mr Recorder of London and received 10£ in pres Rest due to me the tombe bing sett up and finished.'[40]

5. A.188–1969 (fig. 16).

Monument to Emily Georgiana, Countess of Winchilsea and Nottingham (died 1848). By Lawrence Macdonald.

The effigy, in white Carrara marble, is reclining on a classical day-bed. She is wearing a loose robe, and

16. Monument to Emily, Countess of Winchilsea and Nottingham by Lawrence Macdonald, 1850. A.188–1969.

holds a scroll of paper. The bed is raised upon a high marble base.

Lettered (in capitals) on the plinth:

SACRED

TO THE MEMORY

OF

EMILY GEORGIANA

THE BELOVED WIFE

OF

GEORGE WILLIAM

EARL OF WINCHILSEA AND NOTTINGHAM

WHO

DIED JULY THE 10TH 1848

AGED 39 AND WAS

BURIED IN THE CHANCEL OF EWERBY CHURCH

LINCOLNSHIRE

I

When the knell rung for the dying
Soundeth for me
And my corse coldly is lying
Neath the green tree

II

When the turf strangers are heaping
Covers my brest
Come not to gaze on me weeping
I am at rest

III

All my life coldly and sadly
The days have gone by
I who dreamed wildly and madly
Am happy to die

IV

Long since my heart has been breaking
Its pain is past
A time has been set to its aching
Peace comes at last

E.G.   W. & N.

Signed in capitals on the couch:
L. MACDONALD. FECIT. ROMAE. 1850.

Inscribed in capitals on the scroll:
I AM HAPPY INDEED HAPPY IN THE WORD
GOD IS WAITING FOR ME.

Lawrence MacDonald (1799–1878), born in Perthshire, worked from 1832 in Rome, and enjoyed a reputation for portrait sculpture. Rupert Gunnis, in his *Dictionary*, considers this elegant and graceful figure of the Countess of Winchilsea to be Macdonald's most successful statue.

At Eastwell the statue was placed in the south porch, which was then converted into a chapel. It was not damaged by the fall of the nave roof in 1951, but was exposed to the weather on its north side (front) until 1968.

IV. AUTHORSHIP OF THE MONUMENTS TO FRANCES, LADY FINCH, AND TO SIR MOYLE FINCH.

Of the three early 17th century monuments at Eastwell, that to Sir Heneage Finch is a certain work of Nicholas Stone. Is it possible to name a sculptor for the other two?

(a) *Frances, Lady Finch, A.185–1969.*

There is no documentary evidence that the memorial to Sir Heneage's wife is by Stone, but it may safely be attributed to him on stylistic grounds. The cartouche of arms (surely not meant to rest upon the pediment, but to be above it) is typical of his work, and the unusual garlanded capitals are to be found also on a monument by Stone to Sir Charles Morrison at Watford, which is of about the same date. In the agreement of March 3, 1628, between Stone and Lady Morrison, the garlanded capitals are mentioned.[41] The sculptor undertook to 'rayse and place fower pillers of touchstone, or black marble, to containe in height, with their bases and capitals, six foote and a halfe; the bases of the same pillars to be of white marble, and the same to be fairly wrought, polished and glazed, and their capitalls to be fairly carved in a composative manner, with festoons of leaves and flowers . . . "[42] The garlands on the Lady Finch monument are also closely similar to those beneath one of the Heneage Finch cartouches.

(b) *Sir Moyle Finch and his wife*

The first thing to establish is the date of the monument. Sir Moyle died in 1614, his wife early in 1634. On the monument Finch is depicted with closed eyes, whilst those of the Countess are open. It is, therefore, reasonable to suppose that her effigy was carved during her lifetime.

It will be noted that the Dering drawing shows Lady Winchilsea wearing a countess's coronet (presumably of metal) and that the same insignia surmounts the carved heraldic achievement on the canopy. As

Elizabeth Finch was created Countess of Winchilsea on July 12, 1628, we might presume that the monument was constructed between mid-1628 and the beginning of 1634. However, the drawing is on the page following that on which is a sketch of the tomb of Sir Thomas Moyle, dated August 30, 1628, and the inscriptions recorded, on the canopy, refer only to Viscountess Maidstone. This implies that at least the structure had been completed by August 1628, but it is hardly likely that Lady Winchilsea would have ordered, and a carver and metal-worker produced, new coronets in the space of six weeks. A possible explanation of this discrepancy is that the artist drew

18. Monument to Bishop Montague by William Cure II, Bath Abbey. (National Monuments Record.)

coronets of a countess, rather than a viscountess, to conform to the new peerage, about which he would naturally have been informed.

At least two sculptors have been suggested as the author of this monument. Nicholas Stone, and William Cure II.[43] The attribution to the latter was based on similarity to Southwark work, particularly in the strapwork decoration and the putti[44] on the now destroyed canopy, illustrated in the Dering drawing.

However, although Cure succeeded his father Cornelius as Master-Mason to the Crown in 1605, only four monuments so far are definitely known to be connected with him; he died in 1632, and was succeeded as Master-Mason by Nicholas Stone. The first monument is that to Mary, Queen of Scots, in Westminster Abbey (fig. 17), on which he worked jointly with his father; secondly, that to Sir Roger Aston, at Cranford, Middlesex[45]; thirdly to Bishop Montague in Bath Abbey (fig. 18), for which both Cure and Nicholas Johnson jointly signed the contract in November, 1618,[46] and lastly, to the second Earl of Bedford, erected in 1619 at Chenies, Buckinghamshire. In none of these are the effigies so fine as the two now in the Museum, which are obviously portraits.

As far as is known, Cure did not attempt portraiture in monuments, not even for that of Mary, Queen of Scots. The contract for Bishop Montague's monument stipulates no more than 'one similitude or figure representing the said Ld Bishop of Winchester in his robes as late prelate of the Garter well laid in oyle

17. Monument to Mary, Queen of Scots, by Cornelius and William Cure II, Westminster Abbey. Plate to Dart's *Westmonasterium*.

colours' and when agreeing to carve the monument to Sir Roger Aston, his wives and their daughters, Cure mentioned only the 'seven pictures to be kneeling upon the same'.

The Finch effigies bear no relationship to the style of carving by the Johnsons, Cure or even Evesham during the early 17th century; they are altogether much more distinguished. An inspection of the marble effigies of this period in Westminster Abbey demonstrates that none approaches them in quality. Naturally, then, one is bound to return to Nicholas Stone as the possible sculptor. There is a distinct similarity between the figure of Lady Winchilsea and that of Stone's Lady Carey (c.1617) at Stowe-Nine-Churches, Northamptonshire (fig. 13), which, too, must be a portrait.

Can it be proved that any monument by Nicholas Stone contains portraiture? The answer is yes. That to Sir Heneage Finch is certainly one example; the half-length figure must be based on a painting.

It must be admitted, however, that in the contract for the Morrison tomb at Watford, Stone makes no clear mention of a definite portrait for any of the effigies:

'. . . one faire ledger or table, of touchstone or black marble, alsoe of seven foote and three ynches in length, and two foote in breadth, to be raised yt in height six inches above the other table, to the end that it may give a better prospect or viewe of the statue of the said Sir Charles Morrison, which is to be placed thereon: which said statue, or picture, is to be royally and artificially carved, polished, glazed, and made of good and pure white marble, in compleat armour, with sword and spurs, according to the life, to consist of six foote in length of one entire piece of stone: and shall make a statue, or picture, for and of the same worthy lady [Lady Morrison], to be laid upon the table, or ledger-stone . . . And, at the West end of the same monument, shall raise a kind of basement of allablaster . . . on which is to be placed the statue or portraighture of Mrs. Elizabeth Capell, daughter of the said Sir Charles Morrison . . . and at the East end . . . the statue, or picture, of the two Sonns deceased.'[47]

The carving of the Finch effigies is by a first-rate artist. The hands are superbly executed,[48] the faces are realistic and full of character, and especially noteworthy is the sculpting around the eyes. The cushions are loosely filled and consequently depressed by the heads resting upon them. This feature occurs elsewhere in Stone's earlier work, as on, for instance, Lady Carey's monument; eventually the cushions become harder and rigid, and perhaps are the work of his assistants, as at Great Brington, Northamptonshire. It is, therefore, highly likely that the Eastwell effigies are both from Stone's own hand.

Is there any evidence to show that Lady Winchilsea would have known of Nicholas Stone's monumental sculpture during the 1620s? The Finches maintained a close relationship between branches, so we must examine the memorials to members of that family, and also to the Moyles and their relatives.

Not far from Eastwell, Stone erected the monument at Mersham to Bridget, Lady Knatchbull, who died in 1625, and was connected by marriage to the Finch family.[49] It may be thought, as the connection was through her husband's grandmother, who had married a Finch as a second husband, that it was not a very close one. But a reading of Finch wills reveals that the two families kept in touch for at least two generations,[50] as well as the fact that Sir Norton Knatchbull's sister, Mary, also married a Thomas Finch. Stone worked also, c.1631, on the monument to Mary (Kemp), Lady Digges at Chilham, only about five miles from Eastwell. Not only was Lady Digges, the grand-daughter of Amy Moyle,[51] Lady Winchilsea's aunt, but when Sir Dudley Digges was sent, in 1618, to Russia by James I to negotiate a loan to the Emperor, he took a secretary named Finch with him.[52]

At the beginning of the 18th century John Le Neve published several volumes of monumental inscriptions under the title of *Monumenta Anglicana*. In the volume dealing with the memorials of the first half of the 17th century, many of the entries were compiled from the records of Peter Le Neve, Norroy King of Arms, and it is worth noting that several of these are by Nicholas Stone; among them are the monuments to Sir Heneage Finch; Sir Robert Drury (Hawstead, Suffolk); Sir Charles Morrison; Martha Palmer (Enfield, Middlesex); Arthur Coke (Bramfield, Suffolk); Edward Coke (Tittleshall, Norfolk), and others.

These are noted in either Stone's Note-book or Account-Book. The opinion has been expressed that it would have been 'inconceivable'[53] that Stone could have forgotten to mention the Eastwell effigies in either of them. Of the surviving books, the Account-Book does not begin until 1631, and the Note-Book was compiled

late in life, apparently from memory.[54] There is no reference to the sculptor's part in the tomb of Sir Thomas Lucy (died 1640) at Charlecote, Warwickshire,[55] the monument in Portsmouth Cathedral to the Duke of Buckingham (died 1628), nor to two monuments at Riddlesworth, Norfolk, to Sir Dru Drury (died 1617) and his son Dru (died 1632).[56]
The mural monument to the elder Sir Dru consists of a tented canopy, under which kneels a man in

19. Monument to Lord Spencer by Nicholas Stone, Great Brington, Northamptonshire. (Author.)

armour, the curtains being held back by two angels.[57] This monument is virtually identical with that to Lady Knatchbull at Mersham, and must be by Stone. Moreover, Drury had married Catherine Finch, of Lynsted[58] (where she is buried), only a few miles to the north of Eastwell. This does not prove that Lady Winchilsea knew Drury, but she did, and well enough for him to be godfather to her son Francis (born 1586), while a neighbour of his, Lady Sondes, daughter of George Finch, of Norton,[59] was godmother to William (born 1591).[60]
Surely it would have been found as natural in the 17th century as today, for recommendations to pass between members of a family. As far as monuments are concerned we know that Gerard and Nicholas Johnson made three for the Earls of Rutland at Bottesford; Nicholas Stone carved two for the Morrisons at Watford; and later, the Ishams of Lamport, the Brownlows of Belton, and the Bagots of Blithfield, used William and Edward Stanton on more than one occasion. As Penelope (Wriothesley), wife of Lord Spencer, was the stepniece of Lady Winchilsea, might not the Eastwell monument have inspired her to ask Stone to execute her husband's monument at Great Brington in Northamptonshire, when he died in 1636?[61] Another monument there is by Stone's son John.
In view of the several monuments by Nicholas Stone for members of the Finch family and their close relatives it is, therefore, extremely probably that the Winchilsea monument is also by him, though in collaboration with another craftsman, probably from the Johnson workshop, as it has been noted that the canopy, with its putti, is much more characteristic of the Southwark school. Much research still remains to be done on sculptors of the 17th century; from our knowledge at present it seems that of them only Stone could be capable of producing such superb effigies. Recorded works by Stone, which were executed in association with other sculptors, are the monuments to the Earl of Northampton, c.1616, formerly at Dover Castle, and now in the Trinity Hospital at Greenwich (with Isaac James); to Sir Nicholas Bacon and his wife, c.1616, with not dissimilar effigies (with Bernard Johnson) at Redgrave in Suffolk, and that to Thomas Sutton (1616) in the Charterhouse, London[62] (with Nicholas Johnson and Thomas Kinsman). The last has a large superstructure above the canopy, and another example with this feature, with which Stone

beneath the hollowed-out bases of the flanking pillars –
a curious and original feature. Perhaps this monument
may also be connected with Nicholas Stone (fig. 21).[63]
The Eastwell monuments have now become part of
the national collection of English sculpture and the
effigies of Sir Moyle Finch and the Countess of
Winchilsea, which are among the finest English
carvings of their date, look entirely appropriate in
front of the great Rood Screen from 's Hertogenbosch
(fig. 22). It will be remembered that an important
part in the execution of the Rood Screen was played
by Hendrik de Keyser, former master and father-in-law
of Nicholas Stone.[64]

20. Monument to Henry, Lord Norris, attributed to Isaac
James, Westminster Abbey. Plate to Dart's *Westmonasterium*.

21. Monument to Amy (Moyle) (died 1631), wife of Josias Clarke,
Boughton Aluph Church, Kent. (National Monuments Record.)

would have been familiar, is the monument to Lord
Norris (fig. 20), in Westminster Abbey, which has
been attributed to Isaac James, Stone's one-time
master.

As a postscript, it is worth recording that in Boughton
Aluph Church is the monument to Amy Moyle, wife
of Josias Clarke, and daughter of Robert Moyle of
Buckwell. She died in 1631 at the age of 31, and her
effigy has very much the same feeling as that displayed
by the Winchilsea figure. A sheet is thrown over her
body, and falls naturally about her, and the head is
inclined to the right. There are two putti huddled

Notes

1. *The History of Kent*, 1719 (printed and sold by D. Midwinter, at the Rose and Crown, St. Paul's Church-yard), p. 111.

2. *The History and Topographical Survey of the County of Kent*, III, 1790, p. 202.

3. C. R. Councer, F.S.A. 'The Medieval and Renaissance painted glass of Eastwell.' *Archaeologia Cantiana*, LIX, 1946, pp. 109–113.

4. As Challock Church, like Eastwell, is also inside the Park, it too suffered from wartime neglect.

5. The lettering is 'On this site lay the effigies of Moyle Finch Baron Fordwich and his wife Elizabeth Countess of Winchilsea. Removed to the Victoria and Albert Museum London for preservation 1968.' Sir Moyle Finch was not Baron Fordwich. His brother was Sir Henry Finch (died 1625), Sergeant-at-Law, whose son Sir John Finch (1584–1660), Speaker of the House of Commons, and Lord Keeper, was created Baron Finch (of Fordwich) in 1640. The title became extinct on his death.

6. Philip Parsons. *The Monuments and Painted Glass of upwards of one hundred churches, chiefly in the eastern part of Kent*, Canterbury, 1794, pp. 20–24; the well is still marked on Ordnance Survey maps.

7. R. H. D'Elboux. 'Some Kentish Indents.' *Archaeologia Cantiana*, LIX, 1946, p. 99.

8. W. A. Scott Robertson. 'Coulyng Castle.' *Archaeologia Cantiana*, XI, 1877, p. 143.

22. General view of the Eastwell monuments in Gallery 50 (West) of the Victoria and Albert Museum.

9. See under Monument 1.

10. About 1580 Sir Thomas Heneage was keeping a watchful eye on his son-in-law's inheritance. 'Note that Sir Thomas Heneage demands the manors of Beameston and Shottenden, parcel of the inheritance of Lady Finch, to be assured in reversion to Moyle Finch and his heirs. Nicholas Sentleger, from love to Sir Thomas Heneage, and good will to Moyle Finch, has persuaded Lady Finch to yield to such an assurance and promises to win his wife to pass it. Nicholas Sentleger will give bond that neither he nor his will take any benefit of the said manors after the decease of his wife, but leave them to the children of Sir Thomas Finch and his lady.
'If Sir Thomas Heneage will consent to refer the hearing of the matter to Sir Thomas Walsingham, Sentleger promises to agree to any reasonable order that Sir Francis shall make.' *Calendar of State Papers (Domestic) 1580–1625*, 1872, p. 31 (no. 77).

11. An illustration of Heneage's monument is on p. 110 of *The History of St. Paul's Cathedral in London* by Sir William Dugdale, 1761. Damaged effigies, salvaged after the Great Fire, are now in the cathedral crypt.

12. 'Of creations there is now spoken of but one and that at the Count Palatine's suit, to benefit some of his for a gratuity. I think that it will be Sir M. Finche.' Letter from John Thorys to William Trumbull, 1613. *Historical Manuscripts Commission, Downshire MSS.*, IV, p. 68.

13. There is an engraved view of Copped Hall by J. Mynde in *The History of the ancient Town and once famous Abbey of Waltham*, by J. Farmer, 1735.

14. *The Complete Peerage*, XIII, p. 755, quotes a letter from John Chamberlain to Sir Dudley Carleton (November 7, 1618) in which the former expressed the opinion that James I's creation of the Countess of Buckingham 'hath drawne on the Lady Finche to become a countess, yf the bargain go betwixt her and the Lord of Doncaster for Copt-hall, and all the land about yt in Essex.'

15. 'Six wills relating to Cobham Hall', *Archaeologia Cantiana*, XI, 1877, p. 228.

16. William, Baron Grey of Warke was the husband of Lady Finch's grand-daughter, and later, his grandmother's executor. In her will she refers to him as her 'noble sonne', and a year after her death he purchased the manor of Epping from his uncle, the 2nd Earl of Winchilsea.

17. Domestic State Papers, James I, vol. clx, no. 4.

18. Nicholas Herman to the Earl of Middlesex, July 18, 1628, *Historical Manuscripts Commission*, 4th Report, 1874, p. 288. Sir John Finch was Member of Parliament for Winchelsea, and later for Kent. Knighted in 1609, he succeeded his elder brother Sir Theophilus Finch, c.1619, as the second Baronet, and his mother as the 2nd Earl of Winchilsea. He died in 1639.

19. Frances Bell, daughter of Sir Robert Bell, sister of Sir Edmund Bell, and consequently aunt of Lady Finch, was the second wife of Sir Anthony Dering, and mother of Sir Edward.

20. 'Tracing the work of William Stanton.' John Physick, *Country Life Annual*, 1968, pp. 90, 91.

21. The blues are in one or two instances, rendered as green. This seems to be due, as it is more apparent on the former south side of the monument, to the action of sunlight.

22. In *The Visitation of Kent* by Robert Cooke, Clarenceux, Harleian Society, LXXV, 1924, p. 3, this is given as a mullet.

23. *Op. cit.*, pp. 12, 13.

24. *Op. cit.*, pp. 3, 62, 63.

25. 'Amye' on the monument now in the Museum. On another, formerly in Wye Church, but destroyed by the fall of the tower in the late 17th century, was: 'Sir Tho. Kempe of Olantigh Knt Heir Male of the Kempes of Olantigh by dame Evelyn Daur and Coheyr of Sr Valentine Chich by the Heir of Sr Robt Chicheley, left his Heyre Sr Wm Kempe that by dame Eleanor Widdow of Sr Thos Fogge being ye Heir of Browne by an Heir of Sr Thos Arundel left his Heyr Sr Thomas Kempe Knt that by Dame Amie Daur and coheyr of Sr Thos Moyle left his Heyr this last Sr Thos Kempe,' in 'Family Chronicle of Richard Fogge, of Danes Court in Tilmanstone,' *Archaeologia Cantiana*, v, 1862/3, p. 117.

26. Principal Probate Registry, Somerset House (5 Rudd).

27. 'There is no Amy Moyle of Eastwell about that date but Anne Moyle married Sir Thomas Kempe of Wye on January 19, 1550,' letter from Mr. David Winters, M.B.E., of Boughton Aluph.

28. The arms of Peplesham on some 15th century glass in Nettlestead Church, Kent, were *Sable, three pelicans per pale argent*, see W. E. Ball, 'The stained glass windows of Nettlestead Church,' *Archaeologia Cantiana*, XXVIII, 1909, p. 197, and plate facing p. 179. For some reason, these pelicans are always referred to in the heraldry of the Finch family as 'shovellers'.

29. This seemingly rather ambiguous alliance is, in fact, that between John Moyle and a daughter of Sir Robert Darcy, who were Sir Thomas Moyle's parents. The fact that the lady's name was unknown, and also was not given in the 1574 Visitation, gives strength to the supposition that the monument was not erected until some years after the death of Sir Thomas Moyle in 1560, otherwise someone would have been sure to remember the lady's name.

30. Sir Walter Moyle and Margaret Lucomb, Sir Thomas Moyle's grandparents.

31. The inscription is to be found in *Monumenta Anglicana: being Inscriptions on the Monuments of Several Eminent Persons* by John Le Neve, I, 1719, p. 107, and also in Philip Parsons, *op. cit.*, p. 22, who was able only to record part as he found the lettering 'very much obliterated by the damp'.

32. The Herbert quartering seems an exceptional use, and is not given in John Philipot's genealogy in *Miscellanea Genealogica et Heraldica*, II, 1876, opposite p. 325, but in the *Visitation of Kent, 1619*, Harleian Society, XLII, p. 67, there is a note which states that a later hand tricks *Gules, three lioncels rampant or, a mullet argent for difference*, for insertion between the first and second quarterings, adding that it should be the second quartering. The genealogies of the earlier members of the family refer to them as 'Herbert alias Finch'.

33. Will (P.C.C., 132, St. John) quoted by Bryan l'Anson, *op. cit.*, p. 50.

34. In her will Lady Winchilsea makes no reference to the monument, but states 'My bodie I desire may bee buried and layd in Eastwell Church as neare as may bee to the bodie of my husband ml. ffinch with such funerall show as shall bee thought convenient by my Executors.' She asked her executors to provide black gowns for 'three score and tenne poore woemen' to follow her body from Eastwell House to the church. Principal Probate Registry, Somerset House, 23 Seager.

35. *Loc. cit.*, p. 202.

36. MS.497A, with Sir Edward Dering's bookplate, engraved with the date 1630.

37. Neither of these inscriptions remains, nor do we know what others there once were. At least one other is shown on the Dering drawing beginning 'Hic jacet . . . ', but he did not record it. The only lettering now remaining are the names of the twelve children.

38. This portrait bequeathed to the Kent Archaeological Society by Sir John Twisden, Bart. in 1929, see *Archaeologia Cantiana*, LVIII, 1945, p. 63, was sold at Sotheby's, June 7, 1967, as Lot 58.

39. This epitaph is recorded in both *Monumenta Anglicana*, I, 1719, pp. 131, 132, and in Philip Parsons, *op. cit.*, p. 23.

40. *Walpole Society*, VII, 1919, p. 88 and pl. XXXVII(b).

41. Illustrated on plates XIX, XX, *Walpole Society*, VII.

42. R. Clutterbuck. *The History and Antiquities of the County of Hertford*, I, 1815, p. 263.

43. Mrs. K. Esdaile. 'Notes on three monumental drawings from Sir Edward Dering's collections in the Library of the Society of Antiquities,' *Archaeologia Cantiana*, XLVII, 1935, pp. 230–234; 'thanks to the Dering-Philipot drawing we are able for the first time . . . to envisage the work as it was, and to assert that it has nothing to do with Nicholas Stone.'

44. Rather similar putti, though standing, are to be found on the monument to Sir George Hart (*c.*1613), attributed by Mrs. Esdaile to Nicholas Johnson, at Lullingstone, Kent, illustrated in J. G. Mann, 'English Church Monuments 1536–1625,' *Walpole Society*, XXI, 1932, pl. XXI (b).

45. *Gentleman's Magazine*, February 1800, LXX, p. 105.

46. Thomas Dingley. *History from Marble*. Facsimile for the Camden Society, 1868, p. 155.

47. R. Clutterbuck, *op. cit.*

48. A curious and unnatural aspect of the hands, which are not in the usual attitude of prayer, is the position of the fingers. A conscious effort is needed to place the two middle fingers together whilst opening out the remainder. Yet this convention is found almost invariably throughout the 17th century in the work of Gibbons, Nost and the two Stantons, and others. A monument by Nicholas Stone which has equally finely carved hands, is that to Sir Thomas and Lady Merry, Walthamstow, Essex.

49. 'In 1626 I mad a tomb for Ser Norton Katchbill's lady in Kent and sett it up at Mersomhacs for the which I had 30£.' W. L. Spiers, *Walpole Society*, VII, p. 71, pl. XXVI (c). 'This virtuous Lady named Bridget, descended from the auncient family of the Barons of Astley, was the second daughter of John Astley, Esqr., who whilst he lived was the chief gentleman of the privy chamber to Queen Elizabeth, and master

and treasurer of Her Majesty's jewels and plate. She was married to Sir Norton Knatchbull, Knt. with whom she had lived for 33 years and 3 months, she departed this life the 4th of November, 1625, in the 55th year of her age, and in the 1st yeare of the raigne of King Charles, and here lies interred, to whose memory the said Sir Norton Knatchull her husband, has caused this monument to be made.' P. Parsons. *Op. cit.*, p. 137.

50. John Finch, of Milton-next-Sittingbourne, married Alice (Fowle), widow of John Knatchbull, and Finch's will of 1549 declared 'I bequethe vnto Thomas ffynche my son part or halfendle of all such ynnestuf or householde stuf and plate remaignynge in the custodye of one Thomas ffowle of Mersham hatch which late was Alyce Snachbulles, lady wydowe of John Snachbull (and after my wife), and dyvyson thereof made betwyne the said Alyce my wyfe and Rychard Snachbull [father of Sir Norton Knatchbull], according to the last will of John Snachebull his father . . . I gyve unto Wyllyam Snachbull my beddynge and bedstedles . . . ' When his son Thomas Finch died in 1615, his will shows that the two families were still close because he mentions his 'brother Reignold Knatchbull' and his 'nephew Thomas Knatchbull'. James Greenstreet. 'Wills and other records relating to the Family of Finch,' *Archaeologia Cantiana*, XIII, 1880, pp. 329, 330.

51. Illustrated in *Walpole Society*, VII, pl. XXXVII (a), and described on p. 86. 'Mary Kempe, Lady Digges, daughter and coheir of Sir Thomas Kempe of Ollantigh, Knight, by Sir Thomas Moyle's daughter and coheir, sonne of Sir Thomas Kemp, Knight, by an heir of Browne and Arundel, son of Sir William Kemp, Knight, who by Emmeline, daughter and coheir of Sir Valentine Chich, and Philip (*sic*) daughter and heir of Sir Robert Chicely, Mayor of London and brother to Henry the Archbishop, was sonne of Sir Thomas Kemp, Knight, nephew to Thomas Kemp, Bishop of London, the nephew of John Kemp, Archbishop of York, then of Canterbury, Cardinal, Lord Chancellor, &c. lies buried together with Francis her fourth and Richard her eighth sonne.' P. Parsons. *Op. cit.*, p. 75.

52. 'About 10,000l. with the King's letter sent to Moscow by Mr. Finch, Digg's Secretary . . . Finch commanded by the Emperor to deliver up the money without further capitulation, and licensed to depart with letters to his Majesty.' Sir Dudley Digges had been sent by the King with about £20,000 which had been raised by the Muscovy and East India Companies. *Calendar of State Papers . . . East Indies, 1617–1621*, 1870, p. 448, no. 1080.

53. Mrs. Esdaile, *loc. cit.*

54. The only monuments listed by Stone for the years between 1623 and 1628 are to Lord Knyvett (Stanwell); Sir Thomas Palmer (Wingham); Sir Richard Coxe (Westminster Abbey); Sir Edward Pinchon (Writtle); Sir John Monson (South Carlton); Lady Knatchbull (Mersham); Orlando Gibbons (Canterbury Cathedral); Sir George Coppin (St. Martin-in-the-Fields); and a son of Sir Robert Naunton (? Letheringham). This is not a large output for the man who, in 1632, was eventually to succeed William Cure II as Master-Mason to the Crown.

55. According to Sir N. Pevsner and Alexandra Wedgwood in *Warwickshire*, 1966, p. 227, Stone received payment for the Lucy monument.

56. Another monument, probably a ledger-stone, which might be from the Stone workshop, is to Anne St. Leger, mother of Sir Dudley Digges, and niece of Sir Moyle Finch's stepfather, Nicholas St. Leger. No location for this is given by Le Neve, *op. cit.*, I, 1719, p. 170.

57. Sir N. Pevsner. *North-West and South Norfolk*. 'Very good tablet with kneeling knight and two splendidly Mannerist angels . . .'

58. 'Condignae Famae & memoriae sacrum Nobilis & illustris viri Drugonis Drury Militis, silij tertij Roberti Drury de *Egerly* in Comitatu *Bucks*. filij secundi Roberti Drury de *Hasted* in Comitatu *Suff*. Militum; Reginae Elizabethae a primo Regni Anno solius Silentarij; deinde Jacobo Regi nostro; & Anno 1596. Praesidis turris *Londinensis*. (Annos 99 summa cum laude & integritate complevit) Bis conjugio connexi, primo, Dnae. Eliz. Woodhouse, filiae Philippi Calthorp Militis; secundo, Dnae. Catharinae Finch filiae & heredi Gulielmi Finch de *Lynsted* in Comitatu *Cantab*. Armigeri, per secundam uxorem relictae. Drugo Drury Unicus filius ejus duxit Annam aetate primam & unam ex cohaeridibus Edvardi Walgrave de *Lawford* in Comitatu *Essex* Armigeri. Eliz. prima ejus filia nupta Venerabili Thomae Wingfield Militi de *Leveringham* in Comitatu *Suff*. Anna filia secunda Johanni Dean de *Dean Aula* in Co. *Essex* praedict. et Francisca filia tertia Roberto Butler de *Woodhall* in Com. *Hertford* Militibus. Ipse Drugo Drury Miles praeclarus, singulari pietate, integritate, virtute, & (nulli terris inferior) charitate, praecipue praecellens, apud *Riddlesworth* in Comitatu *Norff*. 29°. Aprilis 1617. mortem subijt.' J. Le Neve. *Op. cit.*, I p. 58. The other mural monument at Riddlesworth, to the younger Sir Dru Drury, is an architectural type tablet, also in the Stone style.

59. Her monument at Throwley, Kent, is illustrated in fig. 2 in *Designs for English Sculpture, 1680–1860*, H.M.S.O., 1969. Norton is the parish bordering Lynsted, to the west of Faversham.

60. From a manuscript record of Lady Winchilsea's children, among the papers of the Twisden family (Anne, daughter of Sir Moyle Finch, married Sir William Twisden, Bart.), now in the British Museum (Add. MS.34177, f. 16), and quoted by Bryan l'Anson, *op. cit.*, p. 41.

61. The contract for this monument is still in the possession of Earl Spencer, at Althorp.

62. Lady Winchilsea might also have known of this monument, as her husband in his will mentions 'my mansion house . . . situate . . . on the East side of the ground comonlie called Charterhouse church yarde . . .' The tomb, illustrated by Dr. Whinney, *Sculpture in Britain, 1530 to 1830*, pl. 18A, also has a putto with a spade and another with an inverted torch.

63. At Exton, Rutland, is the shrouded effigy of Lady Kinlosse, died 1627. This also, could well have come from Stone's workshop.

64. Charles Avery. 'The Rood-Loft from Hertogenbosch,' *Yearbook*, 1968, pp. 110–136.

English silver — new pieces and new facts

PERHAPS the rarest and most beautiful of all the pieces of English silver recently acquired by the Museum is a small Elizabethan state salt consisting of a nautilus shell (*nautilus pompilius*) mounted in silver-gilt to represent a bird (fig. 1). The practice of mounting rare and exotic shells in plate is at least as old as the 13th century in Western Europe, probably older, and continued into the 17th century. The salt was held in the silver-gilt container fitted into the shell. The upper part of the body forms a separate cover, which was removed when the salt was in use, and this explains why the lower part is designed as an elegantly conceived form in itself. The neck unscrews: its lower part forms a container, probably for

1. Salt. Nautilus, mounted in silver-gilt. Unmarked, English c.1570–80. M.13–1969.

spices, which were poured into the upper part and then scattered over the food through the beak. The base is decorated with sea-monsters and with a little frog who crouches between the bird's legs.

The bird is too stylized for precise identification, but the Natural History Museum suggest that it was probably intended for a game-cock. Bird forms were used in the design of plate at least as early as the 14th century: in 1328 the plate of Clémence de Hongrie, Queen of France, included an ewer shaped as a cock and another shaped like a grouse. Such designs continued popular throughout the Renaissance and are known to have been used for salts. A 'Sault of mother of pearle garnisshid with siluer guilt the Couer made like a Swanne of siluer guilt' is recorded in Queen Elizabeth's inventory of 1574. Another salt 'the body and couer of Agath being a Turqueycocke garnisshed with golde pearle and stone'[1] was given by Lord Keeper Bacon to Elizabeth, probably in May 1577, when the Queen visited Gorhambury. Besides our salt, the Glynne Cup of 1579–80, at present on loan to the Museum, is the only other example known to survive of the use of a bird-motif in Elizabethan plate (fig. 2). It represents a pelican in her piety: unfortunately the original body, almost certainly a shell, has been destroyed and the present body of silver-gilt is a 19th century restoration.

The salt is unmarked, but is a characteristic Elizabethan work of c.1570–80. The fashion of decorating plate with naturalistic frogs and reptiles was German in origin and was probably brought to England by one of the many foreign goldsmiths working in London. In 1584 Queen Elizabeth bought from the goldsmith Sir Richard Martin 'oone great faire standing cup guilt with a Couer the body garnisshid with sundrey vermen as Snakes Ewetes Frogges and others the said body and foote also laid with sundrey collours and couer garnisshid with sundrey men and beastes hunting with a Stagge in the top thereof'.[2] The 'vermen' were enamelled naturalistically, and the whole was German in inspiration and quite possibly in origin. In 1588 the Queen was presented with two crystal cups whose gold covers were decorated with frogs. One was 'Garnisshid with Frogges, waspes and deyses', on the other the frogs had 'Sparkes of Rubyes in their noses'.[3] In plate this use of naturalistic animal motifs is especially associated with the great goldsmiths Wenzel and Albrecht Jamnitzer of Nuremberg, who decorated pieces with motifs of 'little animals, worms,

2. The Glynne Cup. Maker's mark, a bird in a shaped shield. Silver-gilt. London hall-mark for 1579–80 (the body a 19th century restoration). Lent to the Museum by Mr. H. N. Gladstone.

weeds and snails' cast in silver from life. A comparable German piece to ours is now in the Kunsthistorisches Museum, Vienna. It dates from the third quarter of the sixteenth century, and has been attributed to Wenzel Jamnitzer's workshop. Its base – a piece of earth decorated with grass and lizards – is rigorously appropriate in its naturalism.[4] By contrast, the Elizabethan goldsmith was incoherent and fantastic in his choice of motifs for the salt. This base is smooth and symmetrical in form, and its stylized sea-monsters and waves, ultimately of Flemish origin, are those frequently found on Elizabethan basins. To a container for salt these marine ornaments are appropriate, but that freshwater animal the frog hardly accords with them, especially when so naturalistically treated.

The ceremonial importance of the salt in Elizabethan and earlier times is well-known. This beautiful object, the only known example of its kind, is of incomparable perfection in execution as well as in design: the cast-work is of exceptional quality, and has been chased and engraved with consummate taste and precision. This superlative quality, coupled with its weight and the absence of hallmarks suggest that it was made for some personage of high rank at the Elizabethan court. Unfortunately all that is known of its history is that it was recently in the collection of the Marquess of Scarisbrick. The National Art-Collections Fund made an important and greatly appreciated contribution to its purchase.

The very generous bequest made to the Museum in 1968 by Mrs. Douglas Ives of New York has provided funds for the purchase of two important examples of Huguenot plate. The first of these is a two-handled cup and cover by David Willaume (fig. 3). The piece was a duty-dodger bearing transposed hall-marks for 1706, which have now been removed;[5] its real date of manufacture was after the passing of the Wrought Plate Act of 1719. This act imposed a tax of sixpence on each ounce of wrought silver, which was payable at the time of assay. The tax added considerably to the cost of large objects, and in order to evade payment a silversmith sometimes cut out the marks from a piece of old-fashioned plate that was to be melted down and, as in this instance, inserted the resulting disc of silver at the junction of the bowl and the foot, where it formed a false bottom.[6] On stylistic grounds, it is possible to date the cup to the years 1720–25. The elaborate pierced straps with shell-heads on a shaped and matted ground which are applied to the lower part of the body and the dome of the cover are in the French *Régence* manner. Paul de Lamerie used a similar combination of pierced straps with shells and a matted ground on a cup and cover of 1723, illustrated in John Hayward, *Huguenot Silver in England.*[7]

An additional point of interest is that the museum cup was once in the possession of a member of the Royal family. The engraved crest added to the upper part of the body in about 1800 is that of a Royal prince, so that it almost certainly belonged to one of the sons of George III. Probably it was the Royal owner who gave it as an archery prize at Bayswater on July 22, 1830, the nature of the contest being indicated by an arrow laid across the outline of a target, with the motto, PETE G(C)ENTRUM, engraved on the reverse side of the cup, while the date is inscribed on the foot. Of George III's sons, only two are known to have been associated with the archery societies that proliferated throughout England in the late eighteenth and early nineteenth centuries. George IV was a noted toxophilite and had been Captain-General of the Royal Kentish Bowmen while Prince of Wales,[8] but he died on June 26, 1830, almost a month before the contest at Bayswater. His brother and successor, William IV, was a patron of the Royal Toxophilites, who were so styled because the king presented an

3. Cup and cover. H: 18·2 cms. London *c.*1720–25. Maker, David Willaume. M.15–1969.

annual prize to their society.[9] It seems reasonable to suggest, therefore, that the museum cup and cover was the inaugural prize of his reign.

The second acquisition from the Ives Bequest is a pair of sauceboats of 1755 (fig. 4) by Philip Bruguier the elder, who entered a mark in 1738 from an address in St. Martin's Lane, Leicester Fields. Little else is known about this silversmith except that he had

4. Pair of sauceboats. L. of largest: 14·5 cms. London 1755. Maker's mark of Philip Bruguier the elder. Purchased from the funds of the Ives Bequest. M.94 and a – 1969.

5. Two of the marks on one of the Bruguier sauceboats; the other two occur in another depression.

served an apprenticeship to Philip Rainaud, who had in turn been apprenticed to Pierre Platel in 1700, so that his Huguenot connections are well-established.[10]
The sauceboats are not identical, for one is slightly larger than the other, which indicates that they might once have formed part of a larger set. Their design shows a highly developed sense of naturalism unusual in English rococo silver; they are cast and chased in the form of vine leaves on which a butterfly and other insects are scattered at intervals; and their feet and handles are rusticated. Even the hall-marks applied by Goldsmiths' Hall are in keeping with the calculated asymmetry of the design, for they are placed in the voids created by the overlapping leaves (fig. 5).[11]
The concept of organic naturalism, in which plant or animal forms provide the structure as well as the ornament of an article, came from France, where it was an integral part of the rococo. Juste-Aurèle Meissonier exploited it in his published *Oeuvre*,[12] which illustrated naturalistic plate made to his design, including a great centrepiece executed for the Duke of Kingston in 1735 (fig. 6), with tureens shaped like shells and surmounted by fish, game and vegetables. Most English silversmiths were reluctant to adopt the full repertory of the rococo manner, contenting themselves with a few of the motifs, principally scrolls and small naturalistic details. Those who experimented with the style in its most complete form were often, although not invariably, Huguenots; on the other hand, it must be said that there were many Huguenots who preferred the more moderate English version of the style.
One of the few outstanding exercises in organic rococo to be produced in England is a service based wholly on natural forms which was made in the early 1740's

6. Plate from *L'Oeuvre de Juste-Aurèle Meissonier*, c.1745, showing the engraved design for the centrepiece for the Duke of Kingston, 1735. E.262–1967.

Projet de Sculpture en argent d'un grand Surtout de Table, et les deux Terrines qui ont été executée pour le Millord Duc de Kinston en 1735.
A Paris chez Huquier rue St Jacques au coin de celle des Matburins CPR.

7. Sauceboat and stand. Porcelain. Longton Hall, c.1755–60. C.1242–1924.

for Frederick, Prince of Wales, by Nicholas Sprimont,[13] who came from Liège. It is significant that Sprimont left the silver trade at the end of the same decade to direct the Chelsea Porcelain factory, for it is recognized that shell and vegetable forms occur more frequently in ceramics produced in this country during the 1750's than in plate of the same date. As the example of Chelsea spread to other new porcelain factories, it becomes still easier to find parallels for the design of the Bruguier sauceboats. There is a clear correspondence, for instance, between the silver sauceboats and a porcelain sauceboat formed of overlapping cabbage leaves from the Longton Hall factory, dating from about 1755–60 (fig. 7).[14]

If we seek the reason why Bruguier was one of the Huguenots who were prepared to explore naturalism, a possible clue lies in his address at the time he first entered a mark. His workshops in St. Martin's Lane must have been near Old Slaughter's Coffee House, the resort of a group of people which has recently been credited with the introduction and popularization of the rococo from France.[15] The artists in this group included Hogarth, G. M. Moser and H.-F. Gravelot, all of whom had associations with either the silver-

smithing or the jewellery trades; moreover, all three taught at the St. Martin's Lane Academy, where it is believed that amongst their pupils was John Linnell some of whose rococo designs for furniture and metal-work have survived.[16] While we cannot yet attribute the name of a designer to the Bruguier sauceboats, there seem to be grounds for suggesting that the silver-smith was well aware of the work of Hogarth and his friends in the late 1730's and the 1740's.

In contrast to the Bruguier pieces, the recent purchase of an unmarked silver-gilt cup and cover with applied vine decoration, dating from about 1760–61 (fig. 8), brings into the collections a dignified example of the English rococo manner in one of its last stages of development. The piece is probably unmarked because it was fashioned to order from old plate provided by the client for the purpose, and as a private transaction would have by-passed the normal trade channels, thus obviating the risk of discovery and prosecution by the Goldsmiths' Company.[17]

The cup is engraved with the arms of Charles Powlet, 5th Duke of Bolton, who succeeded his father in 1759 and died by his own hand in 1765. The Duke was Bearer of the Queen's Crown at the Coronation of

8. Cup and cover. Silver-gilt. H: 41·5 cms. London, c.1761. Probably made by Thomas Heming as a gift from George III to the 5th Duke of Bolton. M.9–1970.

George III in 1761,[18] and it has been suggested that the cup was a royal gift to mark the occasion.[19] There is circumstantial evidence to support this contention in a trade card made in about 1765 for Thomas Heming, the Royal Goldsmith,[20] which is decorated with a rococo cartouche supporting examples of some of his patterns. The cup and cover illustrated in the top left-hand corner of the card (fig. 9) bears a marked resemblance to the museum piece. The profiles of the body and of the cover are virtually identical, with the exception of the finial on the cover, which in the case of the museum example takes the form of a ducal coronet in deference to its first owner. Vine decoration is applied in much the same way, trailing in a naturalistic manner across the body. The foot of the cup in the trade card, however, has an outline broken by scrolls. In this respect, and in the handles surmounted by a Bacchus and a female figure with a tambourine, the illustration is closer to another cup and cover by Heming in the museum collections. This is a silver-gilt piece of 1759, also encased in vine trails, but with a fluted and slightly elongated body.[21]

While a plausible case can therefore be made for attributing our new acquisition to the workshop of Thomas Heming, we cannot as yet accept that he was the only silversmith to specialize in cups of this

9. Detail from Thomas Heming's trade card, c.1765.

type. A cup and cover in private possession unites many of the features of the two museum pieces; the cup itself is unmarked, but the cover, assayed in London in 1761, bears the maker's mark ER, which is thought to be that of the Norwegian-born silversmith Emich Romer. Romer, of course, may have added a cover to a cup made by Heming;[22] it is also possible that the works discussed above were adapted from a published design not yet identified.

The major Victorian acquisition of the last few years is the Inventions Vase (fig. 10), designed and embossed by the French artist-craftsman Léonard Morel-Ladeuil (1820–88)[23] for the Birmingham firm of Elkington & Company. The piece was made specially for the International Exhibition held in London in 1862; its theme, a celebration of Science and Industry, was clearly chosen so that the piece should be a worthy successor to a vase with a similar subject which Elkington's showed at the Great Exhibition in 1851.[24]

The difference between the two works is one of treatment as well as of style. The earlier piece was designed and modelled by an English sculptor, William Beattie, and had a huge and somewhat cumbersome body decorated with Renaissance motifs popular in the

10. The Inventions Vase. H: 40·4 cms. Birmingham, 1863. Signed by L. Morel-Ladeuil. M.37–1968.

reign of England's first great queen, Elizabeth; its cover was surmounted by a figure of the Prince Consort, President of the 1851 Commissioners. More important, for such tributes to Victoria and Albert were a commonplace of the British Section of the exhibition, the vase was neither cast nor raised by hand, but electrotyped. For this form of manufacture, negative moulds were made from the artist's original model, and the required thickness of silver (or copper, if a cheaper object was demanded) was deposited into the moulds by electrical action.[25]

Elkington's electrotyped several works specially designed by contemporary artists for their display at the Great Exhibition. They were the patentees of the electro-plating process, which had been developed as a cheap substitute for Sheffield plate, and they were therefore anxious to offset their somewhat commercial image by emphasizing the artistic potential of the related technique of electrotyping. They went to great lengths to recruit modellers who were prepared to work in the medium: the most distinguished of these was Pierre-Emile Jeannest,[26] a French bronzist and designer of both plate and ceramics who came to work in this country in the mid-1840's.

Jeannest died suddenly in 1857 and thereafter Elkington's gave up the struggle to establish the electrotyping process as a medium for original modern design and employed it mainly for the purpose of making reproductions of historic metalwork. Quite apart from the loss of their most able designer, the firm had come to recognize that since 1851 a reaction had set in against techniques which demonstrated industrial ingenuity, and that despite all the lauded advantages of the Industrial Revolution, the form of production most admired by contemporary critics was repoussé or embossed work, painstakingly carried out without the aid of any machinery.

Antoine Vechte (1799–1867) (Vechte le repousseur, as he styled himself), Morel-Ladeuil's master, had been largely responsible for the change. Vechte left France during the aftermath of the French Revolution of 1848, which had brought the luxury trades in Paris to a standstill, and arrived in London to work for Hunt and Roskell of New Bond Street.[27] His ambitious works in the Renaissance style, embossed and chased with remarkable virtuosity, enjoyed a tremendous success at the Great Exhibition,[28] and he became the most celebrated artist-craftsman of his day. As Elkington's were unable to recruit him, they turned to his

11. Detail from an embossed plaque on the Inventions Vase, showing the 1862 exhibition building designed by Francis Fowke in South Kensington.

pupil, bringing Morel-Ladeuil over from Paris to Birmingham in 1859, in time for him to produce some prestige pieces for the 1862 exhibition.

Morel-Ladeuil found the abrupt change of environment distressing and plunged into a demanding programme of work in an attempt to overcome his unhappiness.[29] He designed and made an embossed silver table with the theme of dreams[30] and worked on other pieces for the exhibition, including the

Inventions Vase, a characteristic exercise in the translation of eighteenth and nineteenth century achievements into emblems inspired by the Renaissance. The piece is surmounted by a youthful 'Genius of Mechanical Science' standing on a terrestrial globe; the winged figures forming the handle of the vase hold a locomotive engine and a Siemens' electric telegraph apparatus for transmitting and receiving. The four putti on the foot were designed to grasp respectively a voltaic pile (a tribute to Elkington's, it is unfortunately now missing), a screw propeller, a camera and a card from a Jacquard loom.[31] All these figures are cast, but there are two embossed figurative panels, one on each side of the vase. These represent 'Abstract Science emerging from Chaos' and 'Science as applied to Industry', mainly by means of symbolic putti, but with an endearing admixture of direct representation. It is clear from some of the inventions portrayed that Morel-Ladeuil remained a Frenchman at heart, for in the panel to be seen in the illustration a putto holds a roll of honour inscribed with the names of one Englishman and two Frenchmen; Watt, Daguerre and Jacquard. The background of this

12. The Communion Plate of St. Peter le Poer, Muswell Hill.

13. Alms-dish (originally a secular basin). Silver-gilt. Maker's mark: IS above a crescent. London hall-mark for 1607–08. Inscribed on the boss: *S.P.P. Ex dono Gulielmi. Cockaine Junior. 1626.*

14. Ewer and basin. Silver-gilt. Maker's mark, FT in monogram. London hall-mark for 1618–19. M. 13, 13a – 1964.

panel contains an appropriate reference to the 1862 exhibition, as may be seen from the detail in fig. 10, which shows the exterior of the exhibition building.

The vase was not finally hall-marked at Birmingham until 1863. For this reason, together with a passing reference in a notice of the exhibition to its unfinished state,[32] it has been assumed that the piece was not shown in 1862. Happily George Wallis, a former headmaster of the Birmingham School of Design who had recently joined the staff of the Science and Art Department at South Kensington, was commissioned to write a series of articles on the exhibition for the *Midland Counties Herald*. These articles were subsequently re-printed in pamphlet form under the title, *The Art-Manufactures of Birmingham and the Midland Counties, in the International Exhibition of 1862*. His survey of the Elkington display, a prominent feature of the Midland exhibits, includes a long description of the vase, which he closes by remarking that even the unworked parts were of interest, for they demonstrated the method of 'hammering out the forms from flat silver, sufficiently raised at the back; the details being finished, with infinite care and skill, with small tools adapted to the various effects it is desirable to produce upon the upper surface of the work.'[33]

Frederick Elkington[34] served on the jury of the goldsmithing section of the 1862 exhibition, and the firm were in consequence precluded from receiving an award. But Morel-Ladeuil was awarded a medal for 'artistic excellence in design and repoussé work, as shown in the Table and Cups exhibited by Messrs. ELKINGTON'.[35] The Inventions Vase was shown for the second time at the Paris Universal Exhibition of 1867[36] and on this occasion it appeared with the artist's Milton Shield, executed between 1864 and 1867. This second piece, perhaps the most famous of his works, has been in the possession of the Victoria and Albert Museum since the time of the exhibition.[37] It is appropriate that it has been rejoined by the Inventions Vase.

For many years now the Museum has accepted on loan from all denominations church plate whose beauty and value make it unsuitable for ordinary use. Among recent loans is a set of communion plate from the church of St. Peter le Poer, Muswell Hill (fig. 12). This is an old city church which was refounded in the suburbs at the turn of the century in order to serve a new and more populous parish. Its plate is, therefore, that of an ancient and well-endowed

15. Alms-dish. Silver-gilt. Maker's mark of John Eckfourd. London hall-mark for 1744–45. Inscribed: *Ex dono Gulielmi Iliffe Anno 1744.*

foundation. It comprises two communion cups, one of 1560–61 and one of 1620–21, both with paten covers, and both of standard type, a pair of Caroline flagons of 1630–31, whose fine plain form is that generally current at the period, a paten of 1623–24, a strainer-spoon of 1726–27, and a pair of alms-dishes. It is the alms-dishes that are the exceptional pieces. The first (fig. 13) is hall-marked 1607–8, and has the maker's mark IS above a crescent. The embossed and engraved decoration of strapwork panels containing sea-monsters, bunches of fruit and floral scrolls reveals that it first began life as a secular basin and once had a matching ewer. A basin and ewer of 1618–19 (fig. 14) in the Museum's collection illustrate the sort of ensemble. The basin was converted to its present function in 1625, when William Cockayne presented it to the Church. The presentation of secular plate for use in churches dates back into the High Middle Ages and beyond, and continued after the Reformation, especially as the Reformers, for doctrinal reasons, were anxious to blur as much as possible distinctions of form between secular and ecclesiastical plate.

The other alms-dish (fig. 15) has the maker's mark of John Eckfourd, is hall-marked 1744–45, was presented to the church by William Iliffe in 1744, and is remarkable in that it is a careful copy of the Jacobean alms-dish. Only the greater smoothness and precision of chasing and engraving give it away as being of later date. Georgian self-confidence normally refused to countenance older styles; no doubt conservatism on the part of the donor or churchwardens and a desire that the plate should match when set out on the

communion table were responsible for this exceptional departure. All the plate belonging to the church was repaired and regilded in 1792 and 1831.[38]

Lord Caledon has generously allowed the Museum to borrow the beautiful set of silver-gilt communion plate (figs. 16–17) made by Robert Timbrell in 1714–15 for the chapel of Tyttenhanger House, Ridge, Hertfordshire. The chalice is inscribed BIBITE EX HOC and the paten HOC EST CORPUS MEUM, while the alms-dish is finely engraved with the Sacred Monogram and the cross and nails of the Passion in a radiant aureole – according to a design standard at this time. There appears to be no record of the flagon that normally completed such sets. The austerely rich style is one that was first introduced into England by the Huguenots. French motifs and techniques are first recorded in church silver in the 1680's, in the plate furnished in 1683 for St. James's Piccadilly and in 1688 for the Royal Hospital, Chelsea, by the goldsmith whose mark was *RL with a fleur-de-lis*. By 1699 the style was fully developed. In the chalice of that year made by John Chartier for Christ Church Cathedral, Oxford,[39] the graceless conical or cylindrical bowls and stubby trumpet-shaped feet accepted by the Restoration's undemanding taste have been replaced by a noble design in full French classical baroque style. The oval bowl, baluster stem and circular foot are elegantly proportioned and contrasts of surface are obtained by setting off plain areas against bold gadrooning, simple mouldings and the severe delicacy of cut card work. Only the size of the bowl makes it plain that we are not confronted by a French Roman Catholic chalice but by an Anglican communion vessel. In English church plate the style is rare, and evidently it was confined to a small circle of wealthy clergy and aristocracy. By 1714, the date of the Tyttenhanger pieces, it was losing its last vestiges of Baroque elaboration but had not yet shrunk to the spiritless simplicity of succeeding decades.

The communion set has been very little used, so that it is as sharp and brilliant as when it left the hands of the silversmith. It is still preserved in its original morocco-cases, blind tooled, and lined with marbled paper. The present Tyttenhanger House was erected by Sir Henry Pope Blount (1602–82) the traveller, who 'built here a fair Structure of Brick, made fair Walks and Gardens to it, and died seiz'd hereof'.[40] The chapel was licensed during the Great Rebellion by Ralph Browrigg (d. 1659), who was consecrated Bishop of Exeter in 1642. Now disused, it is intensely

evocative of seventeenth century High Anglican devotion. 'The walls are covered from floor to ceiling with "linen" panels. In the north-east angle is an oak-panelled pulpit, with an old bracket for an hour-glass, and at the west end of the chapel are two rows of pews, with panels having arched heads. On the north side, under a picture of the Last Supper, is a small communion table, and against the opposite wall is a vestment cupboard, on the doors of which are written the Lord's Prayer and the Commandments.' The plate must have been made for Sir Thomas Pope-Blount (1670–1731) second baronet, son of the learned Sir Thomas,[11] and Sir Henry's grandson, who inherited Tyttenhanger in 1697. Its superlative condition is explained by the history of Tyttenhanger. On the death in 1751 of Sir Henry Pope-Blount, Thomas's son, the family became extinct, and the estate passed to the Earls of Hardwicke, who had their own magnificent house at Wimpole in Cambridgeshire. And when Tyttenhanger came to the Caledon family in 1835, the custom of maintaining private chaplains was already beginning to die out.

16. Chalice. Silver-gilt. Maker's mark of Robert Timbrell, London hall-mark for 1714–15. Lent by Lord Caledon.

17. Paten and alms-dish. Silver-gilt. Maker's mark of Robert Timbrell, London hall-mark for 1714–15. Lent by Lord Caledon.

Notes

1. A. J. Collins, *Jewels and Plate of Queen Elizabeth I*, London 1955, p. 465, no. 981; p. 563, no. 1475.

2. Collins, *op. cit.*, p. 578, no. 1541.

3. Collins, *op. cit.*, p. 589, nos. 1573–74.

4. See J. F. Hayward, 'The Mannerist goldsmiths: 5 Germany, Part II, Wenzel Jamnitzer of Nurnberg', in *The Connoisseur* clxiv, 1967, pp. 148–54.

5. This has been done through the kindness of the Antique Plate Committee of Goldsmiths' Hall, to whom we are greatly indebted.

6. Other reasons for the evasion of tax by goldsmiths are discussed by J. F. Hayward in his *Huguenot Silver in England, 1688–1727*, 1959, p. 29.

7. *Ibid.*, pl. 8.

8. G. A. Hansard, *The Book of Archery*, 1840, p. 268.

9. *Ibid.*, pp. 282, 284–85. The headquarters of the society were in Bayswater from 1821 until 1834. The motto on the cup is a variant of the one in current use by the Society. We are indebted to Lt.-Col. H. Boehm, Hon. Secretary of the Royal Toxophilite Society, and to Mr. F. H. Lake for their assistance.

10. We are indebted to Miss Susan Hare, Librarian of Goldsmiths' Hall, for supplying this information, and we are also grateful to Mr. David G. Udy, without whose co-operation it would have been impossible to acquire the sauceboats from the Ives Bequest.

11. M. J. C. Furmedge, of the Assay Office, Goldsmiths' Hall, has kindly informed us that it was not unknown for marks to be positioned in accordance with the wishes of the maker.

12. *Oeuvre de Juste Aurele Meissonier Peintre Sculpteur Architecte &c.* 1 ed. 1734. The museum possesses a later edition of *c.*1745. The Kingston tureens were sold in Paris at the Galerie Georges Petit, Polovtsoff sale, December 2–4, 1909 (lot 18).

13. E. A. Jones, *The Gold and Silver of Windsor Castle*, Letchworth 1911, pls. XXXVI, L, LI.

14. We are grateful to our colleague Mr. J. V. G. Mallet for his help in providing this parallel.

15. M. Girouard, 'English Art and the Rococo', in *Country Life*, CXXXIX, 1966, pp. 58–61, 188–90, 224–27.

16. Linnell's work is discussed in P. Ward-Jackson, *English Furniture Designs of the Eighteenth Century*, HMSO, 1958, pp. 54, 55.

17. The Company's legal powers to seize and assay unmarked wares were exercised more stringently from 1675 onwards after a period of laxity. See Sir C. J. Jackson, *English Goldsmiths and Their Marks*, new ed. 1921, p. 45.

18. See 'Procession to the Coronation of their Majesties', in *Gentleman's Magazine*, XXI, 1761, p. 419.

19. See the description of the piece in Christie's sale catalogue, *Important Old English Silver*, December 3, 1969, lot 28. The first suggestion, that it was made in about 1765 by Wakelin & Taylor, is less likely in view of the illustration in the Heming trade card, cited below.

20. Sir A. Heal, *The London Goldsmiths 1200–1800*, OUP, 1935, pl. XXXVIII.

21. The cup was given by the ESSO Petroleum Company Ltd. (M.41–1959). See C. Oman, *English Silversmiths' Works. Civil and Domestic*, HMSO 1965, pl. 144.

22. It is worth pointing out in this connection that the ancestor of the present owner of the cup with the cover by Romer was also a court official who took part in the Coronation of George III.

23. A biography of Morel-Ladeuil was written by his son: L. Morel, *L'Oeuvre de Morel-Ladeuil*, Paris, 1904.

24. *Great Exhibition of the Works of Industry of all Nations. Official Illustrated Catalogue*, II, 1851, Class XXIII, p. 671, pl. 11; *Art Journal Illustrated Catalogue*, 1851, p. 195.

25. 'Electro-metallurgy' in C. Tomlinson, ed.; *Cyclopaedia of Useful Arts*, 1852, pl. 566, 582.

26. H. Bouilhet, *L'Orfèvrerie française aux XVIIIe et XIXe siecles*, 3 vols., Paris, 1908–13, II, 1910, p. 203; *Art Journal*, 1857, p. 227.

27. H. Bouilhet, *op. cit.*, p. 211.

28. Vechte's two 1851 exhibits, his Jupiter vase of 1847 and his Shakespeare, Milton and Newton shield (unfinished at the time of the exhibition) were acquired by the Goldsmiths' Company in 1890. See J. B. Carrington and G. R. Hughes, *The Plate of the Worshipful Company of Goldsmiths*, OUP, 1926, pp. 121–25 (*ill.*).

29. L. Morel, *op. cit.*, p. 12.

30. *Ibid.*, p. 14, pl. II. The Dreamers' Table was purchased at the reduced price of £1500 in 1863 for presentation by the City of Birmingham to the Prince of Wales (later Edward VII) and Princess Alexandra of Denmark on the occasion of their marriage.

31. *Ibid.*, pp. 13, 14 (*ill.*). Morel claims that the cup was shown in 1862, but in view of the notorious unreliability of biographies written long after the event by descendants of the subject, it was thought best to query his statement.

32. *Cassell's Illustrated Family Paper Exhibitor*, 1862, p. 152.

33. G. Wallis, *op. cit.* (1862?), p. 30.

34. Frederick Elkington was the eldest son of George Richards Elkington, the founder of the firm.

35. *Reports by the Juries*, 1863, Class XXXIII, p. 3.

36. *Art Journal Illustrated Catalogue, Paris Universal Exhibition*, 1867, p. 9 (*ill.*).

37. The shield was purchased for the sum of £2000 (546–1868). With the sanction of the museum Elkington's made hundreds of reproductions of this piece, in two qualities.

38. The plate is illustrated and catalogued in E. Freshfield, *The Communion Plate of the City of London*, London 1894, pp. 92–93, who failed to realize the nature of the 1607 alms-dish, and the interest of the 1744 one.

39. Repr. in C. C. Oman, *English Church Plate*, London 1957, pl. 92a, 93b, 94b, 115, 244. See his discussion pp. 211–12.

40. Chauncy, *Antiquities of Hertfordshire*, ii, ed. of 1826, p. 388; *Victoria County History: Hertford*, ii, p. 389.

41. For Sir Henry and Sir Thomas Pope-Blount, see the *Dictionary of National Biography*.

Index